Getting Started in

CURRENCY TRADING

THIRD EDITION

Winning in Today's FOREX Market

Michael Duane Archer

WILEY

John Wiley & Sons, Inc.

Published by John Wiley & Sons, Inc., Hoboken, New Jersey.

Published simultaneously in Canada.

For general information on our other products and services or for technical support, please contact our Customer Care Department within the United States at (800) 762-2974, outside the United States at (317) 572-3993 or fax (317) 572-4002.

Wiley also publishes its books in a variety of electronic formats. Some content that appears in print may not be available in electronic books. For more information about Wiley products, visit our web site at www.wiley.com.

Library of Congress Cataloging-in-Publication Data:
Archer, Michael D. (Michael Duane)
    Getting started in currency trading : winning in today's Forex market /
Michael Duane Archer. – 3rd ed.
        p. cm. – (Getting started in series)
    Includes index.
    ISBN 978-0-470-60212-6 (pbk.)
    1. Foreign exchange market. 2. Foreign exchange futures. I. Title.
    HG3851.A739 2010
    332.4'5–dc22

                                                    2009043706

Printed in the United States of America

10 9 8 7 6 5 4 3 2 1

To my friend, Frank Semone

Contents

PART 1

THE FOREIGN EXCHANGE MARKETS

Chapter 1

Chapter 2

PART 2

GETTING STARTED

Chapter 8

Chapter 9

PART 3
THE TOOLS OF THE TRADE

Chapter 10

Chapter 11

Chapter 12

Chapter 13

Chapter 14

PART 4

THE COMPLETE FOREX TRADER

PART 5

EXTRA FOR EXPERTS

Chapter 19

Chapter 20

Introduction

About This Book

This book is intended to introduce the novice investor to the exciting, complex, and potentially profitable realm of trading world currencies on the foreign exchange markets (FOREX). It also serves as a reference guide for stock and futures traders who wish to explore new trading opportunities. My primary focus is on the rapidly expanding and evolving online trading marketplace for spot currencies, generally referred to as *retail FOREX.*

From the beginning I must emphasize that currency trading may not be to everyone's disposition. The neophyte investor must be keenly aware of all the risks involved and should never trade on funds he or she deems necessary for survival. Currency trading is a form of speculation—attempting to profit by absorbing a risk that already exists. This differs from gambling in which one creates a risk in order to take it. Savings and investment should be covered before considering speculation.

If you have some experience with leveraged markets such as futures or options, you owe yourself a look at FOREX. Those who have never traded will find it the most laissez-faire of all speculative adventures.

How This Book Is Organized

There are six main parts to this book:

1. Part 1—The Foreign Exchange Markets

    The FOREX Landscape, A Brief History of Currency Trading, Two Ways to Trade FOREX.

    I open the book with a brief overview of the FOREX markets, an event-by-event–based historical overview of currency trading, and the two primary methods for participating in the markets as a retail trader. I hope to dispel any myths the reader has about FOREX.

2. Part 2—Getting Started

Regulation: Past, Present, and Future, The FOREX Lexicon, Trading Tables, A Guide to FOREX Brokers, Opening a FOREX Account, and Making the Trade.

Regulation has been slow to come to retail FOREX, but it is making up for lost time.

Every lucrative industry has its own gamut of highly specialized terms or jargon, and currency trading is no exception. You must thoroughly comprehend this jargon before attempting to initiate any trades. With a little familiarization, the language of currency trading will become second nature.

I assist the new trader in selecting a reputable online currency dealer and explain the steps involved in opening a trading account. The actual step-by-step processes of initiating and liquidating a trade are examined in detail with a complete explanation of each order type.

This section must be understood before the reader proceeds to the later sections.

3. Part 3—The Tools of the Trade

Fundamental Analysis, Technical Analysis, A Trader's Toolbox, The FOREX Marketplace, and Retail FX Platforms.

Historically, there have been two major schools of thought in analyzing markets whether they are stocks, commodity futures, or currencies: fundamental analysis and technical analysis. I explore the advantages and disadvantages of both schools in the chapters in this section. I offer ideas on selecting from these trading tools to assemble a basic, personal trading approach that you can easily build upon with experience. A full chapter reviews the wealth of FOREX products and services now available from third-party vendors. Detailed study of several popular online trading platforms completes the section.

4. Part 4—The Complete FOREX Trader

The Plan, The Plan!, Money Management Simplified, Psychology of Trading, Improving Your Trading Skills.

The prospective trader is given the outline of a trading plan. I place much emphasis on money management, the art and science of avoiding losses; and I offer a technique the new trader can use easily and effectively.

I expose the trader to the psychology of trading and the stresses that may accompany same. I place much emphasis on money management and psychology—two key topics vital to success but often neglected in the search for the holy grail of trading methods. Improving Your Trading Skills proffers a series of techniques and skills from which you can pick and choose to flesh out your own trading program.

5. Part 5—Extra for Experts

   Options and Exotics, Computers and FOREX.

   A single chapter covers options and exotics, two areas of FOREX trading that have blossomed recently. Computer trading is big business in all the organized markets. A final chapter briefly discusses the use of computers to assist in and automatically execute trading decisions. It is important for even the small retail trader to understand how the "big guns" trade FOREX and to understand the impact of computers on the markets, directly and indirectly.

6. Appendixes

   The appendixes are a ready reference of FOREX-specific information, much of which the trader finds useful to have at hand while learning and trading. I point you to Appendix A, How the FOREX Game Is Played. The web sites in Appendix F are meant to offer a self-guided tour of the world of currency trading.

The author's attempt has been to make *Getting Started in Currency Trading* an all-in-one introduction as well as a handy computer-side reference guide. Alas, only you, gentle reader, may judge the level of my success.

Companion Web Site

This edition of *Getting Started in Currency Trading* offers a *Getting Started* companion area on the author's web site, www.goodmanworks.com.

You can find all of the tables in this book in downloadable format. You can customize them to your own needs and either print or work with them in MS Word or MS EXCEL.

A *What's New* section keeps readers up-to-date on the ever-changing retail FOREX landscape and the *Getting Started Blog* offers additional learning ideas from the author.

Disclaimer

Neither the publisher nor the author is liable for any financial losses incurred while trading currencies. FOREX is the ultimate caveat emptor marketplace.

Part

The Foreign Exchange Markets

The FOREX Landscape

Introduction—What Is FOREX?

Foreign exchange is the simultaneous buying of one currency and selling of another. Currencies are traded through a broker or dealer and are executed in currency pairs; for example, the Euro Dollar and the U.S. Dollar (EUR/USD) or the British Pound and the Japanese Yen (GBP/JPY).

The FOReign EXchange Market (FOREX) is the largest financial market in the world, with a volume of more than $2 trillion daily. This is more than three times the total amount of the stocks and futures markets combined.

Unlike other financial markets, the FOREX spot market has neither a physical location nor a central exchange. It operates through an electronic network of banks, corporations, and individuals trading one currency for another. The lack of a physical exchange enables the FOREX market to operate on a 24-hour basis, spanning from one time zone to another across the major financial centers. This fact—that there is no centralized exchange—is important to keep in mind as it permeates all aspects of the FOREX experience.

What Is a Spot Market?

A spot market is any market that deals in the current price of a financial instrument. Futures markets, such as the Chicago Board of Trade, offer commodity contracts whose delivery date may span several months into the future. Settlement of FOREX spot transactions usually occurs within two business

TABLE 1.1 Major FOREX Currencies		
Symbol	Country	Currency
USD	United States	Dollar
EUR	Euro members	Euro
JPY	Japan	Yen
GBP	Great Britain	Pound
CHF	Switzerland	Franc
CAD	Canada	Dollar
AUD	Australia	Dollar

days. There are also *futures* and *forwards* in FOREX, but the overwhelming majority of traders use the spot market. I discuss the opportunities to trade FOREX futures on the International Monetary Market.

Which Currencies Are Traded?

Any currency backed by an existing nation can be traded at the larger brokers. The trading volume of the major currencies (along with their symbols) is given in descending order: the U.S. Dollar (USD), the Euro Dollar (EUR), the Japanese Yen (JPY), the British Pound Sterling (GBP), the Swiss Franc (CHF), the Canadian Dollar (CAD), and the Australian Dollar (AUD). See Table 1.1. All other currencies are referred to as *minors* and those from smaller countries, *exotics*.

FOREX currency symbols are always three letters, where the first two letters identify the name of the country and the third letter identifies the name of that country's currency. (The "CH" in the Swiss Franc acronym stands for Confederation Helvetica.)

A FOREX transaction is always between two currencies. This often confuses new traders coming from the stock or futures markets where every trade is denominated in dollars. The price of a pair is the ratio between their respective values. *Pairs, crosses, majors, minors,* and *exotics* are terms referencing specific combinations of currencies. I discuss these terms in Chapter 5, "The FOREX Lexicon." They are defined in the Glossary.

Who Trades on the Foreign Exchange?

There are two main groups that trade currencies. A minority percentage of daily volume is from companies and governments that buy or sell products and services in a foreign country and must subsequently convert profits made in foreign currencies into their own domestic currency in the course of doing business. This is primarily hedging activity. The majority now consists of investors trading for profit, or speculation. Speculators range from large banks trading 10,000,000 currency units or more and the home-based operator trading perhaps 10,000 units or less. Retail FOREX, as much as it has grown in the past 10 years, still represents a small percentage of the total daily volume but its numbers and significance are growing rapidly.

Today, importers and exporters, international portfolio managers, multinational corporations, high-frequency traders, speculators, day traders, long-term holders, and hedge funds all use the FOREX market to pay for goods and services, to transact in financial assets, or to reduce the risk of currency movements by hedging their exposure in other markets.

A producer of widgets in the United Kingdom is intrinsically *long* the British Pound (GBP). If they sign a long-term sales contract with a company in the United States, they may wish to buy some quantity of the USD and sell an equal quantity of the GBP to *hedge* their margins from a fall in the GBP.

The speculator trades to make a profit by purchasing one currency and simultaneously selling another. The hedger trades to protect his or her *margin* on an international transaction (for example) from adverse currency fluctuations. The hedger has an intrinsic interest in one side of the market or the other. The speculator does not. Speculation is not a bad word. Speculators add *liquidity* to a market, making it easier for everyone to transact business by setting efficient prices. They also absorb risks that exist in the marketplace. This latter differs from the gambler who creates risks in order to take them.

How Are Currency Prices Determined?

Currency prices are affected by a large matrix of constantly changing economic and political conditions, but probably the most important are interest rates, economic conditions, international trade, inflation or deflation, and political stability. Sometimes governments actually participate in the foreign exchange market to influence the value of their currencies. Governments do this by flooding the market with their domestic currency in an attempt to lower the price or, conversely, buying in order to raise the price. This process is known as central bank intervention. Any of these factors, as well as large market orders, can cause high volatility in currency prices. Reports of sudden changes in such factors as unemployment can drive currency prices sharply higher or lower for a short period of time. In fact, news traders specialize in attempting to capitalize on such surprises. Technical factors, such as a well-known chart pattern, may also influence currency prices for brief periods. However, the size and volume of the

FOREX market make it impossible for any one entity to drive the market for any length of time. Crowd psychology and expectations also figure in the equation determining the price of a currency relative to another currency. There are an enormous number of correlations between all these factors and they are almost certainly nonlinear in nature. That means they are constantly changing and rearranging themselves, sometimes in nonpredictive ways. Now you see it, now you don't. If you focus on one or a few of them, the others might change unnoticed. Quantum theory comes to mind.

Why Trade Foreign Currencies?

In today's marketplace, the dollar constantly fluctuates against the other currencies of the world. Several factors, such as the decline of global equity markets and declining world interest rates, have forced investors to pursue new opportunities. The global increase in trade and foreign investments has led to many national economies becoming interconnected with one another. This interconnection, and the resulting fluctuations in exchange rates, has created a huge international market: FOREX. For many investors, this has created exciting opportunities and new profit potentials. The FOREX market offers unmatched potential for profitable trading in any market condition or any stage of the business cycle. These factors equate to the following advantages:

- *No commissions.* No clearing fees, no exchange fees, no government fees, no brokerage fees if you trade with a market maker.

- *No middlemen.* Spot currency trading does away with the middlemen and allows clients to interact directly with the market maker responsible for the pricing on a particular currency pair, if you trade with an Electronic Communications Network (ECN).

- *No fixed lot size.* In the futures markets, lot or contract sizes are determined by the exchanges. A standard-sized contract for silver futures is 5,000 ounces. Even a "mini-contract" of silver, 1,000 ounces, represents a value of approximately $17,000. In spot FOREX, *you* determine the lot size appropriate for your grubstake. This allows traders to effectively participate with accounts of well under $1,000. It also provides a significant money management tool for astute traders.

- *Low transaction cost.* The retail transaction cost (the bid/ask spread) is typically less than 0.1 percent under normal market conditions. At larger dealers, the spread could be as low as 0.07 percent. Prices are quoted in *pips* for currencies. Today pip spreads can be zero at some periods for the most actively traded pairs, but typically range from two to five pips.

- *High liquidity.* With an average trading volume of more than $4 trillion per day, FOREX is the most liquid market in the world. It means that a trader can enter or exit the market at will in almost any market condition. I must note that at the time of the first edition of *Getting Started in Currency Trading* in 2005, the daily volume was slightly less than $2 trillion.

- *Almost instantaneous transactions.* This is an advantageous byproduct of high liquidity.

- *Low margin, high leverage.* These factors increase the potential for higher profits (and losses) and are discussed later. Traders have access to leverage of up to 400 percent although 50 percent to 100 percent is most common. 400:1 leverage means $1 controls $400 of currency.

- *A 24-hour market.* A trader can take advantage of all profitable market conditions at any time. There is no waiting for the opening bell. Markets are closed from Friday afternoon to Sunday afternoon. As the markets transition to the Asian Session, they usually go quiet from 5 P.M. to 7 P.M. Eastern Standard Time.

- *Not related to the stock market.* Trading in the FOREX market involves selling or buying one currency against another. Thus, there is no hard correlation between the foreign currency market and the stock market although both are measures of economic activity in some way and may be correlated in specific respects for a limited period of time. A *bull market* or a *bear market* for a currency is defined in terms of the outlook for its relative value against other currencies. If the outlook is positive, we have a bull market in which a trader profits by buying the currency against other currencies. Conversely, if the outlook is pessimistic, we have a bull market for other currencies and traders take profits by selling the currency against other currencies. In either case, there is always a good market trading opportunity for a trader. Although big price moves occur frequently, a crash is less likely to happen in currencies than stocks because a pair measures relative value. The U.S. Dollar (USD) can be in deep trouble, but so can the European Euro (EUR). The game is the ratio between the two. The top four traded currencies are: the U.S. Dollar (USD), the Euro Dollar (EUR), the Japanese Yen (JPY), and the British Pound (GBP). Fund managers are beginning to show interest in FOREX because of this non-correlation with other investments.

- *Interbank market.* The backbone of the FOREX market consists of a global network of dealers. They are mainly major commercial banks that communicate and trade with one another and with their clients through electronic networks and by telephone. There are no organized exchanges to serve as a central location to facilitate transactions the way the New York Stock Exchange serves the equity markets. The FOREX market operates in a manner similar to that of the NASDAQ market in the United States; thus it is also referred to as an *over-the-counter* (OTC) market. The lack of a centralized exchange permeates all aspects of currency trading.

- *No one can corner the market.* The FOREX market is so vast and has so many participants that no single entity, not even a central bank, can control the market price for an extended period of time. Even interventions by mighty central banks are becoming increasingly ineffectual and short-lived. Thus central banks are becoming less and less inclined to intervene to manipulate market prices. (You may remember the attempt to corner the silver futures market in the late 1970s. Such disruptive excess is not likely in the FOREX markets.)

- *No insider trading.* Because of the FOREX market's size and noncentralized nature, there is virtually no chance for ill effects caused by insider trading. Fraud possibilities, at least against the system as a whole, are significantly less than in any other financial instruments.

- *Limited regulation.* There is but limited governmental influence via regulation in the FOREX markets, primarily because there is no centralized location or exchange. Of course, this is a sword that can cut both ways, but the author believes—with a hearty caveat emptor—less regulation is, on balance, an advantage. Nevertheless, most countries do have some regulatory say and more seems on the way. Regardless, fraud is always fraud wherever it is found and subject to criminal penalties in all countries. Regulatory bodies such as the *Commodity Futures Trading Commission* (CFTC) and *National Futures Association* (NFA) are just now beginning to get a handle on some limited control of the retail FOREX business.

- *Online trading.* The capability of trading online was the impetus for retail FOREX. Today you can select from more than 100 online FOREX broker-dealers. Although none is perfect, the trader has a wide variety of options at his or her disposal.

- *Third-party products and services.* The immense popularity of retail FOREX has fostered a burgeoning industry of third-party products and services.

What Tools Do I Need to Trade Currencies?

A computer with reliable high-speed connection to the Internet, a small grubstake, and the information in this book are all that are needed to begin trading currencies. You do not even need the grubstake to practice on; a free demo

account is offered by all retail FOREX brokers. In fact, I encourage you ˌ
at least one demo account early in this book.

What Does It Cost to Trade Currencies?

An online currency trading account (a micro-account) may be opened for as little as $1! Mini-accounts start at $400. Do not laugh—micro- and mini-accounts are a good way to get your feet wet without taking a bath. Unlike futures, where the size of a contract is set by the exchanges, in FOREX you select how much of any particular currency you wish to buy or sell. Thus, a $3,000 grubstake is not unreasonable as long as the trader engages in appropriately sized trades. FOREX mini-accounts also do not suffer the illiquidity of many futures mini-contracts, as everyone essentially feeds from the same interbank currency "pool."

   Market maker brokers take their expenses and profit by marking up the bid-ask spread. ECN brokers charge a flat lot fee to trade. As an example, if you buy and then later sell 100,000 EURUSD and the spread is two pips, you pay a total of four pips or approximately $40. ECN lot fees vary from $15 to $40 for a 100,000 lot. If you trade a larger lot size and/or frequently you will be able to negotiate these costs.

FOREX versus Stocks

Historically, the securities markets have been considered, at least by the majority of the public, as an investment vehicle. In the past 10 years, securities have taken on a more speculative nature. This was perhaps due to the downfall of the overall stock market as many security issues experienced extreme volatility because of the "irrational exuberance" displayed in the marketplace. The implied return associated with an investment was no longer true. Many traders engaged in the *day trader* rush of the late 1990s only to discover that from a leverage standpoint it took quite a bit of capital to day trade, and the return—while potentially higher than long-term investing—was not exponential, to say the least.

   After the onset of the day trader rush, many traders moved into the futures stock index markets where they found they could better leverage their capital and not have their capital tied up when it could be earning interest or making money somewhere else. Like the futures markets, spot currency trading is an excellent vehicle for the pattern day trader that desires to leverage his or her current capital to trade. Spot currency trading provides more options and greater volatility while at the same time stronger trends than are currently available in stock futures indexes. Former securities day traders have an excellent home in the FOREX market.

There are approximately 4,000 stocks listed on the New York Stock Exchange. Another 2,800 are listed on the NASDAQ. Which one will you trade? Trading just the seven major USD currency pairs instead of 6,800 stocks simplifies matters significantly for the FOREX trader. Fewer decisions, fewer headaches. The trader can specialize in one, two, or three currency pairs and have a full plate offering all the opportunity he or she can seize.

FOREX versus Futures

The futures contract is precisely that—a legally binding agreement to deliver or accept delivery of a specified grade and quantity of a given commodity in a distant month. FOREX, however, is a spot (cash) market in which trades rarely exceed two days. Many FOREX brokers allow their investors to *rollover* open trades after two days. There are FOREX futures or forward contracts, but almost all activity is in the spot market facilitated by rollovers.

In addition to the advantages listed, FOREX trades are almost always executed at the time and price asked by the speculator. There are numerous horror stories about futures traders being locked into an open position even after placing the liquidation order. The high liquidity of the foreign exchange market (roughly three times the trading volume of all the futures markets combined) ensures the prompt execution of all orders (entry, exit, limit, etc.) at the desired price and time.

The caveat here is something called a requote or dealer intervention, which I discuss in a later chapter.

The Commodity Futures Trading Commission (CFTC) authorizes futures exchanges to place daily limits on contracts that significantly hamper the ability to enter and exit the market at a selected price and time. No such limits exist in the FOREX market.

Stock and futures traders are used to thinking in terms of the U.S. Dollar versus something else, such as the price of a stock or the price of wheat. This is like comparing apples to oranges. In currency trading, however, it is always a comparison of one currency to another currency—someone's apples to someone else's apples. This paradigm shift can take a little getting used to, but I will give you plenty of examples to help smooth the transition.

The author was a commodity futures trader and registered trading advisor for many years but has found currency trading much more to his liking for many of the reasons listed above.

I must reiterate: There is always some risk in speculation regardless of which financial instruments are traded and where they are traded, regulated or unregulated. Leverage is a door that swings both ways.

Both stock and futures traders must make a similar adjustment to currency trading: In stocks and futures the specific investment vehicle is denominated in dollars or local currency. In FOREX the underlying vehicle is a *pair*—the relative value of one currency to another.

Summary

FOREX means FOReign EXchange. The FOREX (FX) market is more than a $4 trillion-a-day financial market, dwarfing everything else, including stocks and futures. Because there is no centralized exchange or clearinghouse for currency trading the FOREX market is currently less regulated than other financial markets.

There are a wide variety of reasons to consider FOREX trading, including high leverage and low costs. Access to the FOREX markets via the Internet has resulted in a great deal of interest by small traders previously locked out of this enormous marketplace. Getting started requires only this book, a review of the FX landscape, a computer and Internet connection, and a small grubstake.

Chapter

2

A Brief History of Currency Trading

Introduction

This material may not seem relevant to trading currencies today, but even a modest perspective adds substance and depth to a trader. "He who knows only his own generation remains always a child," George Norlin once said.

Ancient Times

Foreign exchange dealing can be traced back to the early stages of history, possibly beginning with the introduction of coinage by the ancient Egyptians, and the use of paper notes by the Babylonians. Certainly by biblical times, the Middle East saw a rudimentary international monetary system when the Roman gold coin *aureus* gained worldwide acceptance followed by the silver *denarius*, both a common stock among the money changers of the period. In the Bible, Jesus becomes angry at the money changers. I hope His wrath was directed at the poor exchange rates and not the profession itself!

By the Middle Ages, foreign exchange became a function of international banking with the growth in the use of bills of exchange by the merchant princes and international debt papers by the budding European powers in the course of their underwriting the period's wars.

The Gold Standard, 1816–1933

The gold standard was a fixed commodity standard: participating countries fixed a physical weight of gold for the currency in circulation, making it directly redeemable in the form of the precious metal. In 1816, for instance, the pound sterling was defined as 123.27 grains of gold, which was on its way to becoming the foremost reserve currency and was at the time the principal component of the international capital market. This led to the expression "as good as gold" when applied to Sterling—the Bank of England at the time gained stability and prestige as the premier monetary authority.

Of the major currencies, the U.S. dollar adopted the gold standard late in 1879 and became the standard-bearer, replacing the British pound when Britain and other European countries came off the system with the outbreak of World War I in 1914. Eventually, though, the worsening international depression led even the dollar off the gold standard by 1933; this marked the period of collapse in international trade and financial flows prior to World War II.

The Fed

As an investor, it is essential to acquire a basic knowledge of the *Federal Reserve System* (the Fed). The Federal Reserve was created by the U.S. Congress in 1913. Before that, the U.S. government lacked any formal organization for studying and implementing monetary policy. Consequently, markets were often unstable and the public had little faith in the banking system. The Fed is an independent entity, but is subject to oversight from Congress. This means that decisions do not have to be ratified by the president or anyone else in the government, but Congress periodically reviews the Fed's activities.

The Fed is headed by a government agency in Washington known as the Board of Governors of the Federal Reserve. The Board of Governors consists of seven presidential appointees, each of whom serve 14-year terms. All members must be confirmed by the Senate, and they can be reappointed. The board is led by a chairman and a vice chairman, each appointed by the president and approved by the Senate for four-year terms. The current chair is Ben Bernanke, who was sworn in on February 1, 2006, to a 4-year term.

There are 12 regional Federal Reserve Banks located in major cities around the country that operate under the supervision of the Board of Governors. Reserve Banks act as the operating arm of the *central bank* and do most of the work of the Fed. The banks generate their own income from four main sources:

1. Services provided to banks.

2. Interest earned on government securities.

3. Income from foreign currency held.

4. Interest on loans to depository institutions.

The income generated from these activities is used to finance day-to-day operations, including information gathering and economic research. Any excess income is funneled back into the U.S. Treasury.

The system also includes the Federal Open Market Committee, better known as the FOMC. This is the policy-creating branch of the Federal Reserve. Traditionally the chair of the board is also selected as the chair of the FOMC. The voting members of the FOMC are the seven members of the Board of Governors, the president of the Federal Reserve Bank of New York, and presidents of four other Reserve Banks who serve on a one-year rotating basis. All Reserve Bank presidents participate in FOMC policy discussions whether or not they are voting members. The FOMC makes the important decisions on interest rates and other monetary policies. This is the reason they get most of the attention in the media.

The primary responsibility of the Fed is "to promote sustainable growth, high levels of employment, stability of prices to help preserve the purchasing power of the dollar, and moderate long-term interest rates."

In other words, the Fed's job is to foster a sound banking system and a healthy economy. To accomplish its mission the Fed serves as the banker's bank, the government's bank, the regulator of financial institutions, and as the nation's money manager.

The Fed also issues all coin and paper currency. The U.S. Treasury actually produces the cash, but the Fed Bank then distributes it to financial institutions. It is also the Fed's responsibility to check bills for wear and tear, taking damaged currency out of circulation.

The Federal Reserve Board (FRB) has regulation and supervision responsibilities over banks. This includes monitoring banks that are members of the system, international banking facilities in the United States, foreign activities of member banks, and the U.S. activities of foreign-owned banks. The Fed also helps to ensure that banks act in the public's interest by helping in the development of federal laws governing consumer credit. Examples are the Truth in Lending Act, the Equal Credit Opportunity Act, the Home Mortgage Disclosure Act, and the Truth in Savings Act. In short, the Fed is the police officer for banking activities within the United States and abroad.

The FRB also sets margin requirements for stock investors. This limits the amount of money you can borrow to purchase securities. Currently, the requirement is set at 50 percent, meaning that with $500 you have the opportunity to purchase up to $1,000 worth of securities.

Most people accept the Fed without question. But a growing minority has concluded that the economy would be better off without it. Let the market decide the ratio between spending and savings, they say. The Fed ultimately acts to redistribute wealth by increasing the money supply and "lending" it cheaply to banks, which in turn lend it back to the people who created the wealth in the first place.

Securities and Exchange Commission, 1933–1934

When the stock market crashed in October 1929, countless investors lost their fortunes. Banks also lost great sums of money in the Crash because they had invested heavily in the markets. When people feared their banks might not be able to pay back the money that depositors had in their accounts, a "run" on the banking system caused many bank failures.

With the Crash and ensuing depression, public confidence in the markets plummeted. There was a consensus that for the economy to recover, the public's faith in the capital markets needed to be restored. Congress held hearings to identify the problems and search for solutions.

Based on the findings in these hearings, Congress passed the Securities Act of 1933 and the Securities Exchange Act of 1934. These laws were designed to restore investor confidence in capital markets by providing more structure and government oversight. The main purposes of these laws can be reduced to two commonsense notions:

1. Companies that publicly offer securities for investment dollars must tell the public the truth about their businesses, the securities they are selling, and the risks involved in investing.
2. People who sell and trade securities—brokers, dealers, and exchanges— must treat investors fairly and honestly, putting investors' interests first.

The Bretton Woods System, 1944–1973

The post–World War II period saw Great Britain's economy in ruins, its infrastructure having been bombed. The country's confidence with its currency was at a low. By contrast, the United States, thanks to its physical isolation, was left relatively unscathed by the war. Its industrial might was ready to be turned to civilian purposes. This then has led to the dollar's rise to prominence, becoming the reserve currency of choice and staple to the international financial markets.

Bretton Woods came about in July 1944 when 45 countries attended, at the behest of the United States, a conference to formulate a new international financial framework. This framework was designed to ensure prosperity in the postwar period and prevent the recurrence of the 1930s global depression. Named after a resort hotel in New Hampshire, the Bretton Woods system formalized the role of the U.S. dollar as the new global reserve currency, with its value fixed into gold. The United States assumed the responsibility of ensuring convertibility while other currencies were pegged to the dollar.

Among the key features of the new framework were:

- Fixed but adjustable exchange rates.
- The International Monetary Fund.
- The World Bank.

The End of Bretton Woods and the Advent of Floating Exchange Rates

After close to three decades of running the international financial system, Bretton Woods finally went the way of history due to growing structural imbalances among the economies, leading to mounting volatility and speculation in a one-year period from June 1972 to June 1973. At the time the United Kingdom, facing deficit problems, initially floated the Sterling. Then it was devaluated further in February of 1973, losing 11 percent of its value along with the Swiss Franc and the Japanese Yen. This eventually led to the European Economic Community floating their currencies as well.

At the core of Bretton Woods' problems were deteriorating confidence in the dollar's ability to maintain full convertibility and the unwillingness of surplus countries to revalue for its adverse impact in external trade. Despite a last-ditch effort by the Group of Ten finance ministers through the Smithsonian Agreement in December 1971, the international financial system from 1973 onward saw market-driven floating exchange rates taking hold. Several times efforts for reestablishing controlled systems were undertaken with varying levels of success. The most well known of these was Europe's Exchange Rate Mechanism of the 1990s, which eventually led to the *European Monetary Union.*

International Monetary Market

In December 1972, the International Monetary Market (IMM) was incorporated as a division of the Chicago Mercantile Exchange (CME) that specialized in currency futures, interest-rate futures, and stock index futures, as well as futures options.

Into the Millennium

Until the arrival of the *Euro* in 2002 (see next subsection), the international scene has remained essentially unchanged for more than 30 years, although the volume of transactions in foreign exchange has increased enormously. Electronic trading has made it possible to initiate instantaneous trades in the billions of dollars. That has introduced the fragile nature of technology with its lack of redundancy, but no fallout from that has yet to be seen. China's emergence as a world power has focused attention on its economy and its currency, the yuan, which at the present time is controlled and does not float. The author believes it will be impossible to continue the tight control over the yuan, and floating rates will be inevitable.

Arrival of the Euro

On January 1, 2002, the Euro became the official currency of 12 European nations that agreed to remove their previous currencies from circulation prior to February 28, 2002. See Table 2.1.

The Euro was considered an immediate success and is now the second most frequently traded currency in FOREX markets behind the USD. Not coincidently the EURUSD is the most traded currency pair.

Since 2002, 10 more countries have adopted the Euro: Andorra, Cyprus, Malta, Monaco, Montenegro, San Marino, Slovakia, Slovenia, Spain, and Vatican City.

More details on the Euro can be found in Appendix C of this book.

TABLE 2.1 European Original Monetary Union

Austria	Schilling
Belgium	Franc
Finland	Markka
France	Franc
Germany	Mark
Greece	Drachma
Ireland	Punt
Italy	Lira
Luxembourg	Franc
Netherlands	Guilder
Portugal	Escudo
Spain	Peseta

The CFTC and the NFA

The new kids on the FOREX block for U.S. traders are the Commodity Futures Trading Commission (CFTC) and the National Futures Association (NFA). Previously dedicated to regulating the commodity futures industry, these agencies are becoming quickly and deeply (many say too deeply) involved in regulating the retail FOREX business. In 2009 NFA Compliance Regulation 2-43 went into effect and has made a significant impact on retail FOREX.

Table 2.2 depicts the major events in FOREX history and regulation.

TABLE 2.2 Timeline of Foreign Exchange
1913—U.S. Congress creates the Federal Reserve System.
1933—Congress passes the Securities Act of 1933 to counter the effects of the Great Crash of 1929.
1934—The Securities Exchange Act of 1934 creates the beginnings of the Securities and Exchange Commission.
1936—The Commodity Exchange Act is enacted in direct response to manipulating grain and futures markets.
1944—The Bretton Woods Accord is established to help stabilize the global economy after World War II.
1971—The Smithsonian Agreement is established to allow for a greater fluctuation band for currencies.
1972—The European Joint Float is established as the European community tries to move away from their dependency on the U.S. Dollar.
1972—The International Monetary Market is created as a division of the Chicago Mercantile Exchange.
1973—The Smithsonian Agreement and European Joint Float fail, signifying the official switch to a free-floating system.
1974—Congress creates the Commodity Futures Trading Commission to regulate the futures and options markets.
1978—The European Monetary System is introduced to again try to gain independence from the U.S. Dollar.
1978—The free-floating system is officially mandated by the International Monetary Fund.
1993—The European Monetary System fails to make way for a worldwide, free-floating system.
1994—Online currency trading makes its debut.
2000—Commodity Modernization Act establishes new regulations for securities derivatives, including currencies in futures or forwards form.
2002—The Euro becomes the official currency of 12 European nations on January 1.
2009—The CFTC and NFA implement NFA Compliance Rule 2-43.
2009—The NFA sets minimum margin requirements for retail FOREX.

Summary

Until the late 1960s the currency markets were extremely stable and very much a closed club. Things were about to change rapidly! Currency trading is probably the world's *second*-oldest profession!

The Euro, introduced in 2002, is the official currency of 22 European countries: Andorra, Austria, Belgium, Cyprus, Finland, France, Germany, Greece, Ireland, Italy, Kosovo, Luxembourg, Malta, Monaco, Montenegro, the Netherlands, Portugal, San Marino, Slovakia, Slovenia, Spain, and Vatican City. Lithuania will convert in 2010 and Estonia is expected to convert in 2011.

NFA Compliance Rule 2-43 has in many ways changed how the game is played at the retail level.

Some key dates and events—1973, 1978, 1994, 2002, 2009.

Two Ways to Trade FOREX

Introduction—Futures Contracts

The overwhelming majority of currency trading volume is in the spot market. FOREX inevitably means spot trading to most participants. But it is possible to trade FOREX as a futures vehicle. The primary advantage of *FOREX futures* lies in the fact that the futures markets are centralized and as such are more heavily regulated. Traders leery of market maker practices in retail spot FOREX may find comfort and a better sleep by trading currencies on a centralized, heavily regulated futures exchange. Indeed, an increase in futures FOREX has been identified in the past two years although volume continues to be dwarfed by the spot market. The selection of traded currency pairs with reasonable liquidity is also smaller in the futures arena. A secondary advantage is that many popular technical trading methods use volume of trading and open interest. While aggregate volume is known in FOREX, daily figures are unobtainable because of the decentralized nature of the business. Attempts are under way, including those by the author, to synthesize spot FOREX volume and open interest statistics from other data using statistical methods. The correlation of spot FOREX data to futures FOREX data has not been promising.

A *futures contract* is an agreement, or *contract*, between two parties: a *short position*, the party who agrees to deliver a commodity, and a long position, the party who agrees to receive a commodity. For example, a grain farmer would be the holder of the short position (agreeing to sell the grain) while the bakery would be the holder of the long (agreeing to buy the grain).

In a futures contract, everything is precisely specified: the quantity and quality of the underlying commodity, the specific price per unit, and the date and method of delivery. The price of a futures contract is represented by the agreed-on price of the underlying commodity or financial instrument that will be delivered in the future. For example, in the grain scenario, the price of the contract might be 5,000 bushels of grain at a price of $4 per bushel and the delivery date may be the third Wednesday in September of the current year.

Options (here meaning delivery months) are staggered throughout the calendar year. Typically the most current option month generates the most trading activity as it is most easily identified with the spot market.

Currency Futures

The FOREX market is essentially a cash or spot market in which more than 90 percent of the trades are liquidated within 48 hours. Currency trades held longer than this are sometimes routed through an authorized commodity futures exchange such as the International Monetary Market (IMM). IMM was founded in 1972 and is a division of the CME Group, formerly the *Chicago Mercantile Exchange*. CME Group specializes in currency futures, interest-rate futures, and stock index futures, as well as options on futures. Clearinghouses (the futures exchange) and introducing brokers are subject to more stringent regulations from the Securities and Exchange Commission (SEC), Commodity Futures Trading Commission (CFTC), and National Futures Association (NFA) agencies than the FOREX spot market (see www.cmegroup.com for more details).

It should also be noted that FOREX traders are charged only a transaction cost per trade, which is simply the difference between the current *bid* and *ask* prices. Currency futures traders are charged a round-turn commission varying from broker to broker. In addition, margin requirements for futures contracts are usually slightly higher than the requirements for the FOREX spot market.

Contract Specifications

Table 3.1 is a list of currencies traded through IMM at the Chicago Mercantile Exchange and their contract specifications.

Size represents one contract requirement though some brokers offer mini-contracts, usually one-tenth the size of the standard contract. Months identify the month of contract delivery. The tick symbols H, M, U, Z are abbreviations for March, June, September, and December, respectively. Hours indicate the

TABLE 3.1 Currency Contract Specifications				
Commodity	Contract Size	Months	Hours	Minimum Fluctuation
Australian Dollar	100,000 AUD	H, M, U, Z	7:20–14:00	0.0001 AUD = $10.00
British Pound	62,500 GBP	H, M, U, Z	7:20–14:15	0.0002 GBP = $12.50
Canadian Dollar	100,000 CAD	H, M, U, Z	7:20–14:00	0.0001 CAD = $10.00
Eurocurrency	62,500 EUR	H, M, U, Z	7:20–14:15	0.0001 EUR = $ 6.25
Japanese Yen	12,500,000 JPY	H, M, U, Z	7:00–14:00	0.0001 JPY = $12.50
Mexican Peso	500,000 MXN	All months	7:00–14:00	0.0025 MXN = $12.50
New Zealand Dollar	100,000 NZD	H, M, U, Z	7:00–14:00	0.0001 NZD = $10.00
Russian Ruble	2,500,00 RUR	H, M, U, Z	7:20–14:00	0.0001 RUR = $25.00
South African Rand	5,000,000 ZAR	All months	7:20–14:00	0.0025 ZAR = $12.50
Swiss Franc	62,500 CHF	H, M, U, Z	7:20–14:15	0.0001 CHF = $12.50

local trading hours in Chicago. The minimum fluctuation represents the smallest monetary unit that is registered as one pip in price movement at the exchange and is usually one ten-thousandth of the base currency.

Currencies Trading Volume

Figure 3.1, FX Futures and Options, summarizes the growth of currency futures trading over five years. Keep in mind that spot trading has also increased in those years.

U.S. Dollar Index

The U.S. Dollar Index (ticker symbol = DX) is an openly traded futures contract offered by the New York Board of Trade. It is computed using a trade-weighted geometric average of six currencies. See Table 3.2.

IMM currency futures traders monitor the U.S. Dollar Index to gauge the dollar's overall performance in world currency markets. If the Dollar Index is trending lower, then it is likely that a major currency that is a component of the

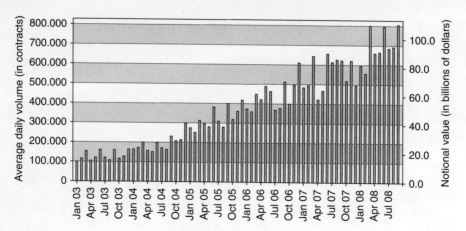

FIGURE 3.1 FX Futures and Options (Jan 2003–Sep 2008)
Source: CME Group, www.cmegroup.com.

TABLE 3.2 U.S. Dollar Index	
Currency	*Weight %*
Eurocurrency	57.6
Japanese Yen	13.6
British Pound	11.9
Canadian Dollar	9.1
Swedish Krona	4.2
Swiss Franc	3.6

Dollar Index is trading higher. When a currency trader takes a quick glance at the price of the U.S. Dollar Index, it gives the trader a good feel for what is going on in the FOREX market worldwide.

For traders who are interested in more details on commodity futures, I recommend Todd Lofton's paperbound book, *Getting Started in Futures* (John Wiley & Sons, 2007).

Volume and Open Interest

Volume and open interest statistics are not available on the spot market as there is no centralized clearinghouse or exchange to collect the data. It is available for currency futures.

Volume is the total number of transactions over a fixed period of time, usually one trading session. Open Interest is the total number of outstanding futures contracts. If a new long buys from a new short, open interest increases by one. If a new long or new short buys or sells to an old short or old long, open interest does not change. If an old long offsets to an old short, open interest decreases by one. Many technical traders in the futures market consider volume and open interest to be useful forecasting information.

Open Interest is further dissected for analysis in some futures markets between commercial interests (hedgers), large speculators, and small speculators as seen on the web site www.timingcharts.com. A government report issues this information as the Commitment of Traders (COT).

Where to Trade

The primary exchange for futures, FOREX is the International Monetary Market division of the CME Group (www.cmegroup.com). ICE FX (www.theice.com), formerly the New York Board of Trade, makes a market in currency futures.

FOREX Futures

Turnabout is fair play. Some retail spot FOREX brokers now offer trading in silver (XAGUSD) and gold (XAUUSD).

TIP: Gold and silver traders with a bent for high risk may find higher leverage available with an overseas retail spot FOREX broker.

Summary

Almost all retail traders prefer spot FOREX. Futures FOREX has its advantages: (1) a centralized exchange, (2) stronger regulation, and (3) availability of daily volume and open interest statistics.

Part

2

Getting Started

4

Regulation: Past, Present, and Future

The foreign exchange market has no central clearinghouse as do the stock market and the commodity futures market. Nor is it based in any one country; it is a complex, often freewheeling, loosely woven worldwide network of banks. This network is referred to as the Interbank system. Retail FOREX brokers—in different ways—tap into this network to fill their customers' orders. These facts permeate every aspect of currency trading, especially the regulatory environment. It is difficult, if not impossible, to get a firm regulatory grip on such an entity. That fact cuts both ways. The market is laissez-faire, but it is also a caveat emptor enterprise. If you wish to trade currencies, you must accept these facts from the beginning.

Regulation in the FOREX Market

In the second edition of *Getting Started in Currency Trading,* I wrote:

> The retail FOREX regulatory picture continues to evolve—slowly. Three years ago some broker-dealers proudly advertised they were not NFA members. Curiously one of those was REFCO, which failed soon thereafter. Today all of the major broker-dealers have joined the NFA (National Futures Association) and come under the watchful government eye of the CFTC (Commodity Futures

Trading Commission). My first advice to you: Do not trade with an unregistered broker-dealer. Every broker-dealer should have his NFA registration number on the web site's home page.

Regulation is seldom proactive; it usually is the result of a crisis. An NFA spokesman confessed to me that their hands were somewhat tied until a crisis provoked additional legislation. The NFA does host a booth at most FOREX trade shows. If you attend one of these, you might want to ask questions or voice your concerns to the people staffing them. They seem to be good listeners and keep close tabs on the pulse of the FOREX marketplace.

Broker-dealers register as Futures Commission Merchants (FCMs). Currently, Introducing Brokers (IBs) can be covered by the FCM or register independently. As below, it is likely that IBs will all soon be required to register.

Times have changed! In 2008 and 2009 the regulatory agencies in the United States have quickly evolved from a Casper Milquetoast to Magilla Gorilla. The CFTC and NFA have acted quite proactively.

Appendix A, "How the FOREX Game Is Played," outlines many of the issues for all parties that have prompted the fast-tracking of regulation in retail FOREX.

Regulation Past

In the beginning of retail FOREX, regulations, other than fraud statutes, were essentially non-existent. This was also true of the commodity futures markets up to the mid-1970s. The regulatory path of retail FOREX is following a remarkably similar path to that of commodity futures in the 1970s and 1980s.

The Commodity Futures Trading Commission (CFTC)

In 1974 Congress created the Commodity Futures Trading Commission as the independent agency with the mandate to regulate commodity futures and options markets in the United States. The agency is chartered to protect market participants against manipulation, abusive trade practices, and fraud.

Through effective oversight and regulation the CFTC enables the markets to better serve their important function in the nation's economy, providing a mechanism for price discovery and a means of offsetting price risk. The CFTC also seeks to protect customers by requiring: (1) that registrants disclose market risks and past performance to prospective customers (in the case of money managers and advisors); (2) that customer funds be kept in accounts separate ("segregated funds") from their own use; and (3) that customer accounts be adjusted to reflect the current market value of their investments at the close of each trading day ("clearing"). Futures accounts are technically safer than securities accounts because brokers must show a zero-zero balance sheet at the end of each trading session.

TIP: The regulatory path of retail FOREX is closely following the path of commodity futures in the 1970s and 1980s—only the pace now has quickened.

National Futures Association

The CFTC was originally created under so-called Sunshine Laws, meaning that its continued existence would be evaluated vis-à-vis its effectiveness. As the futures industry exploded in the late 1970s, not only was its charter renewed but a separate quasi-private self-regulatory agency was created to implement the laws, rules, and regulations. Thus in 1982 was born the National Futures Association (NFA). The NFA is the CFTC's face to the public and directs the regulatory and registration actions of the CFTC into the marketplace.

The NFA stipulates that members cannot transact business with nonmembers. So, for example, if your FOREX broker-dealer is an NFA member, it is not allowed to do business with nonmember money managers (Commodity Trading Advisors or CTAs).

Commodity Futures Modernization Act of 2000

This was the first act by the CFTC pertaining to the then-emerging retail FOREX business. Beginning in the 1980s cross-border capital movements accelerated with the advent of computers, technology, and the Internet—extending market continuum through Asian, European, and American time zones. Transactions in foreign exchange rocketed from about $70 billion a day in the 1980s to more than $2 trillion a day two decades later.

The Patriot Act

A principal feature of the ubiquitous Patriot Act is the desire to limit money laundering so that large transactions might be followed, theoretically ensuring that funds are not headed to finance terrorist activities. It is obvious that such tracking will affect foreign exchange markets. You see reference to the Patriot Act on broker forms when you open an account.

The CFTC Reauthorization Act of 2005

The most critical legislation of interest to U.S. traders is the CFTC Reauthorization Act of 2005; it specifically addresses retail FOREX. The primary thrust of the Reauthorization Act and legislation currently pending is to require retail brokers to meet minimum capital requirements. The new minimum is $20,000,000—up from $5,000,000 just three years ago and no minimum 10 years back. A number of mergers have already taken place. The NFA is also enacting a Know Thy Customer rule for FCMs. This will require them to undertake a more proactive due diligence of prospective clients and their suitability for currency trading. One effect of this will probably be to eliminate account-funding options by PayPal and other electronic transfers except for bank wires.

Traders may wish to periodically check FOREX broker-dealer financials here: www.cftc.gov.

Retail FOREX seems to be following a path parallel to retail futures in the 1970s and 1980s. As predicted in the second edition, Introducing Brokers (IBs) are now required to register and meet minimal capital requirements. I expect mergers between the majors within the next several years as competition, smaller profit margins, and lower growth rates loom.

Similar slow-but-sure regulation of retail FOREX is occurring in other countries. Brokers not domiciled in the United States also should register with the NFA if they desire to prospect and accept accounts from U.S. citizens.

The Financial Markets Association (FMA) has suggested international foreign exchange regulatory standards. FMA's model code currently has regulatory standing in Australia, Austria, Canada, Cyprus, Hong Kong, Malaysia, Malta, Mauritius, the Philippines, Slovenia, and Switzerland.

Countries with specific agencies regulating FOREX: United Kingdom—Financial Services Authority (FSA); Australia—Australian Securities and Investment Commission (ASIC); Switzerland—requires registration as a Financial Intermediary under Swiss Federal Law; Canada—Investment Canada, Federal Competition Bureau.

Regulation Past of the retail FOREX industry could be considered mild and somewhat tentative. But in early 2008 the NFA and the CFTC began to put some teeth into their regulatory oversight with major new compliance rules.

Regulation Present

Government regulation often is an all-or-nothing effort. For the first 10 years of retail FOREX the CFTC and NFA did little. To be sure, part of the reason was that it took time to get a handle on this loose, freewheeling, and widely disseminated business.

In 2008 and 2009 these agencies poured out new regulations at a ferocious pace—usually without requesting much in the way of feedback from market participants. When I discussed the proposed Compliance Rule 2-43 with an NFA representative at a FOREX trade show in August 2008, I was assured it would be slow in coming and there would be a substantial comment period. Not so. To some extent the economic meltdown of 2008 encouraged this fast-track mode.

The new NFA Compliance Rule 2-43 has wrought havoc on brokers as well as traders. The latest regulations concerning hedging, order placement (*First In First Out*, FIFO), and money manager registration has sent U.S.-based brokers scurrying to find overseas affiliates that are beyond the reach of the NFA and CFTC. One incentive for brokers: Traders do not like the new regulations either and many are moving their accounts and their money overseas. To that extent, the regulation's purpose of protecting U.S. citizens who trade FOREX may be partially counterproductive.

In late 2009 brokers found that they had to quickly make major changes to their trading platforms to accommodate the new FIFO and hedging regulations. The sense in the industry was that regulations were made without regard to what was involved in making them work. For example, one of the major independent trading platforms planning to release an updated version in the summer of 2009 was sent "back to the drawing board" at the last minute to implement the necessary code into their software. The situation for most of the summer and fall of 2009 could only be considered as chaotic.

The government often carries a hatchet and meat cleaver when a scalpel and carving knife would have done the job. Nonetheless, those who complain that regulations are typically reactive cannot fault the proactive work of these agencies recently.

TIP: No government, no agency, no regulation can prevent fraud completely. The best protection for traders is knowledge, education, and a firm understanding of what caveat emptor means and implies.

NFA Compliance Rule 2-43

The regulation that has dropped on the industry like a bomb is NFA Compliance Rule 2-43. Although 2-43 addresses many issues, the two most important are Anti-Hedging and FIFO.

Anti-Hedging Anti-hedging has been the most controversial new regulation. It has, in many ways, turned the retail FOREX business on its head—at least for the moment. Traders are prohibited from entering and brokers are prohibited from accepting orders that would place a trader on both sides (buy and sell) of any currency pair. Traders use speculative hedging for a wide range of trading and money management functions, including the popular news trading technique and multiple time-frame systems.

FIFO (First In First Out) Related to anti-hedging, FIFO changes the manner in which open orders are ledgered and closed. Orders entered first must be closed first. Again, this substantially upsets the applecart for many traders, especially those who are short-term traders, those who tier in positions, and those who use automated trading systems.

Price Adjustments Brokers are prohibited from canceling customer orders except under certain conditions. Price adjustments to filled orders may only be made for specific, limited reasons. This part of Rule 2-43, while unpopular with brokers, is generally accepted as positive by traders.

Capital Requirements for Retail FOREX Broker-Dealers Broker-dealers in retail FOREX must meet higher and higher capital requirements. As predicted in the first edition and began in the second edition, mergers are now common in retail FOREX. Small firms, both good ones and bad ones, are getting shut out.

The CFTC Reauthorization Act of 2008 increases the adjusted net capital requirement for certain *counterparty* FCMs to $20 million. This requirement was phased in; it is a quantum leap from the previous $5 million. A counterparty FCM is generally considered to be a market maker—a broker-dealer who trades as counterparty to their customers. The author predicts the entire counterparty paradigm will be revisited by the CFTC and NFA soon. *Introducing Brokers* (IB) who coattail on an FCMs capital base are now also required to meet minimal capital requirements of their own.

Recently, a small broker-dealer with good customer support was shut out by this regulation and, as I write, is looking for a new FCM sponsor. I can hear the conversation with a prospective FCM's CEO: "Sir, we offer our customers terrific customer service. It is the touchstone of our business model." "Go away, kid." Regulations often have unintended consequences.

Registration of FOREX Money Managers The NFA has proposed to the CFTC that every FOREX money manager must register as a Commodity Trading Advisor (CTA) in the same manner and with the same process as those who manage money in commodity futures.

It is assumed the CFTC will oblige, but final regulations, at the time of this writing, have not been passed or implemented. Nonetheless, most retail FOREX broker-dealers are now requiring that money managers who work with their customers must go ahead and register as a CTA. It is possible that FOREX money managers who have been in business for a certain number of years might be grandfathered—but no one is counting on this. It is likely that exemptions from registration similar to those for commodity futures CTAs will stand. The most important of those are: (1) your primary business is not that of a CTA and you do not hold yourself out to the public as a CTA, and (2) you manage fewer than 15 accounts.

To provide for the new registration requirements a separate test has been created, the Series 34 examination. FOREX CTAs will be required to pass the Commodity Futures Series 3 examination as a prerequisite. Again, at the time of this writing, final rules have not been released.

As mentioned earlier, many brokers—including the majors—are affiliating with overseas broker-dealers who are not obligated to comply with NFA and CFTC regulations. One broker told me that two of their best money managers will leave if they are required to register as a CTA. File this one also in the unintended consequences folder. As a former CTA I can attest that regulation is an expensive proposition. If you manage $20 million per year, $100,000 to meet all the requirements to sustain an audit is doable. If you manage $2 million, it makes no sense at all.

TIP: This bears some watching because it involves a small loophole through which a few brokers are driving large trucks. One suspects that the CFTC and NFA will become interested soon.

Another area continuing to receive regulatory attention is graciously called a "harmonization issue" by the industry.

Suitability/Know-Your-Customer Requirements This is NFA Compliance Rule 2-30. This basically requires broker-dealers to determine suitability to trade retail FOREX on a customer-by-customer basis, not, as in the old days, with a simple acknowledgment on the account form, "You understand the risk of FOREX trading." But there is still little specific guidance and enforcement by the NFA. One may expect that to change soon.

Some brokers still allow a customer to deposit and withdraw funds with services such as PayPal and eGold. One strongly suspects Know-Thy-Customer will bring those methods to a close in the not-too-distant future. FOREX brokers now typically do withdrawals in kind: If you made a wire deposit, your withdrawal will be sent by wire.

Margin Requirements In late 2009 the NFA also mandated minimum margin requirements for retail FOREX positions: 1 percent for any pair containing one or both of what the NFA labels as "majors"—USD, GBP, CHF, CAD, JPY, EUR, AUD, NZD, SOK, NOK, DKK. All others now require a 4 percent margin. This means that for U.S. traders the maximum leverage is 100:1 and 25:1, respectively.

Many U.S. broker-dealers have already established overseas offices to stem the tide of customers leaving in droves because of Rule 2-43 and the new margin requirements. Few will want to trade exotic currency pairs at 25:1 leverage.

Foreign Regulation

Many foreign countries also regulate retail FOREX, though typically not at the level of the NFA and CFTC in the United States. The United Kingdom's Financial Services Authority (FSA) bears the most similarity to the NFA and CFTC.

Regulation Future

Only time will tell if the current pace of regulation will continue, or if it will slow down, allowing participants to digest what they currently have on their plate. But, clearly, the regulatory cat is out of the bag in retail FOREX. Regulation Future bears watching by all players in the retail FOREX space. As we go to press there are rumors that some factions in the CFTC want to force retail FOREX into an exchange environment similar to commodity futures. As mentioned above, the market-making paradigm may be on the chopping block soon. We shall see.

Summary

The FOREX forums are a good place to find updated regulatory information as well as traders' (and sometimes brokers') take on them. Both the CFTC web site, (www.cftc.gov) and the NFA web site (www.nfa.futures.org) are worth a peek on a monthly basis. For those who wish to dig deeper, I recommend www.forexlawblog.com. As the Madoff case demonstrates, regulations sometimes miss the forest for the trees; security is truly in your hands and knowledge is still king.

Fraud is always fraud, irrespective of specific industry regulations. I recommend FOREX traders keep copies of *everything* as well as screenshots of relevant web pages and communication logs.

Chapter 5

The FOREX Lexicon

A s in any worthwhile endeavor, each industry tends to create its own unique terminology. The FOREX market is no different. You, the novice trader, must thoroughly comprehend certain terms before making your first trade. As your eighth-grade English teacher taught you in vocabulary class—to use them is to know them.

Currency Pairs

Every FOREX trade involves the simultaneous buying of one currency and the selling of another currency. These two currencies are always referred to as the *currency pair* in a trade.

Major and Minor Currencies

The seven most frequently traded currencies (USD, EUR, JPY, GBP, CHF, CAD, and AUD) are called the *major currencies*. All other currencies are referred to as minor currencies. The most frequently traded minors are the New Zealand Dollar (NZD), the South African Rand (ZAR), and the Singapore Dollar (SGD). After that, the frequency is difficult to ascertain because of perpetually changing trade agreements in the international arena.

Cross Currency

A *cross currency* is any pair in which neither currency is the U.S. Dollar. These pairs may exhibit erratic price behavior since the trader has, in effect, initiated two USD trades. For example, initiating a long (buy) EUR/GBP trade is equivalent to buying a EUR/USD currency pair and selling a GBP/USD. Cross currency pairs frequently carry a higher transaction cost. The three most frequently traded cross rates are EUR/JPY, GBP/EUR, and GBP/JPY.

Exotic Currency

An *exotic* is a currency pair in which one currency is the USD and the other is a currency from a smaller country such as the Polish Zloty. There are approximately 25 exotics that can be traded by the retail FOREX participant. Liquidity—the ability to buy and sell without substantial *pip* spread increases; a willing buyer or seller is always available at or near the last price—is not good. Whereas a EUR/USD pair may be traded at two pips at almost any time, the EURTRY may balloon to 30 pips or more during the Asian session.

Base Currency

The *base currency* is the first currency in any currency pair. It shows how much the base currency is worth as measured against the second currency. For example, if the USD/CHF rate equals 1.6215, then one USD is worth CHF 1.6215. In the FOREX markets, the U.S. Dollar is normally considered the base currency for quotes, meaning that quotes are expressed as a unit of $1 USD per the other currency quoted in the pair. The exceptions are: the British Pound, the Euro, and the Australian Dollar. If you go long the EUR/USD, you are buying the EUR.

Quote Currency

The *quote currency* is the second currency in any currency pair. This is frequently called the pip currency and any unrealized profit or loss is expressed in this currency. If you go short the EUR/USD, you are buying the USD.

Pips

A *pip* is the smallest unit of price for any foreign currency. Nearly all currency pairs consist of five significant digits and most pairs have the decimal point immediately after the first digit, that is, EUR/USD equals 1.2812. In this instance, a single pip equals the smallest change in the fourth decimal place, that is, 0.0001. Therefore, if the quote currency in any pair is USD, then one pip always equals $\frac{1}{100}$ of a cent.

One notable exception is the USD/JPY pair where a pip equals $0.01 (one U.S. Dollar equals approximately 107.19 Japanese Yen). Pips are sometimes called *points*.

Ticks

Just as a pip is the smallest price movement (the y-axis), a *tick* is the smallest interval of time (the x-axis) that occurs between two trades. When trading the most active currency pairs (such as EUR/USD or USD/JPY) during peak trading periods, multiple ticks may (and will) occur within the span of one second. When trading a low-activity minor cross pair (such as the Mexican Peso and the Singapore Dollar), a tick may only occur once every two or three hours.

Ticks, therefore, do not occur at uniform intervals of time. Fortunately, most historical data vendors will group sequences of streaming data and calculate the open, high, low, and close over regular time intervals (1-minute, 5-minute, 30-minute, 1-hour, daily, and so forth). See Figure 5.1.

Pips are a function of price; ticks are a function of time. Any location on a chart is effectively a Cartesian coordinate of Price, read vertically from bottom to top and Time, read horizontally from left to right.

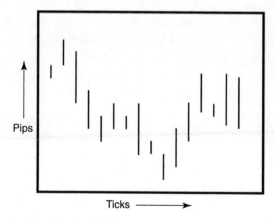

FIGURE 5.1 Pip-Tick Relationship

Margin

When an investor opens a new *margin* account with a FOREX broker, he or she must deposit a minimum amount of monies with that broker. This minimum varies from broker to broker and can be as low as $100 to as high as $100,000.

Each time the trader executes a new trade, a certain percentage of the account balance in the margin account will be earmarked as the initial margin requirement for the new trade based on the underlying currency pair, its current price, and the number of units traded (called a *lot*). The lot size always refers to the base currency. An even lot is usually a quantity of 100,000 units, but most brokers permit investors to trade in odd lots (fractions of 100,000 units). A mini-lot is 10,000 units and a micro-lot is generally considered to be 1,000 units. A standard lot is 100,000 and a bank lot is 250,000 units.

For U.S. retail FOREX traders the minimum margin has been set by the NFA to 1 percent (100:1 leverage) for major currency pairs and 4 percent (25:1 leverage) for exotics.

Margin Calls

Nearly all FOREX brokers monitor your account balance continuously. If your balance falls below 4 percent of the open margin requirement, they will issue the first margin call warning, usually by an online pop-up message on the screen and/or an e-mail notification. If your account balance drops below 3 percent of the margin requirement for your open positions, they will issue a second margin warning. At 2 percent, they will liquidate all your open trades and notify you of your current account balance. These percentages may vary from broker to broker. You may not even be able to execute a trade that exceeds certain capital and risk parameters. Brokers today are able to closely watch customer accounts to prevent them from getting to the point of requiring a margin call. You can be assured that as a new customer your account will be initially monitored with higher precision until the broker has a sense of how you trade.

Leverage

Leverage is the ratio of the amount used in a transaction to the required security deposit (margin). It is the ability to control large dollar amounts of a security with a comparatively small amount of capital. Leveraging varies dramatically with different brokers, ranging from 10:1 to 400:1. Leverage is frequently referred to as gearing. Typical ranges for trading are 50:1 to 100:1. The formula for calculating leverage is:

$$\text{Leverage} = 100/\text{Margin Percent}$$

The most typical leverage used by traders in retail FOREX is 50:1 to 100:1. Some brokers offer up to 400:1. A new trader should start with very low leverage, perhaps 20:1 and certainly no higher than 50:1.

To some extent FOREX traders set their own leverage insofar as they determine the lot size to trade. But your broker-dealer will set a maximum.

Bid Price

The bid is the price at which the market is prepared to buy a specific currency pair in the FOREX market. At this price, the trader can sell the base currency. It is shown on the left side of the quotation. For example, in the quote USD/CHF 1.4527/32, the bid price is 1.4527, meaning that you can sell one U.S. Dollar for 1.4527 Swiss Francs.

Ask Price

The ask is the price at which the market is prepared to sell a specific currency pair in the FOREX market. At this price, the trader can buy the base currency. It is shown on the right side of the quotation. For example, in the quote USD/CHF 1.4527/32, the ask price is 1.4532, meaning that you can buy one U.S. Dollar for 1.4532 Swiss Francs. The ask price is also called the offer price.

Bid-Ask Spread

The spread is the difference between the bid and ask price. The "big figure quote" is the dealer expression referring to the first few digits of an exchange rate. These digits are often omitted in dealer quotes. For example, a USD/JPY rate might be 117.30/117.35, but would be quoted verbally without the first three digits as "30/35." You *buy the ask* and *sell the bid*.

TIP: Be sure you know to what accuracy your broker provides currency quotes. Many now quote in fractional (⅒) pips. This may be referred to as "Four Digit Pricing" and "Five Digit Pricing."

TABLE 5.1 Examples of Quote Convention	
EUR/USD	1.2604/07
GBP/USD	1.5089/94
CHF/JPY	84.40/45

Quote Convention

Exchange rates in the FOREX market are expressed using the following format:

Base Currency/Quote Currency   Bid/Ask

Examples can be found in Table 5.1.

Normally only the final two digits of the bid price are shown. If the ask price is more than 100 pips above the bid price, then three digits will be displayed to the right of the slash mark (that is, EUR/CZK 32.5420/780). This only occurs when the quote currency is a weak monetary unit.

Market Maker and ECN

Retail brokers are of two types, although some gray areas, terms such as *liquidity provider* and *No Dealing Desk* (NDD), have appeared recently.

A *market maker* is the counterparty to each transaction. In effect, they are acting as their own mini-exchange. At one end market makers are tapped into the Interbank market—often indirectly—and at the other end are the retail customers. What goes on in-between could be a book unto itself.

An *Electronic Communications Network* (ECN) broker is simply a matchmaker. They also have liquidity providers at one end—usually banks, sometimes other ECNs—and clients at the other. An ECN simply matches orders.

Transaction Cost

The critical characteristic of the bid-ask spread is that it is also the *transaction cost* for a round-turn trade. Round-turn means both a buy (or sell) trade and an offsetting sell (or buy) trade of the same size in the same currency pair. In the case of the EUR/USD rate as seen earlier in Table 5.1, the transaction cost is three pips. The formula for calculating the transaction cost is:

Transaction Cost = Ask Price − Bid Price

In FOREX you buy the ask and sell the bid. You offset a trade by closing the trade, not executing the opposite action—buy if you are short, sell if you are long.

Market-maker brokers add their profit into the spread. Electronic Communication Network brokers (ECNs) charge a small commission per lot.

Rollover

Rollover is the process where the settlement of an open trade is rolled forward to another value date. The cost of this process is based on the interest rate differential of the two currencies. Rollover cost is not significant for the short-term trader but impacts cost for the long-term trader who might hold a position for several days. If you intend to do long-term trading, be sure to shop rollover costs among several broker-dealers.

Summary

Trading currencies on margin lets you increase your buying power. If you have $2,000 cash in a margin account that allows 100:1 leverage, you could purchase up to $200,000 worth of currency because you only have to post 1 percent of the purchase price as collateral. Another way of saying this is that you have $200,000 in buying power.

With more buying power, you can increase your total return on investment with less cash outlay. To be sure, trading on margin magnifies your profits *and* your losses.

A detailed description on how to calculate profit and loss of leveraged trades occurs in Appendix G, "FOREX Calculation Scenarios."

An extensive Glossary of FOREX terms is provided at the end of this book.

Trading Tables

OREX is truly a numbers game with pips, dollars, lot size, stop-loss, take-profit, leverage, margin, profit and loss, transaction costs, and more to know. Separately they are not difficult to understand but the interrelationships involving various mathematical formulas, ratios, decimals, and fractions can be difficult to master. For example, the pip amount of your take-profit divided by the pip amount of your stop-loss is the profit-to-loss ratio. It, in turn, is closely related to the ratio of winners to losers over a fixed number of trades. The new trader has a big plate, as is, even before considering these myriad mathematical mechanizations.

All of the mechanics are important and worth knowing. But I have found over years of mentoring new traders that they are best learned by practice. Your broker's trading platform and/or tools on their web site should allow you to calculate most of these values. Simply using your demo account diligently can, over time, make most of these clear to you. As you calculate the values make an effort to see the relationship between each of the numbers, essentially reverse-engineering them.

TIP: All calculations involve two or more factors. Change only one of them at a time, up and down, and see how they affect the others. Excellent calculation tools are available on www.goforex.net, www.forexcalc.com, and www.oanda.com.

For those who have a penchant for math, I have included most of the key calculations with examples in Appendix G. For those who do not, I offer Trading Tables. These are the key calculations and ratios you should know for getting started. Most of them are related to converting pips to dollars, profit and loss, and money management. In Chapter 16, "Money Management Simplified," you learn how to put these tables to good use. You can use these computer-side as you trade. All of them are available for download from the Getting Started section of www.goodmanworks.com.

For the Trading Tables, pip values have been rounded off slightly in some cases to make them easier for the student to use.

Pips

A *pip* is the smallest price increment that any currency pair can move in either direction. In the FOREX markets, profits are calculated in terms of pips first, then dollars second. See Tables 6.1 and 6.2. The conversion of pips to dollars may be considered the base FOREX calculation. Calculate that against your lot size and you are halfway home already.

Approximate USD values for a one-pip move per contract in the major currency pairs are shown in Table 6.2, per 100,000 units of the base currency.

TIP: On a typical day, actively traded currency pairs like EUR/USD and USD/JPY may fluctuate 100 pips or more. Table 6.2 is based on a margin requirement of 100 percent (leverage = 1:1). To calculate actual profit (or loss)

TABLE 6.1 Single Pip Values	
USD = Quote Currency	
EUR/USD	.0001 USD
GBP/USD	.0001 USD
AUD/USD	.0001 USD
USD = Base Currency	
USD/JPY	.01 JPY
USD/CHF	.0001 CHF
USD/CAD	.0001 CAD
Non-USD Cross Rates	
EUR/JPY	.01 JPY
EUR/CHF	.0001 CHF
EUR/GBP	.0001 GBP
GBP/JPY	.01 JPY
GBP/CHF	.0001 CHF
CHF/JPY	.01 JPY

TABLE 6.2 Full Lot Pip Values	
Currencies	*1 Pip Value per Full Lot (100,000 units)*
EUR/USD	EUR 100,000 × .0001 = USD 10.00
GBP/USD	GBP 100,000 × .0001 = USD 10.00
AUD/USD	AUD 100,000 × .0001 = USD 10.00
USD/JPY	USD 100,000 × .01 = JPY 1,000 / USDJPY spot (105.50) = USD 9.47
USD/CHF	USD 100,000 × .0001 = CHF 10.00 / USDCHF spot (1.2335) = USD 8.11
USD/CAD	USD 100,000 × .0001 = CAD 10.00 / USDCAD spot (1.3148) = USD 7.61
EUR/JPY	EUR 100,000 × .01 = JPY 1,000 / USDJPY spot (105.50) = USD 9.47
EUR/CHF	EUR 100,000 × .0001 = CHF 10.00 / USDCHF spot (1.2335) = USD 8.11
EUR/GBP	EUR 100,000 × .0001 = CHF 10.00 × GBPUSD spot (1.8890) = USD 5.2
GBP/JPY	GBP 100,000 × .01 = JPY 1,000 / USDJPY spot (105.50) = USD 9.47
GBP/CHF	GBP 100,000 × .0001 = CHF 10.00 / USDCHF spot (1.2335) = USD 8.11
CHF/JPY	CHF 100,000 × .01 = JPY 1,000 / USDJPY spot (105.50) = USD 9.47

in leveraged positions, multiply the pip value per 100k times the leverage ratio (margin percentage divided by 100).

Note that the EUR/GBP cross rate pair in Table 6.2 uses multiplication with the USD spot price instead of division. This is because the USD is the quote (second) currency in the spot conversion pair.

Profit and Loss

Table 6.3 allows you to see your profit or loss in dollars for various pip amounts and lot sizes. A micro-lot is 1,000 (1k) Units; a mini-lot is 10,000 (10k) Units; a standard lot is 100,000 (100k) Units; a bank lot is 250,000 (250k) Units. Some of these have been rounded off to make easier reading; they are close enough to serve the purpose for a quick in-trade status check.

Margin

Margin-per-trade is the amount of dollars you must put into play to control a larger amount of currency pair. *Margin* is a bit of a misnomer in FOREX. If you open a trade on a 100,000 lot of EURUSD and the broker requires $2,000 to accept the trade, your margin is $2,000. Brokers do set maximum margins. If you have multiple open positions your margin is the sum total of all of them; this is your aggregate margin. See Table 6.4.

TABLE 6.3 Profit and Loss

PROFIT AND LOSS IN DOLLARS
Lot Size

Pips	1,000	10,000	100,000	250,000
1	0.10	1	10	25
2	0.20	2	20	50
3	0.30	3	30	75
4	0.40	4	40	100
5	0.50	5	50	125
6	0.60	6	60	150
7	0.70	7	70	175
8	0.80	8	80	200
9	0.90	9	90	225
10	1.00	10	100	250
15	1.50	15	150	375
20	2.00	20	200	500
25	2.50	25	250	625
30	3.00	30	300	750
35	3.50	35	350	875
40	4.00	40	400	1000
45	4.50	45	450	1125
50	5.00	50	500	1250
75	7.50	75	750	1875
100	10.00	100	1000	2500
125	12.50	125	1250	3125
150	15.00	150	1500	3750
175	17.50	175	1750	4375
200	20.00	200	2000	5000
225	22.50	225	2250	5625
250	25.00	250	2500	6250
300	30.00	300	3000	7500
400	40.00	400	4000	10000
500	50.00	500	5000	12500

TABLE 6.4 Margins

MARGIN
Value of Trade

Leverage	$1,000	$2,500	$5,000	$10,000	$25,000	$50,000	$100,000	$250,000	$500,000	$1,000,000
10:1	100	250	500	1000	2500	5000	10000	25000	50000	100000
20:1	50	125	250	500	1250	2500	5000	12500	25000	50000
30:1	33	83	167	333	833	1667	3333	8333	16667	33333
40:1	25	63	125	250	625	1250	2500	6250	12500	25000
50:1	20	50	100	200	500	1000	2000	5000	10000	20000
60:1	17	42	83	167	416	833	1667	4167	8333	16667
70:1	14	36	63	143	357	714	1429	3571	7143	14286
80:1	13	31	71	125	313	625	1250	3125	6250	12500
90:1	11	28	63	111	278	556	1111	2778	5556	11111
100:1	10	25	50	100	250	500	1000	2500	5000	10000
150:1	7	17	33	67	167	333	667	1667	3333	6667
200:1	5	13	25	50	125	250	500	1250	2500	5000
250:1	4	10	20	40	100	200	400	1000	2000	4000
300:1	3	8	17	33	83	167	333	833	1667	3333
400:1	3	6	12	24	63	125	250	625	1250	2500

	TABLE 6.5 Leverage						
	LEVERAGE						
	Amount Traded						
Margin Required	5000	10000	25000	50000	100000	250000	500000
1000	5:1	10:1	25:1	50:1	100:1	250:1	500:1
2000	2.5:1	5:1	12.5:1	25:1	50:1	125:1	250:1
3000	1.66:1	3:1	8:1	17:1	33:1	83:1	167:1
4000	1.25:1	2.5:1	6:1	12.5:1	25:1	63:1	125:1
5000	1:1	2:1	5:1	10:1	20:1	50:1	100:1
25000	1:5	1:2.5	1:1	2:1	4:1	10:1	20:1
50000	1:10	1:5	1:2	1:1	2:1	5:1	10:1
100000	1:20	1:10	1:4	1:2	1:1	2.5:1	5:1
250000	1:50	1:20	1:10	1:5	1:2.5	1:1	2:1

Leverage

Leverage is margin-per-trade quoted as a ratio. In the above example, leverage is 50:1 (100,000/2,000). The higher the ratio, the higher your profit (or loss) potential.

As you can see in Table 6.3, on a 100,000 lot a pip is worth $10. With leverage at 50:1 if prices go for (or against) you by 200 pips, you have made (or lost) your entire margin of $2,000, a 100 percent profit (or loss). See Table 6.5 for profit or loss in dollars of margin against different leverage ratios.

The Bid-Ask Spread

FOREX prices are always quoted in the form of Bid-Ask-Last Trade. If you are a potential buyer, the Ask is the price someone will sell to you. If you are a potential seller, the Bid is what someone is willing to buy from you. You Buy the Ask and Sell the Bid in FOREX.

Market-maker brokers add their transaction costs to this bid-ask spread. By knowing how many pips are in the spread you are able to calculate your costs for the trade, exclusive of any other factors such as slippage, commissions, or rollover costs. Typically only ECNs charge commissions and, therefore, their bid-ask spreads are tighter. Bid-ask spreads typically range from 0 pips to 10 pips in most pairs but can balloon much higher during fast markets and slow markets,

	TABLE 6.6 The Bid-Ask Spread									
	PIP SPREAD COSTS IN DOLLARS									
	Lot Size									
Pips	*1000*	*2500*	*5000*	*10000*	*20000*	*25000*	*30000*	*50000*	*100000*	*250000*
1	0.10	0.25	0.50	1.00	2.00	2.50	3.00	5.00	10.00	25.00
2	0.20	0.50	1.00	2.00	4.00	5.00	6.00	10.00	20.00	50.00
3	0.30	0.75	1.50	3.00	6.00	7.50	9.00	15.00	30.00	75.00
4	0.40	1.00	2.00	4.00	8.00	10.00	12.00	20.00	40.00	100.00
5	0.50	1.25	2.50	5.00	10.00	12.50	15.00	25.00	50.00	125.00
6	0.60	1.50	3.00	6.00	12.00	15.00	18.00	30.00	60.00	150.00
7	0.70	1.75	3.50	7.00	14.00	17.50	21.00	35.00	70.00	175.00
8	0.80	2.00	4.00	8.00	16.00	20.00	24.00	40.00	80.00	200.00
9	0.90	2.25	4.50	9.00	18.00	22.50	27.00	45.00	90.00	225.00
10	1.00	2.50	5.00	10.00	20.00	25.00	30.00	50.00	100.00	250.00
12	1.20	2.40	4.80	9.60	19.20	30.00	36.00	60.00	120.00	300.00
15	1.50	3.75	7.50	15.00	30.00	37.50	45.00	75.00	150.00	375.00
18	1.80	3.60	7.20	14.40	28.80	45.00	54.00	90.00	180.00	475.00
20	2.00	5.00	10.00	20.00	40.00	50.00	60.00	100.00	200.00	500.00
25	2.50	6.25	12.50	25.00	50.00	60.00	75.00	125.00	250.00	625.00

as well as before, during, and after news releases. The information in Table 6.6 is given for the purpose of calculating the dollar value of the bid-ask spread and, if you trade with a market maker, the majority of your cost to trade that currency pair.

Profit Threshold

This is a little more complex, but important for money management over the longer term.

When you enter a trade you will also want to enter a stop-loss and a take-profit order. Almost all traders seek a ratio higher than 1:1 between these two, with take-profit as the larger number for a profit/loss ratio. A 3:1 ratio means you risk one unit to make three units. For example, if your stop-loss (S/L) is 50 pips, your take profit (T/P) is 150 pips. Table 6.7 shows the basic Profit-Loss ratios for T/P and S/L pip values. Ninety percent of profit-loss ratios fall in the shaded area.

TABLE 6.7	Profit-to-Loses Ratios					
	Profit-to-Loss Ratios					
P/L Ratio	*Profit/Loss (Pips or Dollars)*					
1:3	10/30	25/75	50/150	75/225	100/300	200/600
1:2	10/20	25/50	50/100	75/150	100/200	200/400
1:1	10/10	25/25	50/50	75/75	100/200	200/200
2:1	10/5	25/12	50/25	75/37	100/50	200/100
3:1	10/3	25/8	50/17	75/25	100/33	200/67
4:1	10/3	25/6	50/13	75/19	100/25	200/50
5:1	10/2	25/5	50/10	75/15	100/20	200/40

Once you make 10 trades you will know how many were winners and how many were losers. Over the long haul it is difficult to sustain more than 60 percent winners. Most traders are happy to get 40 percent winners. This can also be quoted as a ratio of winners/losers. For example, if out of 10 trades you have five winners and five losers, the ratio is 1:1. This is a relatively high ratio for winners/losers but relatively low for profit/loss. Table 6.8 shows the basic Winners-Losers ratios.

As you can intuitively see, the two are inversely correlated. To achieve a profit in the long term, the higher the profit/loss ratio, the lower the

TABLE 6.8	Winners-to-Losers Ratios	
WINNERS-TO-LOSERS RATIOS		
Winners	*Losers*	*Ratio*
0	10	TRY DOUBLE EXEMPT MUNICIPAL BONDS
1	9	1:9
2	8	1:4
3	7	1:2.3
4	6	1:1.5
5	5	1:1
6	4	1:5:1
7	3	2.3:1
8	2	4:1
9	1	9:1
10	0	LOOK OUT, WARREN BUFFETT!

	TABLE 6.9 Profit Threshold						
	PROFIT THRESHOLD						
			W/L Ratio				
P/L Ratio	5:1	4:1	3:1	2:1	1:1	1:2	1:3
1:2	+	+	+	=	−	−	−
1:1	+	+	+	+	=	−	−
2:1	+	+	+	+	+	=	−
3:1	+	+	+	+	+	+	=
4:1	+	+	+	+	+	+	+
5:1	+	+	+	+	+	+	+

winner/loser ratio can be. Conversely, the lower the profit/loss ratio, the higher the winner/loser ratio must be to keep you in the black.

TIP: The higher your winners-to-losers ratio is, the lower your profit-loss ratio can be to meet the Profit Threshold. Conversely, the higher your profit-loss ratio, the lower your winners-to-losers ratio can be to meet the Profit Threshold. Short-term traders—guerillas and scalpers—typically have high winners-to-losers ratios, but low profit-to-loss ratios. Long-term traders—day traders and position traders—typically have high profit-to-loss ratios, but low winners-to-losers ratios. There is more than one way to skin the FOREX cat.

An example of this: If I hit three winners out of every 10 trades (seven losers) and achieve a 3:1 profit-to-loss ratio of $300/$100, I lost $700 but made $900 so I am okay. Table 6.9 shows the intersections of these two ratios as Positive, Negative, or Neutral (Profit Threshold). Chapter 16, "Money Management Simplified," discusses the profit threshold in relation to the Campaign Trading Method.

TIP: Depending on your own selected T/P-S/L (Profit-Loss Ratio) you must know the Profit Threshold Winners-to-Losers Ratio. Where does the black end, the red begin? You do not want to cross that line; if possible, not even come close to it.

The light gray areas are losing and danger-zone combinations. The dark gray area of both high profit-to-loss and high winners-to-losers is difficult to maintain for any significant number of trades. Going there typically means the trader is using high leverage, investing most of his or her margin, and trading frequently. Such behavior is not sustainable over long periods of time.

For each trade you enter you must consider three factors: Leverage, Account Traded, and Required Margin. The information in Table 6.10 is also in Tables 6.7, 6.8, and 6.9 but is presented here for ready reference.

TABLE 6.10 Leverage, Lot Size, Margin		
Leverage, Lot Size, Margin		
Leverage	Lot Size	Margin
1:1	1000	1000
10:1	1000	100
20:1	1000	50
50:1	1000	20
100:1	1000	10
200:1	1000	5
300:1	1000	3.33
400:1	1000	2.5
1:1	10000	10000
10:1	10000	1000
20:1	10000	500
50:1	10000	200
100:1	10000	100
200:1	10000	50
300:1	10000	33.33
400:1	10000	25
1:1	100000	100000
10:1	100000	10000
20:1	100000	5000
50:1	100000	2000
100:1	100000	1000
200:1	100000	500
300:1	100000	333.33
400:1	100000	250

For Futures Traders

Futures traders tend to think in dollars versus a commodity asset (silver, soybeans, pork bellies, etc.). The switch to co-relational values with ratios—one currency against another—can be a bit trying at first. The trick is to practice calculating profit and loss for fictitious trades. Again, use any of the online calculators available for practice. Change each parameter in turn and observe how it alters the others as well as the outcome. It may help to think of a currency pair as a spread.

Summary

Don't panic! It is copasetic to learn the various numeric values, calculations, and formulas along the way. Practice on your demo account is the way to go for most new traders. The most critical at the outset are Profit-and-Loss and Profit Threshold.

Chapter 16, "Money Management Simplified," shows how to put these many factors together into a sustainable plan of action.

But the math is not nearly as complex as it may appear at first. In fact I can reduce it all to the following cheat sheet. Tables 6.1 through 6.10 are available for download from the Getting Started section of www.goodmanworks.com.

Basic FOREX Calculations

Price Change = Exit Price − Entry Price
Leverage = 100 / Margin Percent
Margin Percent = 100 / Leverage
Profit in Pips = Price Change × Pip Factor

If the Quote Currency in a trade = USD, then

Profit in USD = Price Change × Units Traded

If the Base Currency in a trade = USD, then

Profit in USD = Price Change × Units Traded/Exit Price

When the profit for non-USD cross rates is being calculated, the following applies: The conversion rate is the currency pair with the USD and the quote currency of the cross rate pair.

If the base currency of the conversion rate = USD, then

Profit in USD = Price Change × Units Traded/Conversion Rate

If the quote currency of the conversion rate = USD, then

Profit in USD = Price Change × Units Traded × Conversion Rate

You can now calculate profit and loss during open positions.

Learning these basic calculations will endow you with confidence, something you will need in substantial measure to succeed as a currency trader. But take your time; full understanding is not mission-critical at the outset. Use the Trading Tables for getting started.

Chapter

7

A Guide to FOREX Brokers

While regulation has indeed increased, it remains much less robust than it is in either the securities or commodity futures industries. FOREX has no central clearinghouse, making it a substantially different space from commodity futures or listed securities. Prospective traders need to understand the differences and ramifications when selecting a FOREX broker.

At last count I found more than 100 FOREX broker-dealers with online retail platforms. Although some of them are Introducing Brokers (IBs) for other companies, there remain many full Futures Clearing Merchants (FCM) brokers from which to choose.

One big improvement since the last edition: Several third-party trading platforms with a full complement of features are now offered by multiple brokers. Previously, moving brokers meant learning a new platform. But now, if you find a trading platform you like, you can have a wide selection of brokers to choose for your trading activities. The most popular platforms are discussed in Chapter 14, "Retail FX Platforms."

Broker-Dealer Due Diligence

Retail brokers can be divided into market makers (dealers) and ECNs (Electronic Communications Networks). ECN is the way the true Interbank market operates. ECN brokers can have from one to a dozen liquidity providers. Market makers now also speak in terms of liquidity providers to avoid the stigma of the market-maker moniker. Each approach has advantages and disadvantages. Most retailers are still market makers, but more and more are venturing into the ECN world. The Big Three (see below) now offer a market-maker venue to small traders and an ECN venue for their larger and institutional clients. Market makers are going to be better at providing liquidity in slow or fast markets; ECNs are perceived as more legitimate in not engaging in activities market makers have at least been accused of—stop harvesting, ballooning spreads, and requoting. ECN platforms are somewhat more difficult to use and require more diligence on the part of the trader.

The beginner should first determine what tools he or she will need to trade. Of course, the more you study, the more you learn and the more you want. Your needs may change. Download and conduct due diligence on *at least* five of these broker-dealers' demo platforms. Today, many brokers provide a variety of different platforms to even small traders. Use the checklist I provide to research their services in the categories noted and how they relate to your needs. Keep notes. I answer some of the questions for you; more can be found on their web sites, in their documents, and on the FOREX Internet review boards and forums.

I like to send an e-mail question or two to sales to gather information but also to see if and how they respond. Ask to be contacted back by e-mail. Most sales reps will ignore your request and call you, a few will e-mail you, and many will not contact you at all or simply add you to an automated mailing list. Six years after writing the first pages of the first edition of *Getting Started in Currency Trading*, I continue to be amazed by the inability of many broker-dealers to answer an e-mail at all—much less in a timely manner!

Increasing capital requirements for retail broker-dealers will continue to shake up the retail FOREX industry. I also expect mergers between major players to continue and even a musical chairs effect is on the horizon as smaller firms jockey for position vis-à-vis increasingly onerous regulations. The entire market-making paradigm may be in a fast fade. Most traders now have multiple brokers—typically a primary and two secondary broker-dealers. Given the flux of the industry, this seems like a good idea.

Traders have vastly different experiences with brokers. Listed below are some that I would not fund with five cents but that receive wonderful reviews from others. Certainly study the reviews—but in the end, make your own call.

Use the Broker Due Diligence form to keep track of the brokers you review and or test. The reader can download this from the Getting Started section of www.goodmanworks.com.

TIP: The author has used 14 FOREX brokers in the past 10 years of trading. No broker is even close to perfect. Dealing with a FOREX broker—no matter how good they are—is part of the business of trading. Use at least one primary broker and two back-ups. Do not let poor communication from brokers distract you. Do not be surprised when a previously great broker turns mediocre for no apparent reason. Keep your eye on the ball.

Demo Accounts

Always start with a Demo Account! All retail FOREX brokers offer these accounts. This account allows you to preview most of the broker's platform features and become familiar with how charting, indicators, order placement, and accounting are handled. Do one survey of demos to decide which brokers to take to the next level with a micro-account or mini-account. Typically a micro-account allows for trades of as little as 1,000 units; a mini-account, for 10,000 units. There may be some difference between the demo account and a real-time account, especially in the data-feed and order types; make an effort to find out what these are for each broker on which you do due diligence.

Market Maker or ECN?

Market maker or ECN is the single most critical distinction between FOREX broker-dealers. A market maker, or dealer, is always the counterparty to your trades; an ECN requires an actual counter order for execution. Given the liquidity of the FOREX markets a counter order is only a problem in a very fast or very slow market or if you place an extremely large order. An ECN cannot play many of the games that market makers do—in large part they do not need to because they have no book to balance. But ECN trading also requires a more accurate and delicate trading touch—an additional skill that the trader must acquire.

Regarding market makers: Some are good, even very good; many are awful. Keep in mind what "counterparty to your trade" means. Then remember that market makers hold all the cards—the data stream, the dealing desk, or control via their liquidity providers with an NDD (No Dealing Desk), the trading platform, and all the tools—requoting, pip spreads, trading rules, dealer intervention, accepting or canceling trades—all for the supposed purpose of maintaining an orderly market. National Futures Association (NFA) Compliance Rule 2-43 has minimized some of these factors—but not eliminated them by any means. Progress is being made but continued excesses will make them the dinosaurs of the industry.

ECNs have their own issues—the biggest one is that their platforms are more difficult to learn and use effectively. They are often bare bones and require integration of third-party charting and technical services. But they have much less leeway because they are functionally trade matchers. In fast or slow markets liquidity may actually be worse with an ECN because they do not have many of the orderly market tools at their disposal. But on balance, I feel that once you have gotten your feet wet in FOREX shop for an ECN. Several retail brokers are offering ECN trading to even mini-accounts. How they bundle 10k lots into a 250k bank lot without intervention I have not fully determined.

The core issue—and the reason the author predicted in the second edition that market makers would lose ground to ECNs—is that market makers manipulate the book to maintain order. This involves a number of activities such as requoting, dealer intervention, and setting pip spread—as and when they please. Market makers trade against their customers—it is why and how they are what they are. A profit for you may well be a loss for them. What would *you* do with a customer who cost you money on a consistent basis?

Market makers set, manipulate, or control pip spreads usually as legitimate operations of the market-making process; ECNs generally do not. Many trading platforms—both market maker and ECS—provide depth of market (DOM): the ability to see standing buy and sell orders, the quantities and prices bid and asked. This can be valuable information if you learn how to use it properly.

To complicate matters some firms that are obviously market makers now advertise a no dealing desk. The author is unsure how such a hybrid operates; in some instances it appears to be nothing more than semantics in an effort to shake the market-maker moniker. Lack of regulation makes knowing how a broker-dealer processes trades difficult if not impossible. The author queried five such brokers about this process and received no response from four of them and what can only be described as "mumbo-jumbo" from the other one. More and more brokers are attempting to distance themselves from the market-maker label, but whether they are actually making any significant changes to how they execute trades remains a question in many instances. You will hear the term *liquidity provider* from both ECNs and market makers. For a market maker it really has little meaning but it sounds good. It does not matter how many liquidity providers a broker-dealer has if it stops the feed to sniff and/or manipulate it before passing it through to the customer.

In reviewing the fine print of account forms you notice that even ECNs withhold the right to intervene as market makers. Yes, it is confusing! In FOREX, ultimately, "You pay your money and you take your pick."

FCM or IB?

A Futures Clearing Merchant (FCM) is a full, licensed broker-dealer who has met the current $20 million NFA capital requirement.

An IB (Introducing Broker) is an independent who routes trades and uses the trading platform and clearing services of a larger FCM (Futures Clearing Merchant) broker-dealer. IBs now must also meet a modest capital requirement but they are still essentially a coattail on the FCM.

The rationale for using an IB is that they may offer a higher level of customer care or value-add services you want and cannot get from the broker-dealer. An example of a value-add IB is HawaiiFOREX (GFTFOREX), which offers a structured educational program currently based on the work of Joe DiNapoli; www.atcbrokers.com (FXCM) with a variety of platforms. Service can also be a legitimate reason to prefer an IB over its own FCM as in the instance of www.tradeviewforex.com (IKONGM) although in this particular case the FCM also offers excellent customer care. Of course, everyone in the chain wants to get fed although markups are generally quite small.

No two traders are alike, and the landscape is constantly changing. Broker recommendations per se are risky business. That said, the author's consensus opinion is that the new trader should open a demo account with one of the Big Three, an ECN, a market maker, and perhaps an IB to get a good look at the broker-dealer landscape. If your FOREX career blossoms—and we hope it does—move on to one of the larger ECN brokers. It is now possible to actually start with an ECN, but I still recommend testing the waters with a market maker in the mix. See Appendix A, "How the FOREX Game Is Played," which discusses the current issues of importance to traders with respect to broker-dealer structure and practices.

All of this said, over the past five years things have gotten better, not worse, for the retail FOREX trader. What is true today may not be true tomorrow—one reason most traders hold accounts with multiple brokers.

Platform Capabilities

Perhaps most critical to the trader is a broker-dealer's platform capabilities. Due diligence, vis-à-vis your needs, will take some time and effort on your part. Here is what to look for in several categories. Learn everything possible before making a trade. Demo accounts are ideal for this purpose. Many brokers now offer one of several standard trading platforms from independent vendors. The three most popular platforms are NinjaTrader, MetaTrader, and eSignal. If you find a platform you like (see Chapter 14, "Retail FX Platforms") you will want to endeavor to trade only with brokers offering that platform. The trend today is clearly toward everything under one roof—quotes, charts, indicators, order-entry, and programming.

Trading Tools

Traders are fascinated by charts, numbers, and indicators, and most broker-dealers are happy to accommodate them. Downloading a demo account will give you a good idea of the toolset available. In a few instances the demo does not offer the entire palette so you need a mini-account to see and test drive everything. Not sure? Ask the broker.

Most platforms offer integrated charting and technical studies capability. For those platforms that do not, you need to access a third-party vendor. We recommend an integrated platform for the novice.

Unless you have a unique trading tool, the days of needing to access a broker's platform for order entry and a separate platform for market analysis are coming to an end. Today's platforms do all the integration for you.

Most of the popular indicators are available—moving averages, stochastics, relative strength, oscillators, Bollinger bands, and many others. (See Figure 7.1.)

FIGURE 7.1 Technical Indicators
Source: www.ninjatrader.com

Bar charts with a variety of settings for time frames and units are offered. The new MetaTrader-5 platform has 21 preset time frames and if that is not sufficient, you can custom configure more—as many as you like with NinjaTrader. Be sure the dealer has what you need; integrated charting capability is a must, especially for the new trader. Swing charts, candlesticks, and point and figure charts are also available.

Most platforms offer a palette by which you can customize the look and feel of charts. The size, scale, and coloring of charts can make a big difference to your interpretation of them. As an experiment, take a single pair with the same time scale and unit and make a half-dozen or so charts with different parameters. My advice to the beginner is to keep all charts in the same size and color scheme. Trading is an extremely delicate process, and even small differences matter.

It is best if you have some idea of what you want before beginning your due diligence. Some primary considerations: colors, sizing/scaling, time frames, vertical and horizontal scrolling, printing. As an old-time trader, the author still likes to print charts for analysis.

TIP: Do not let the plethora of indicators and charts overwhelm you. I recommend that you initially work with bar charts, moving averages, and an oscillator. Learn them one at a time. Once comfortable, pick an Indicator of the Week to add to your platform and study.

The Trader's Desktop

How easy is it to place and monitor your orders? View your charts and technical indicators? Most retail dealers do a great job of this but layout and organization vary. Those factors can be important depending on how you trade, especially if you trade frequently. Can that information be easily backed up or saved? Almost all broker-dealers and integrated platform vendors have this process down pat; much of your decision is a matter of personal style. (See Figure 7.2.)

News

Most broker-dealers offer news feeds and news and announcement calendars. There are many third-party providers, but for the average trader what is offered integrated on trader platforms is enough. Do not get mesmerized by the news, but do watch and note how the market reacts to it.

The author uses a small proprietary program for NinjaTrader, which helps track upcoming news announcements. Commercial equivalents are now becoming available.

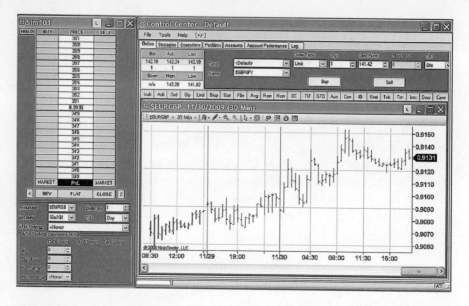

FIGURE 7.2   Trading Platform
Source: www.ninjatrader.com

Platform Stability and Backbone

As we have mentioned above, trading platforms are enormously complex software programs. Real-time delivery of information is also a daunting task. Put those factors together and it is a minor miracle they work as well as they do. But . . . things happen. One of the biggest brokers had their trading platform crash for almost 24 hours in February 2007. Platform stability has improved enormously in the past few years.

What backbone is a prospective broker-dealer using—Windows, Java, Web-based, or Flash? Windows is the most stable, and Java is cross-platform if you are using a Mac computer. At one time Java platforms had a bad habit of crashing under heavy loads but that seems for the most part to have been remedied. If you use Java *do not* install the latest Sun update without getting the okay from your broker-dealer. Updates are supposed to be downwardly compatible, but there is a lot going on in a real-time trading platform. Having owned a web conferencing business, author Archer has been leery of Java, but it has improved a great deal recently.

Flash platforms are available, but they do not have the years of development behind them that Windows and Java platforms do. Flash platforms have potential, once developers in FOREX get a handle on the immense Macromedia tool set.

The Internet is not perfect. You should not trade online unless you have a high-speed Internet connection. A backup connection from a different vendor is a good idea if you are a serious trader. Cable is more reliable than DSL in most locations. Some brokers offer their platforms on multiple backbones and even recommend specific browsers for their Windows-based venues. Traders should also invest in a reliable battery backup power supply for their computer.

Once you are trading with substantial amounts of money and taking larger positions, consider opening a small secondary account with a different broker-dealer in a different country on a different backbone. Should your primary broker go incommunicado and you need to execute a trade, you have an out. In your due diligence process, after you have sampled four or five mini-accounts and select a primary broker you may consider leaving a mini-account open as a hedge.

Trading platform stability has improved enormously in the past few years, but you must still be prepared for the occasional interruption of service.

Historical Data

If you want to look at charts from months and years gone by, you will need historical data. Some brokers offer it in their trading platform, some as a separate service, and some not at all. For comprehensive historical data, you may wish to consider one of the data vendors in Chapter 13, "The FOREX Marketplace." Historical data is available online, for download or on a CD. The vendor www.disktrading.com is a good value.

Both the MetaTrader and NinjaTrader platforms offer excellent tools for integrating historical data—and it is an easy task to import additional data, as needed.

The site www.disktrading.com offers historical data preformatted for all the major platforms—a big time saver!

Historical data is the inexpensive approach for developing and testing trading methods, systems, and theories. See the section Market Environments (ME) in Chapter 18, "Improving Your Trading Skills," for approaches to effectively testing trading methods and systems.

Data Feed

Application Programming Interface (API) is your broker-dealer's price data stream from its liquidity providers—usually banks—made available for custom programming. What sources it is composed of is usually difficult if not impossible to ascertain. No two are identical. Market makers use a composite of sources—that may even include its own micro-ECN. But given the enormous liquidity of the market, they do not usually vary a great deal. The exception is when market makers requote.

Most brokers offer their API as a separate service. A trader would use the API to drive third-party software or his or her own software program. On the flip side, third-party vendors offer their services using various dealers' API. It can be confusing. If you use a third-party program for trading or even just for your charts, be sure it has a one-to-one or close correspondence with your broker-dealer data stream. Rolling your own integration is strictly for experienced programmer gurus. New traders should probably avoid third-party integration, also.

APIs are becoming less and less important as the integrated trading platforms now offer robust scripting languages. NinjaTrader's NinjaScript is a subset of C# with many additional functions, objects, and libraries specifically designed for trading system development.

Orders

Traders use a wide variety of different orders for entry, stop protection, and exit (price objectives). Our advice: Keep it simple. Thoroughly understand what an order does and how it works before using it. Many exotic order types add a level of complexity to the trading process that beginners normally do not need. Some orders also offer an extra license to the broker-dealer to manage their book; ergo, they generally love them and encourage them. Functionality of orders may differ slightly from market makers to ECNs.

You should be able to do everything you want with three types of orders: Market or Instant Execution, Stop, and Limits. Remember, speculative hedging is now prohibited for NFA member broker-dealers. You cannot simultaneously buy and sell the same currency pair.

I offer more detail on order placement and management in Chapter 9, "Making the Trade."

Margin Requirements

Because a trader can open an account from $1 to $1,000,000 and trade any size lot, margins and leverage are something of a misnomer in FOREX.

Broker-dealers allow you to set your own fixed maximum leverage—typically from 10:1 to 100:1. Dealers are mostly concerned that you do not hold open positions in excess of your account balance. If you do—or even come close—you will get a margin call, and you will be expected to meet it immediately. A broker may even liquidate part or all of your position(s) without informing you.

The lower the margin requirement, the higher the leverage factor. Profits and losses are magnified as the leverage is increased.

In reality today margin calls in FOREX are rare. Brokers are able to electronically monitor all parameters based on your account size, trading activity, and experience. If you attempt to enter an order outside of those parameters it will not execute. Big Broker is watching you!

Simple money-management rules—that you implement—are the key to avoiding margin calls and overtrading. In Chapter 16, "Money Management Simplified," I offer the Campaign Trade Method for novices.

I recommend these basic four ideas to new traders: (1) never commit more than one-half of your account balance to open positions, (2) never trade more than two market pairs concurrently, (3) never commit more than 25 percent of your capital to a single position, and (4) never trade over 50:1 leverage. Begin your trading career at 20:1 and work up in increments of 10:1 as you are successful, and start with a demo account, move to a micro-account then to a mini-account before committing your full grubstake. Experienced traders often modulate these parameters according to how confident they are of a trade. But that requires experience to make it an effective tool. New traders should keep the number of money-management parameters simple and to a bare minimum.

Order Backup

Does your broker offer the capability to phone an order if their trader platform goes down or your Internet drops? Be sure that telephone order backup is available, although lines will be swamped if it is a system-wide outage and not your own Internet connection. If you open a mini- or micro-account, ask your broker to let you test a telephone order so that you know it exists and have the process down pat for when and if you need it. Keep in mind that brokers do not expect their platforms to go down often, and when they do, their backup systems tend to be overwhelmed.

TIP: Keep one secondary account with enough funding to cover whatever you expect your maximum exposure to be when trading. Be sure it is on a different FCM and data feed than your primary account.

Account Minimums

Micro-accounts now start at $1—but realistically you need $300 to $400 even to trade 1k lots in FOREX mini-accounts (10k lots) are $1,000 to $3,000 and standard accounts (100k lots) typically begin at $5,000. ECNs tend to have higher minimums. This is a far cry from the days in the commodity futures markets where $5,000 was considered a mini-account and $25,000 was the standard. In FOREX the ability to set your own lot sizes and leverage make smaller accounts justifiable. Account size, leverage, and lot size should all work in harmony and be consistent; your broker-dealer monitors such parameters carefully in an effort to protect both parties.

The new NFA minimum margin requirements may impact minimum account sizes.

TIP: Your grubstake should be at least the equivalent of 30 trade losses and initial margin for a single trade. If you risk $50 per trade (50 pips on a mini-lot), you should have a $1,600 account. How much you risk per trade is determined by money-management parameters; see Chapter 16, "Money Management Simplified."

Pairs, Crosses, and Exotics

A pair is a tradable set of currencies including the USD. A cross is a set without the USD. An exotic is a set with the USD but with an exotic currency such as the Hungarian Forint, Indonesian Rupiah, or Thai Baht. There are 25 or so exotics offered currently. Today's exotic may be tomorrow's pair; the Polish Zloty is considered an exotic, but its rising popularity may move it to a standard pair sometime in the not too distant future. The big banana remains the EUR/USD major pair.

There are eight majors. Mathematically there are 27 different major pairs. The most liquid are listed in Table 7.1.

TABLE 7.1 Most Liquid Currency Pairs
EUR/USD Euro / U.S. Dollar
"Euro"
USD/JPY U.S. Dollar / Japanese Yen
"Dollar Yen"
GBP/USD British Pound / U.S. Dollar
"Cable"
USD/CAD U.S. Dollar / Canadian Dollar
"Dollar Canada"
AUD/USD Australian Dollar/U.S. Dollar
"Aussie Dollar"
USD/CHF U.S. Dollar / Swiss Franc
"Swissy"
EUR/JPY Euro / Japanese Yen
"Euro Yen"

Liquidity in exotics can be poor—especially on ECNs. If there is no buyer or seller an ECN simply runs a market order as high or low as necessary to fill it. The author trades the EUR/TRY and during the North American session inadvertently paid a 55 pip (!) spread on just a 10k lot! Trade only the 5 or 10 most liquid pairs at the beginning of your trading career.

TIP: Liquidity should not be confused with volatility. The most volatile pairs as of this writing are: GBP/AUD, EUR/NZD, GBP/JPY. Insofar as the latter is the most liquid of the three, it gets much attention from short-term traders.

Deposits and Withdrawals

Typically accomplished by check or wire, eGold—www.efundsfinance.com—and PayPal—www.paypal.com—are also used by some broker-dealers for account deposits. These latter two options may disappear as the NFA implements and enforces a Know Your Client regulation for broker-dealers. An attempt to deposit funds for a small account to Oanda via PayPal was difficult and time-consuming. Needless to say, keep complete hardcopy, cross-referenced records of all monetary transactions with your broker. A date log of all transactions and communications is also advised. Beware of brokers who make withdrawals difficult or take an inordinate amount of time to make them.

Note that many brokers require withdrawals in kind. If you deposited a check, you will receive a check.

TIP: Take screenshots, print and/or save important broker web pages, especially those regarding account forms, terms you are agreeing to, and so forth. You may never see that page again! Important web pages have a strange propensity to disappear when you need them most.

Transaction Costs

There are no commissions in FOREX in the form they exist for securities or commodity futures traders if you use a market maker. Similar to the NASDAQ market, FOREX operates on a bid-ask spread. The minimum fluctuation of a currency pair is a pip, and spreads (and just about everything else) are quoted in pips.

The more liquid a market, either with respect to time-of-day (TOD) or pair, the lower will be the pip spread to trade. Temporal conditions of a market maker can also affect spreads. Remember, you pay the spread both going in and going out. The EUR/USD is far and away the most liquid pair. Some ECNs offer it at 1 pip; most retail market makers are now at 1.5 to 3 pips with 2 pips the standard. Again, when markets are illiquid for a market maker or generally because of prevailing fast conditions, pip spreads balloon—sometimes enormously. By following a pair for a few weeks you can *usually* get a good idea of when and under what circumstances this will occur. See Appendix A, "How the FOREX Game Is Played" for more. Spreads will be highest during the session for which the currencies in the pair are not native; in other words, the CHF/JPY during the North American session. Two pips does not sound like much, but for active short-term or high-frequency traders, costs add up quickly. Two pips reduces a 10-pip trade by 20 percent, but a 50-pip trade by only 4 percent. There are now *ultra-high-frequency traders*—we called it churning an account in days gone by—but do not think I could mouse-click that fast. In Chapter 20, "Computers and FOREX," I discuss *high-frequency* and ultra-high-frequency trading, which takes short-term to an entirely new level.

ECNs typically charge a *lot* fee instead of a bid-ask spread mark-up. Calculate the lot fee across the lot size to get the full, correct spread. Lot fees on less than 10,000 size can be expensive—one reason ECNs are most likely to have higher account minimums.

Rollovers—holding a position across multiple sessions—may also be a transaction cost. If you intend to be a longer term *position trader*, be sure to know a prospective broker's rollover policy—some can be pricey.

Trading Hours

FOREX is more or less a round-the-clock activity. The day begins with the Asian session, dovetails to the European session, and ends with the North American session. (See Appendix D, "Time Zones and Global FX Trading Hours.")

The North American session is the most active—and volatile. I have found relatively quieter opportunities, good for beginners, in the other two sessions. But be aware of potentially larger pip spreads, as markets may be thin. All currencies trade in all sessions although they tend to be most active in the session to which the country belongs. I prefer trading the EUR/USD from 8 P.M. to 12 P.M. Eastern time. This may be a function of the markets being less volatile—or the children being asleep!

TIP: The Asian session starts gradually over two hours, 5 P.M. Eastern to 7 P.M. Eastern. Traders often refer to this as *quiet time* as the markets tend to move very little.

Executions of market orders at odd hours can take your breath away! Early in a session, late in the week, and so forth. The market may be thin even though the chart looks fine. I once made the mistake of entering a market order in the EUR/GBP for a small 25,000 lot with a market maker and was filled 12 pips off in a quiet—too quiet—trading market.

The Depth of Market features of some trading platforms such as NinjaTrader and MetaTrader-5 can be a big help, minimizing such occurrences. These allow the trader to see how many orders (bid and ask) are currently placed at prices above and below the last trade.

Customer Service

Some things never change. My rant about customer service in the second edition is still valid.

> As every Boomer knows, the quality of customer service (at least in the United States) has fallen dramatically in the past 30 years. Practices that would have put a company out of business in 1977 are SOP today. Retail FOREX is no different and in my humble opinion is worse than many other industries. If you are old enough to have done business with a retail brokerage firm in the 1960s or 1970s, you are in for a shock.
>
> The actual quality of service varies enormously from broker-dealer to broker-dealer, but the general level in the industry is appalling. My pet peeve: brokers with great trading platforms, good pip spreads, and horrific customer service. Nothing can derail a trader from his trading process faster than poor customer service. The reviews are an essential guide to what people have experienced with sales, customer service, and technical support. Most noncritical support is handled via e-mail. Critical issues warrant a telephone call or an IM-style chat if it is available. Please do not burden your dealer's customer service people with telephone calls for noncritical issues.
>
> If customer service is poor, one would think that at least sales support would be stellar. Not so. I have found sales support at many firms to be perfectly dreadful. Inability to answer e-mail in a timely manner or at all, failure to intelligently address basic questions, and abysmal understanding of what they are selling are typical trader issues.
>
> Retail FOREX is relatively new, and it is still growing rapidly. The number of qualified sales and customer support personnel in relationship to inquiries and customers is currently grossly inadequate. I have found a large number of sales and CS representatives who could only be described as clueless. Better training is one solution to the problem; actually reading an e-mail from a prospect or client before responding is another. Answering e-mail in a timely fashion would be

a nice touch, also. The industry as a whole needs customer service help and desperately. Technical support is generally stronger but still fraught with difficulties. Many tech support representatives feel the customer is always wrong or are simply unqualified for the job.

TIP: If you cannot get a response to a sales inquiry, how will they treat you if you become a customer?

Follow the FOREX review boards for an indication of service. But do not always take them at face value. As they say, "YMMV—Your Mileage May Vary."

Documentation

Most brokers have excellent documentation to protect both them and you. Lawyers are expensive, but there are a lot of them! You may wish to have your accountant or lawyer review the firm's documentation if you do not understand something. But do not expect to get the broker-dealer to make any changes in it for you. Keep hard copies of all documentation and especially those that require your signature.

Do not spare the ink or paper—print all of your broker's documentation and study it in depth.

Similar to securities and futures, you can open an individual account, joint account, partnership account, or corporate account. Beyond the individual account additional paperwork is required. If you have someone manage your money, there is a separate form for that purpose.

Requoting

In the second edition I wrote:

> This can get ugly. Only market makers requote. It is the soft under-belly and Achilles' heel of FOREX. If anything brings in the regulators to control the industry it will be requoting. In requoting, market mak-ers fill your order with prices not seen on their standard online price feed. Fortunately requoting is not nearly the problem it was two or three years ago, but it is out there, and if you are a small trader, you will probably experience it. Broker-dealers are learning that traders run so quickly and complain so loudly about requoting, they are encour-aged to refrain from the practice. Requoting is sometimes equated with dealer intervention and is most typical of market makers.

I am happy to report that while *requoting* still occurs, its frequency has dropped substantially. You may thank both competition and NFA Compliance Rule 2-43, which limits the times and circumstances that prices can be requoted by brokers.

Stop Harvesting

Market makers uniformly deny *stop harvesting*—the practice of running prices to elect a stop-loss order. Traders seem to think otherwise. Troll the review boards for who is hot, who is not with respect to this practice.

Ballooning Spreads

Brokers will often widen the bid-ask spreads on currency pairs when the markets are quiet and illiquid and just before and after a news release. This happens on both market maker and ECN trading platforms. It is a natural occurrence for ECNs, and market makers do it to protect themselves and manage their book. How much it happens and how wide the *ballooning* becomes the question of where management ends and profit incentive takes over. If you know when and under what circumstances it will occur you can act accordingly and not be hurt or surprised.

Financials

The CFTC (Commodity Futures Trading Commission) has raised the capital requirements for a full FCM retail FOREX broker from nothing to $20 million in six years. An overextended broker with a high net worth is not better than a small net-worth broker with a strong balance sheet, as Refco traders learned in 2005. Unfortunately the NFA is not likely to think in that fashion, resulting in the closing or merger of solid small-capitalized firms and allowing relatively anemic big fish to continue to swim. Financial disclosure requirements remain relatively minimal in FOREX but the author believes that too will change over the next two or three years. If you dig deep on some of the forums and on the NFA web site, www.nfa.org, you can find financial information that is difficult to pry from the broker-dealers themselves. At least in theory an ECN should require less capital than a market maker. Because an ECN matches trades for execution, finding themselves on a potentially dangerous large unbalanced position is less likely for them than for a market maker.

Rollovers and Interest

Rollover charges are determined by the difference between U.S. interest rates and the interest rates of the corresponding pair country. The greater the interest rate differential between the two countries in the currency pair or cross, the greater the rollover charge will be. For example, if the British Pound (GBP) has the greater differential with the U.S. Dollar (USD), then the rollover charge for holding the GBP positions would be the most expensive. Conversely if the Swiss Franc (CHF) were to have the smallest interest rate differential to the U.S. Dollar, then the session carryover (*overnight*) charges for the USD/CHF would be the least expensive of the currency pairs.

Rollovers are a complex issue, fortunately of limited importance to the small trader. If you trade intersession a substantial amount of the time, ask for specific broker-dealer policies on rollovers; they do vary, and some are much better than others.

Some dealers offer interest on your unused account balance. Again, policies within those companies differ. If you have a large amount of unused account monies, it can make a real difference. Larger traders tend to get better deals to keep them from shuffling money in and out of their accounts to maximize interest.

FOREX Broker-Dealers

You can please some of the traders some of the time, but you cannot please all of the traders all of the time. As you peruse broker-dealer reviews, you can see many that have both one-star and five-star reviews. Some of these are just plain sour grapes, and some are shills. Look for similar issues mentioned over long periods of time and on different review boards. Focus on the reviews in the context of what you as a trader require. As in anything else, a larger sample is a better indicator than a small sample.

The inclusion of a broker-dealer herein does not constitute a recommendation; exclusion likewise does not imply disapproval. Your experience may differ from mine.

Market Maker Spotlight

Ikon-Royal

www.ikon-royal.com

Ikon-Royal is the primary subsidiary of IkonGM. Both have been players in retail FOREX almost from the get-go. Royal Trading was acquired in 2007. They offer both the Currenex and MetaTrader platforms. As Currenex ventures

Sydney   Tokyo   Dubai   London   New York

| Home | About Us | Education | Accounts | Software | Live News | Promotions | Support | FAQs |

FIGURE 7.3   IKON-GM Royal Division
Source: www.ikon-royal.com

into the retail side of FOREX you will see it offered by other brokers in the near future.

Spreads are excellent, the minimum account is $2,000, and the minimum lot size is 10,000. FX options and other products have been recently added to Ikon's line. They are definitely moving up the ladder!

E-mails are generally answered quickly and, on the occasion that is not the case, a phone call will work. They have an old-fashioned approach to customer service. The reviews for Ikon-Royal are above average. It is an excellent all-around selection for new and intermediate traders.

See Figure 7.3.

ECN Spotlight

www.pfgbest.com

This is an old-line commodity futures house (Peregrine) that moved into FOREX some years ago. They offer MetaTrader, eSignal, NinjaTrader, and Currenex platforms. PFG also offers stock and options trading.

Spreads are excellent. PFG has multiple liquidity providers; the actual number depends on which platform you use. Rollover costs are average.

PFG is a stickler for detail and compliance. It may take you a bit longer to open an account with them than with some other brokers but the process is smooth thanks to quality customer care. The minimum account is $2,500 at the time of this writing and the minimum lot size is a mini (10,000).

You can also trade futures with PFG. I am told they will integrate both FOREX and futures on the new MetaTrader-5 platform but you can currently trade both futures and FOREX with them on the NinjaTrader platform.

PFG now offers retail clients the professional Currenex trading platform with eight liquidity providers. An advanced version offers charting capability, but the platform is not as robust as MetaTrader, eSignal, or NinjaTrader. A trader could well use Currenex for execution of trades and one of the others to do his or her market analysis.

Customer service is above average. E-mail responses can be nearly instantaneous—or occasionally require a re-ping. (See Figure 7.4.)

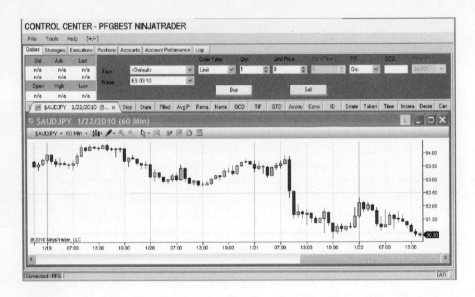

FIGURE 7.4   PFGBest.com

Popular Broker-Dealers

The author has done substantial due diligence on the companies listed below, including downloading and reviewing their platforms, making e-mail contact, and asking a few questions. I have sampled micro- and mini-accounts with a dozen or more brokers. We believe those below are among the best retail broker-dealers in the FOREX industry. But one person's fine wine is another's poison. None are perfect by any stretch of the imagination.

Expectations vary. The more knowledgeable you become, the lower will be your expectations if only because you understand how the game is played. Many of the review board complaints are from traders with limited knowledge and unrealistic expectations—but not all of them. Pip spreads are going to balloon occasionally, prices will be requoted to you, customer service will frustrate you, platforms and the Internet will go down. Make an attempt to build the occasional minor disaster into your trading and into your expectations.

The hot button remains the pitiful sales and customer service in the retail FOREX industry.

You notice references to *news trading* on the review boards. This refers to the practice of attempting to trade on news or announcements. It is a dangerous practice; prices may jump or fall quickly (spikes), and pip spreads will expand enormously. It can be very profitable—or deadly—and is not for the new trader in our humble opinion. Market makers are on the lookout for news traders. The authors believe that many of the negative news trading reviews are sour grapes although market makers do seem to use the occasion to trade against their clients. On the other hand it is ridiculous for market makers to advertise "2 pip spreads" when they regularly balloon to 25 or 30 pips on any pending news. If you must trade the news, do it with an ECN, and do not use market orders. For news trading, an execution tool such as www.secretnewsweapon.com is de rigueur. Perhaps fortunately, the NFA anti-hedging rules are running off the news traders to overseas brokers.

FOREX is the most laissez-faire of all markets, and that cuts both ways. No one wants to be cheated, but if you cannot take the knocks, do not play the game. The profit opportunities are enormous, and that attracts all kinds. Opportunists and strongly driven business people are in plentiful supply in the FOREX market.

ATCbrokers

www.atcbrokers

An ECN, ATC uses the MetaTrader platform but offers other platforms, as well. They have had some difficulties getting their ECN feed to work with MetaTrader but as of this writing seem to have it down to a science.

ATC originally used the feed from HotspotFX but when HotspotFX closed their retail business, they went to FXCM. They continue to add additional liquidity providers for their high-end accounts.

Service is superb; ATC is willing to work with serious traders to an extent most others are not. Costs are average for an ECN. Expect spreads to get even tighter as they add liquidity providers.

Oanda

www.oanda.com

Oanda started with quite a poor reputation in the late 1990s but it now is considered one of the best retail houses. They are extremely well capitalized. There are lots of educational tools on the web site for beginners. Customer service is

FIGURE 7.5 ATC Brokers

adequate; you are a number to Oanda. Telephone support is iffy, but e-mail is often quick and efficient. The platform, Java-based, is extremely clean and easy-to-use, a real boon for a beginner. The technical tool set is good if somewhat limited in comparison to others such as NinjaTrader and MetaTrader. Box options are a unique feature. Their API for developers is excellent but pricey with respect to current industry standards where an account will get it to you no charge.

Oanda claims to have no dealing desk (NDD), which would make it an ECN, if that is the case. But the author's sample trades sure looked like a market maker. The line of demarcation between market maker and ECN is beginning to blur as brokers attempt to distance themselves from the market-maker moniker.

The author uses Oanda to trade micro-lots when he wishes to test a new trading idea.

MB Trading

www.mbtrading.com

This company was originally EFgroup—which was an IB for MB Trading. MB re-acquired EFgroup in 2008. They are an ECN.

They are currently phasing in MetaTrader as their FOREX platform after a trying time with their in-house Navigator. MB Trading offers mini (10,000) lot trading, although the author did not understand the mechanism by which a 10k lot could be fed into or drawn out of an ECN feed. Commissions are low but rollover costs are high.

MB also offers the NinjaTrader platform and a free and good API for developers. (With the power of the programming languages of NinjaTrader's NinjaScript and MetaTrader's MQL5 most traders can develop what they need without an API.)

The reviews indicate different customer service experiences from "gosh-awful" to "they're the greatest." Mine was in-between. The staff is apparently quite young for the most part.

FXDD

www.fxdd.com

FXDD is a market maker. They offer a micro MetaTrader platform for a $400 ante, which may be attractive for openers if the MetaTrader platform appeals to you. FXDD has an extensive web site with a plethora of learning and reference materials.

TradeStation

www.tradestation.com

If the TradeStation software, tool set, and programming script is to your liking, you can trade FOREX with it also. They clear their trades through Gain

Capital at the present time. A number of dealers are said to be integrating TradeStation at some level, including Oanda in association with SnapDragon, www.snapdragon.co.uk, although the author has not seen any as yet in operation. Reviews and customer service are mixed. MetaTrader and NinjaTrader have somewhat eclipsed TradeStation's attraction as a means of developing trading tools and systems and back-testing but their EasyLanguage holds its own and is certainly the easiest to learn.

Deutsches Bank

Now you can trade with the huge Deutsches Bank (DB, www.dbfx.com), a major player in the Interbank market. DB does more than 20 percent of the worldwide FX business. Initial reviews have not been encouraging but may relate to rollout pains as retail FOREX is new to them—worth watching. The account minimum has just been lowered to $5,000 as of this writing.

DBFX partners with FXCM for technology but the author was assured they use their own liquidity providers and data feed. DBFX currently claims to be an ECN.

Customer service is friendly, responsive, and better than industry average.

You can expect to see other banks take advantage of leveraging their FOREX trading to attract retail clients.

The Big Three

These three companies seem to account for perhaps 50 percent of the retail FOREX business. When you are big, you get noticed. These folks are either loved or hated. They all appear to have strong financial positions. All three are primarily market makers to smaller accounts but at varying levels, migrating to ECN, and/or *liquidity provider,* and or *NDD,* and/or *straight-through processing,* for larger accounts and institutional business.

Gain Capital

www.gaincapital.com

Gain Capital is essentially a market maker to small accounts, an ECN to larger and institutional accounts. Their in-house platform is stable but seems quite out-of-date now. They do offer third-party integration with other vendors such as the excellent NinjaTrader, TradeStation, eSignal, and MetaTrader. Gain has recently raised their account minimum to $25,000. You can still trade with them on www.FOREX.com, a wholly owned subsidiary for smaller cap traders. FOREX.com shares data feed and most platform features with Gain; as do all the

Big Three, they have their share of detractors. Customer service is above average. Costs and spreads are about average for a market maker. Fills are satisfactory, at least on the major pairs.

GFTFOREX

www.gftforex.com

GFT has a large palette of products and services for the trader. Their DealBook is a terrific platform although it is complex. GFT allows you to integrate several third-party services and offers alternative platforms. Many IBs use GFT as their backbone.

FOREX Capital Markets (FXCM)

www.fxcm.com

FOREX Capital Markets is the classic love/hate broker-dealer. Everyone goes after the 800-pound gorilla on the street in any business. You will see the FXCM trading platform on many other dealers—typically IBs or partners of FXCM.

For the Professional

When you are ready to enter the big time in FOREX, these broker-dealers are the Gold Standard of the industry.

Dukascopy

www.dukascopy.com

Dukascopy offers a unique centralized-decentralized clearing system but is essentially a large ECN. An interesting article on this new approach is on www.e-FOREX.net in the January 2007 edition. It has enormous potential to revolutionize retail FOREX. They provide a wide variety of FOREX services and products under one roof. Their web site was recently redesigned, vastly improving navigation, which had been an issue. They offer both a Java and web-based platform. The recommended browser for the web-based platform is Firefox. The author did, indeed, have issues with both platforms on Internet Explorer.

If you like their clearing services and trading platform, a great deal of customization is possible with two API packages.

Not for small traders, the minimum account is $50,000. E-mail inquiries regarding sales were answered quickly on one occasion, not at all on another.

Customer service per se was much better. It is a Swiss company but with possible eastern European interests according to some blogs.

Spreads are excellent; costs are attractive to large traders.

English is a second language for most of the customer service and support staff. Communication can be difficult although they seem to try hard to please and accommodate. Sticklers for detail, as would befit a Swiss company.

HotSpotFX

www.hotspotfx.com

HotSpotFX exited the retail FOREX scene in 2008 to concentrate on its institutional and professional trading clientele. They are currently working with FX Bridge (www.fxbridge.com) on a new trading platform, which looks promising. If you have the financial resources it remains an excellent choice. Multiple liquidity providers. Simply unparalleled customer care.

Fraud, Scams, and Off-Exchange

Even though there is no exchange (central clearinghouse) for currency trading, broker-dealers who operate from telephone boiler rooms are still referred to as off-exchange. Beware of these practitioners and avoid them like the plague. Most of them have no web site or a few shoddy pages built in straight HTML and operate primarily via telephone solicitations. They typically sell FOREX options. (See Chapter 19, "Options and Exotics," for information on legitimate FOREX options trading.) They are almost never registered with the CFTC, NFA, or any recognized regulatory body. If in doubt you can always Google their name for more information.

You can spread-bet on FOREX through legitimate, licensed bookmakers. I offer some web site links in Chapter 13, "The FOREX Marketplace." The new online gambling laws may affect the ability of U.S. citizens to participate in spread-betting.

Broker-Dealer Due Diligence Form

You may wish to use the Broker-Dealer Due Diligence Form in your research. (See Table 7.2.) Feel free to customize it to fit your specific needs and wants, for example, adding specific platform features, indicators, currencies, or orders you require. A copy of this spreadsheet in customized .xls format and suitable for printing may be downloaded from the Getting Started section of www.goodmanworks.com.

TABLE 7.2 Broker-Dealer Due Diligence Form

Name				
Web Site				
Contact				
Demo Account	Yes	No		
Mini Account	Yes	No		
Minimum				
Full Account				
Minimum				
Type	ECN	Market Maker	No Dealing Desk	IB
Backbone	Java	Windows	Flash	Other
Recommended Browser				
Charts				
	Bar	Line P&F	Candlestick Swing	Specialty
Indicators				
	Moving Averages	Oscillators	Others	
Chart Tools				
	Scaling	Scrolling	Time Increments	Printing
Platform Customization				
Third-Party Integration				
Historical Data				
Orders	Limit	Stop Market	Combination	Specialty
Order Backup Procedure				
Trading Hours				
Spreads				

TABLE 7.2 (*Continued*)		
Margins		
Leverage		
Currencies Traded		
Exotics	Yes	No
Options	Yes	No
Rollover Policy		
Financials		
Reviews		
Documentation		
Customer Service		
Likes/Dislikes		
Summary		

Summary

It is critical the prospective trader, especially the beginner, perform due diligence on a broker-dealer thoroughly before depositing money and making a trade.

Begin your due diligence with a study of the reviews, and then select several demo accounts to download. The best reviews are www.forexpeacearmy.com and www.goforex.net. Keep in mind four things when reading reviews: (1) Unhappy campers tend to be more vocal than happy campers. This is especially meaningful for the Big Three. The sheer volume of trade will result in a large number of complaints. (2) A large sample (25 reviews) is probably more reliable than a small sample (5 reviews). (3) Note the dates on the reviews. If you see complaints about the same problem over several months, that is probably not good. If a specific complaint is mentioned two or three times, then it disappears, that is probably good. (4) To make the sample more meaningful throw out both the best review and the worst review. The former is probably a shill; the latter, sour grapes.

The recommended process for getting started is:

Due Diligence → Demo Account → Micro-Account →
Mini-Account → Full Account

How long the entire process takes is up to you. Do not be rushed. It is your money so get it as right as you can the first time. Six months from due diligence to full account is not unreasonable in the author's opinion.

Do not leave questions unanswered and hope for the best. On the other hand, do not e-mail a flurry of questions the answers to which are found on the web site or by spending an evening with their demo account and documentation. If your experience is similar to mine, they will not be answered anyway.

Trading is about finding good trades, executing them properly, and following them to—hopefully—a tidy profit. Once you begin trading you will want to devote 100 percent of your effort to those activities, not readjusting your processes because you found out something about your broker-dealer you should have known at the outset. No broker is perfect; do not expect to find one. If you do—call me!

8

Opening a
FOREX Account

In the fall of 1974 I accompanied a friend to the local Denver office of E.F. Hutton to open a new commodity futures account. The broker handed my friend the account form—an 8½ × 5½ card. On the front side one was to enter Name, Address, Telephone, Social Security Number, Employer, Position, and Estimated Net Worth. On the reverse, a two-paragraph disclosure requiring a signature and the date. After filling out the form my friend handed it back to the broker, opened his briefcase and counted out $30,000 in one hundred dollar bills. The broker calmly re-counted the money and handed it to the cashier along with the account card. The cashier issued my friend a receipt and an account number, wished him good trading, and we were done.

Times have changed. Opening an online retail FOREX account is easy business—barring a glitch in the software—but the information required is much more extensive than it was in the halcyon days of 1974.

Do not open a live account until you have completed a thorough due diligence of the broker-dealer and worked several hours with their demo trading platform. Sadly, you will need to follow this entire process even if you are opening a $100 micro-account. Fortunately, you will not need to redo the process if you decide to open your full trading account with the broker-dealer in question.

Account Types

As in other investments, the FOREX trader can open a wide variety of accounts for self-directed trading: Individual Accounts, Joint Accounts (with different flavors), Partnership Accounts, Corporate Accounts, and Retirement/Investment Accounts (also with multiple flavors). The easiest to open is, of course, an individual account or a joint account. All the others require extra documentation: Retirement/Investment accounts the most; and you must confirm the account is eligible for FOREX trading—many are not and need to be amended to do so.

Should you desire to have your account managed by a third party, such as a professional money manager, that also requires additional forms. The due diligence required to select capable money managers is a book in and of itself, beyond the charter of this tome, which assumes you want to make your own trading decisions. Professional accounts may be managed by individual managers or placed in a FOREX trading fund. Many hedge funds now trade currencies, either with other investment vehicles or FOREX-only. Please see Chapter 13, "The FOREX Marketplace," for FOREX management resources.

Be sure you are opening a FOREX spot account and not a FOREX forwards or futures account—unless one of the latter is your choice. Almost all FOREX dealing is in the spot market, both at the institutional and retail level.

The forms for each dealer do vary in number and in specific content—if only slightly. It goes without saying: Read carefully any document before signing. If you have questions, ask the broker for clarification. If in doubt, ask your attorney or your accountant. Like all legal forms today, they are wordy and complex. FOREX can be a dangerous game, and the broker wants to protect your interest and, especially, theirs. As the regulatory environment firms, you can expect forms to get wordier and longer to incorporate the requirements of new laws, rules, regulations—and to cover the broker's back.

Opening the Account: Steps

Attorneys are not cheap, but they are plentiful. You can be assured your broker-dealer's account forms generated substantial fees or hours for their legal team.

Account forms are online and can be printed out in hard copy. The broker may request two sets, one of which is returned to you, or should be. If they only request a single set of account documents, verify that you will receive a copy. Print an extra clean copy for your records in case the online forms change or are modified.

Forms are usually in Adobe Acrobat PDF format. If so, the broker-dealer's Open an Account page will have the link to the PDF reader if it is not already installed on your computer.

TIP: Grab a screenshot of each page you view on your broker's web site for the account registration process. Do this by holding down the ALT+Print Screen keys. You can then copy it to a Word document with CTRL+V.

You will generally encounter four steps to opening an account, although they may go by different names or phrases:

1. *Select an Account Type:* As stated, you must first select the account type. Because most forms are online, the selection of an account type tells the automated registration module what to dish up next.

2. *Personal Information:* This is the bread-and-butter name, address, telephone, fax, e-mail, employer, position, Social Security number. Forms beyond Individual and Joint will require more kinds of personal and account information.

3. *Financial Information:* This step is getting more and more involved. The broker wants to make sure you are qualified to trade currencies— even if it is a $100 mini-account. I am even seeing broker-dealers requiring what could be called mini-financial statements from prospective customers. If you want to play the game, there is no way out, at least legally. A tax form is usually included in this step, also.

4. *Review:* You will be asked to review the documents carefully before submitting. Again—ask the broker any questions you might still have or query your attorney, accountant, and/or financial planner.

Review your documents twice. If the broker finds something wrong at Step 5 you will have wasted a great deal of time. Some brokers accept applications quite quickly, in one or two days. Others, sticklers for details, can take up to a week or longer.

Two threads run through these documents. The desire of the broker to protect both parties and the NFA's Know-Thy-Customer Rules, which are getting stricter.

TIP: Start a folder and keep copies of everything! I like to keep a time log of all communications with the broker including correspondence, telephone conversations, and e-mail. Brokers hold the upper hand, so if there is a dispute you need all the ammunition you can muster.

I have not seen electronic signatures appear in the industry. Given the NFA's Know Thy Customer emphasis of late, I doubt they will appear at all.

You will be asked to snail mail, fax, or scan and e-mail the forms with appropriate information and signatures to the broker. You will need to include a scan of your driver's license or other picture ID. I do not like this either, but it is the way things work with electronic registration; there is a downside to everything.

- *Acceptance:* Once your documents are accepted, you will be notified that your account is ready to fund and trade. Typically acceptance takes only one or two days unless there is a problem.

- *Funding:* Now you are ready to fund your account and begin trading. Funding is either by cashier's check or bank wire. Personal checks may be accepted by some brokers, but they take a long time to clear, and they add a step to the process. Better to take the 30 minutes for a trip to your bank for a cashier's check or a wire transfer. (See Figure 8.1.)

Some brokers have been accepting PayPal and eGold. Yes, they deduct the fee from your opening balance. Again, the KTC rule is probably going to send these methods to the sidelines.

Before actually trading, spend one last hour with the demo account. Keep at the ready a small notebook or document with the following information at your side; it may either be handwritten or copied from the broker web site:

FOREX Broker-Dealer Funding Options

Brokers offer a variety of methods to fund your account.

Your account must first be approved before it can be funded.

When you make withdrawals they will be 'in kind.'

WIRE TRANSFER
The quickest and the safest

CERTIFIED CHECK
A reliable method with hardcopy receipt

PERSONAL CHECK
Funds will be held until they clear

PAYPAL
This can get tricky and PAYPAL Fees are very high.

FIGURE 8.1   Funding Options

- The broker's hours of operation: When you can contact them by e-mail or telephone.
- Pairs traded.
- The bid-ask pip spread for the currencies you intend to trade.
- The amount of margin and leverage ratio you are using.
- The minimum and maximum trading unit size. Some brokers now offer fractional pips, which can be quite confusing.
- Telephone order backup in case you lose connectivity at a critical juncture. Unfortunately there is a recent trend toward not offering such a backup. Know your broker's policies.
- Key e-mails for the broker-dealer.
- Your access information to your account. These are typically: Account number, Login, Password.

Demo Account – Things to Learn

Basic FOREX Calculation, Ratios and Conversions
Reading and Understanding Transaction Reports
Entering a Trade – Market Orders
Entering a Trade – Pending Orders
Entering Stop Loss and Take Profit Orders
Exiting a Trade
Canceling a Trade
Modifying a Trade
Navigating Charts
Annotating Charts
Arranging Workspaces
Applying Indicators
Failsafe Procedures

FIGURE 8.2   Demo Account Functionality

All other primary concerns—requoting practices, stop harvesting, ballooning spreads, communication, platform features, the order entry process, and record keeping—should have been completed long before you decided to open an account.

Summary

The time you spend at the computer should be directed 100 percent to trading decisions, not trying to figure out how many pips equals $100, what your leverage factor will be on a trade, or trying to remember where to find the Close Order button on the trading platform.

Your goal *after you work with a demo account* is to open a mini- or micro-account and get your feet wet. Since you do not have a trading method developed as yet, think in terms of "finger exercises"—getting familiar with basic FOREX calculations, order types and entry, all the platform features—all with a small quantity of real money on the line.

Figure 8.2 shows the basic functionalities you want to learn. They must become second nature to you. It is also important to understand how to manipulate the platform, create charts and indicators, and adjust time scales, colors, and other features—collectively called navigation.

Chapter

9

Making the Trade

With the completion of this chapter, you will be ready to open a few demo accounts and see for yourself why the FOREX markets are so exciting and popular.

Orders

An order is an instruction with defined parameters to your broker to take a specific action in the market, either now or in the future. An order is for immediate execution or pending execution. Pending means prices must behave in some specific way before the order becomes for immediate execution. A market order is for immediate execution, at the best bid or ask the broker can offer to you.

The number and types of currency trading orders that can be used with broker-dealers have expanded substantially in the past few years. Customer demand for more flexibility and trade execution options and competition have been the main driving forces. Broker-dealers, especially market makers, are happy to oblige, since a large palette of orders helps them manage their book.

Orders can be further broken down into three primary categories of functionality—(1) market (immediate execution), (2) limit (pending execution), and (3) stop (pending execution) (see Table 9.1). All broker-dealers offer the basic three, and some brokers have unique in-house specialty orders. Because orders can be classified according to different criteria, they are cross-category. Some orders are not mutually exclusive and can be combined.

TABLE 9.1 Common Broker-Dealer FOREX Orders	
FOREX Order Types	*Combined*
Market	No
Limit	Yes, with Stop
Stop	Yes, with Limit
Combination	Varies from Broker to Broker
Specialty	Varies from Broker to Broker

NFA Compliance Rule 2-43 now prohibits hedging orders—simultaneous orders to buy and sell. If your trading method requires hedging you may still find a foreign broker to accommodate your needs.

The trader's guiding rule should be to keep it simple. Do not use an order simply because it looks fun or interesting. Your trading method should be your primary guide to selecting an order arsenal. Complex orders distract from the primary job of watching and analyzing the markets, are difficult to execute, and increase the chances for error.

Most broker-dealers delineate the various orders they accept in their trading platform documentation; please look there before e-mailing them. Order functionality is typically integrated into the trading platform but some of them can still be difficult to execute. You can Google "FOREX orders" and variations to find some listings of broker-dealer web sites, FOREX portals, and learning web sites.

The exact definitions of many orders may vary slightly from broker to broker. Be sure you know your broker's terms before making any order.

The author has traded online FOREX for 12 years and has never had need for an order beyond the Basic Three palette.

Market Orders

A market order is an order to buy or sell at the market price. The buy may be to initiate a new position or liquidate a previous sell position. The sell may be to initiate a new position or liquidate a previous buy position. A market order may not be at the current price because, like a river, prices are always flowing. Most market makers show you the price you will receive before you execute the order. In requoting, you do not get that price. Large orders and slow, fast, and illiquid (*thin*) markets affect the price you receive on a market order.

A buy adds to aggregate demand and pushes prices up, if only slightly; a sell adds to aggregate supply and has the opposite effect. The bid-ask spread in

FOREX reflects this, as well as protecting your broker and helping him maintain an orderly book—and make a fair profit by serving you.

Limit Orders

A limit order specifies a specific price to execute your order. It may also specify duration, how long you wish to keep the order active. If the price is touched within the specified duration, your order becomes a market order.

There is also a stop-limit order. You specify a price and also a maximum range beyond that price for which the order can be executed. The advantage of a stop-limit order is that you will get the price you want if that price is reached. The disadvantage is that if prices do not trade in your specified range, your order remains unexecuted. In a fast market a stop-limit order may be a complete waste of effort; it simply will not be executed.

TIP: Use market orders in normal markets; use limit orders for large orders and in fast, slow, and thin markets. A market order in a fast market, such as immediately after the release of a news item, can be a disaster. Always use stops with every market order.

Be sure to keep track of all open orders you have in every market. They are *your* responsibility, not the broker's.

Stop Orders

A *stop order* is the terminology used for a limit order that liquidates or offsets an open position.

An automatic trailing stop is offered by several broker-dealers. This raises or lowers your stop by a fixed value as the market goes in your position, thus protecting some of your profits. You can, of course, mechanically apply trailing stops. They are great in theory, not quite so great in practice. They work better with some trading methods than with others. I find automatic trailing stops are too mechanical.

A major debate has raged for years in both futures and FOREX as to whether traders should use stop-loss orders in the market or simply keep them to themselves—mental stops—and wait for the market to reach that price and then use a market order. Many traders believe brokers use stops entered in the market to balance their book. Brokers are occasionally accused of running or harvesting stops—moving their data feed specifically to execute the stop order. This does happen; how often is difficult to say.

Beginners should use stops. Once you have some experience in the market—and if and only if you have good discipline—then keep mental stops. It is easy to ignore a mental stop and hope the market will turn back in your favor—and it usually does not. Yes, by using stops the broker can see your order; and, yes, stops may be harvested; and, yes, stop fills—especially without limits—may be poor. But we still recommend that the new trader use them.

Never leave an open position unattended without a stop. I still remember an incident from when I was a young commodities trader and watched the markets from the local Peavey office. Soybeans were limit up with a profit of $1,000. I left to get a cup of coffee from the cantina, returning in less than five minutes to see the market was limit down—a $1,000 loss. A further discussion of this important topic is included in Chapter 16, "Money Management Simplified."

Stops may also be combined with limit orders. I do not recommend this type of order to the new trader.

You may have difficulty getting comfortable with stops and limits. They are essentially mirror images of each other. See Figure 9.1.

TIP: A stop order is at a worse price than current price. Lower if sell stop for a sell, higher if buy stop for a buy. A limit order is at a better price than current price. Higher if sell limit for a sell, lower if buy limit for a buy.

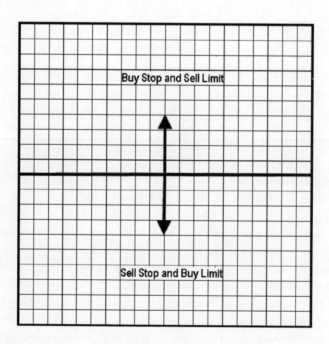

FIGURE 9.1 Stop and Limit Orders

Combination Orders

Many orders are not mutually exclusive and can, if the broker permits it, be combined. A common one is a *one cancels the other* (OCO) order. The execution of one order automatically cancels the other. You might enter both a buy and sell order in a market awaiting a breakout from a narrow trading range. If either is executed, it cancels the other.

Specialty Orders

There are perhaps a dozen or more specialty orders; the beginner is advised to stay away from them. A few brokers offer orders unique to their trading platform. Time triggers specify a time when an order should become active and for how long. A Box-Top is a market order that automatically changes to a limit order if it is not executed at the market price right away. Limit On Close (LOC) and Limit On Open (LOO) are executed at the closing price or the limit price if that price is equal to or better than a specified limit price.

The FOREX forums are a good place to find out how traders use specialty stops as well as the pros and cons. New traders should avoid these modulations.

Order Placement

Order placement will vary from broker to broker, depending on how their trading platform is organized. As of 2009 placing an order is a simple and pleasant experience. Your trading platform really does all the calculation for you. Traders can typically see the various parameters of their orders before executing—leverage, margins, pips-to-dollars (if the dollar is your account-denominated currency), and other pertinent information.

Practice with a broker's order placement system first on a demo account. When you open a mini- or micro-account, practice again with small amounts of real money. I suggest lots of a maximum of 500 units until your process is error-free.

When you enter an order you must specify three pieces of information: (1) the currency pair, (2) buying or selling, and (3) the quantity. If it is a pending order you must also specify how long it will remain in the market. I recommend that the new trader enter both a stop-loss and a take-profit order with every market order. Once a pending order has been filled, then enter a stop-loss and take-profit immediately.

TIP: Practice all the types of orders you intend to use on a demo account until they are second nature to you. Each time you sit down to work with the demo, practice a few orders as your first task. Begin with simple market orders, add stop-loss and take-profit orders, then move on to pending orders.

Order Execution

Traders using an online trading platform click on the "Buy " or "Sell" button after having specified the underlying currency pair, the desired number of units to trade, the price, and the order type. The execution of the order is almost always instantaneous. This means that the price seen at the exact time of the click will be given to the customer. If you leave the order palette or window open too long and prices change you will receive a requote when you actually pull the trigger.

It is still possible with most brokers to place an order by phone in an emergency situation, but this method is almost unheard of today as a standard practice. Some brokers will no longer accept telephone orders. If they do, be sure to have *all* your identification information at the ready. If they do not, you may enter a counter trade in the same amount on your backup broker's platform. Not pretty but it will serve the purpose.

Order Confirmation

Online traders receive a screen message indicating confirmation of an order within seconds after the trade has been accepted and executed, as shown in Figure 9.2. The trade will also show up on the platform's Open Positions page.

FIGURE 9.2   Order Confirmation Screen

Source: TradeviewForex, www.tradeviewforex.com and MetaTrader, www.metaquotes.net

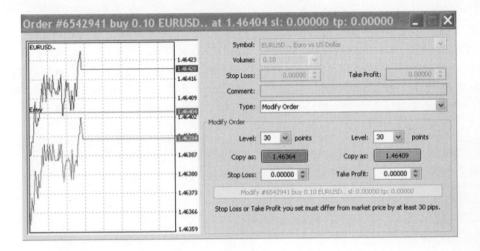

FIGURE 9.3 Order Cancel or Modify
Source: TradeviewForex, www.tradeviewfx.com and MetaTrader, www.metaquotes.net

Traders can also cancel or modify an order that has not been executed at any time. Most brokers respond with a message similar to the one seen in Figure 9.3.

Open Orders

Your broker's trading platform will also inform you of your transaction exposure and details (see Figure 9.4).

Once your trade is executed, it will show on your broker's Open Trades page. When the trade is closed and complete, a summary will show on the Account Summary page. As far as the order and accounting information you require is concerned, almost all brokers have this down pat on their platforms. One of the purposes of the demo account is allowing you to become second nature comfortable with how it all works and ties together.

TIP: Before executing an order review all aspects of the order one last time before clicking "Submit." The two most common order entry errors are selecting "Buy" instead of "Sell" (especially to offset an order) and entering the

ORDER	TIME	TYPE	SIZE	SYMBOL	PRICE	S/L	T/P	PRICE	COMMISSION	PROFIT
17841355	2010.01.14.04	Sell	2	EURUSD	1.4547	1.4611		1.3617	0	18,592.00

FIGURE 9.4 Open Orders Summary

incorrect number of units. Note what values are preset (if any) on your broker's trading platform. Prices are quoted as either to four or five decimals of accuracy.

Remember, to offset an order it must be for the identical currency pair and number of units. Both Buy and Sell are offset with a Close Trade. If you attempt to Sell to liquidate a long or Buy to liquidate a short, you will receive an error message on a U.S. domiciled trading platform and simply have two trades in opposite directions (a hedge) opened on most foreign trading platforms.

If you buy a 50,000 lot and then another 50,000 lot, when you liquidate, the first 50,000 lot—on a U.S. account—will automatically be the one closed. Of course, you can also liquidate them as a single 100,000k lot.

Open a Demo Account

I suggest you open one demo account at this time. You will want to test drive others later. If you wish to begin with a broker and platform good for your entire trading career, I recommend www.pfgbest.com with the Ninja Trader platform. My broker is Tony Alaniz. If you wish to trade a micro-account to begin, www.oanda.com is a good choice.

Summary

The vast majority of traders can fully work their trading method with market, limit, and stop orders. Know which type of orders you need, and know how they work. Make sure that you and your broker are on the same page with respect to what they mean. Test your orders thoroughly in a demo account. A few trading systems require substantial order manipulation, but your time is generally better spent studying the markets than worrying about how to execute complicated order strategies and techniques.

The author strongly recommends that the new trader place a market order to enter a trade and place both a fixed-dollar stop-loss and fixed dollar take-profit order at the same time. Then, sit on your hands. See Chapter 16, "Money Management Simplified," for more on the fixed-dollar technique. The manual, which comes with your broker's trading platform, will detail all the orders available to you.

"Well, doggies," as Jed Clampett would say, you are ready to trade. At this stage in the game only execute trades on a demo account to get a feel for how things work.

TIP: You have three areas of interest in a demo account: (1) the order process, (2) the accounting process, and (3) platform features. Trading, for now, is just a means of learning these processes. After Chapter 15, "The Plan! The Plan!," you should have enough intellectual ammo to test the waters.

Practice, Practice, Practice!

Part

7

The Tools of the Trade

Fundamental Analysis

I t is commonly accepted that there are two major schools when formulating a trading strategy for any market, be it securities, futures, or currencies. These two disciplines are called fundamental analysis and technical analysis. The former is based on economic factors while the latter is concerned with price actions. The trader may opt to include elements of both disciplines while honing his or her personal trading strategy. Typically, fundamentals are about the long term; technicals are about the short term. Keep in mind what Lord Keynes once wrote: "In the long run we are all dead."

Supply and Demand

Fundamental analysis is a study of the economy and is based on the assumption that the supply and demand for currencies is a result of economic processes that can be observed in practice and that can be predicted. Fundamental analysis studies the relationship between the evolution of exchange rates and economic indicators, a relationship that it verifies and uses to make predictions.

For currencies, a fundamental trading strategy consists of strategic assessments in which a certain currency is traded based on virtually any criteria excluding the price action. These criteria include the economic condition of the country that the currency represents, monetary policy, and other elements that are fundamental to economies.

The focus of fundamental analysis lies in the economic, social, and political forces that drive supply and demand. There is no single set of beliefs that guides fundamental analysis, yet most fundamental analysts look at various macroeconomic indicators, such as economic growth rates, interest rates, inflation, and unemployment. Several theories prevail as to how currencies should be valued.

Done alone, fundamental analysis can be stressful for traders who deal with commodities, currencies, and other *margined* products. The reason for this is that fundamental analysis often does not provide specific entry and exit points, and therefore it can be difficult for traders to control risk when utilizing leverage techniques.

Currency prices are a reflection of the balance between supply and demand for currencies. Interest rates and the overall strength of the economy are the two primary factors that affect supply and demand. Economic indicators (for example, gross domestic product, foreign investment, and the trade balance) reflect the overall health of an economy. Therefore, they are responsible for the underlying changes in supply and demand for a particular currency. A tremendous amount of data relating to these indicators is released at regular intervals, and some of this data is significant. Data that is related to interest rates and international trade is analyzed closely.

Interest Rates

If there is an uncertainty in the market in terms of interest rates, then any developments regarding interest rates can have a direct effect on the currency markets. Generally, when a country raises its interest rates, the country's currency strengthens in relation to other currencies as assets are shifted away from it to gain a higher return elsewhere. Interest rate hikes, however, are usually not good news for stock markets. This is because many investors withdraw money from a country's stock market when there is an increase in interest rates, causing the country's currency to weaken. See Figure 10.1.

Knowing which effect prevails can be tricky, but usually there is an agreement among practitioners in the field as to what the interest rate move will do. The producer price index, the consumer price index, and the gross domestic product have proven to be the indicators with the biggest impact. The timing of interest rate moves is usually known in advance. It is generally known that these moves take place after regular meetings of the BOE (Bank of England), Fed (U.S. Federal Reserve), ECB (European Central Bank), BOJ (Bank of Japan), and other central banks.

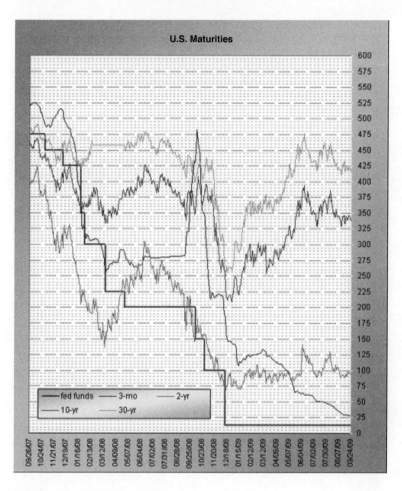

FIGURE 10.1 U.S. Interest Rates
Courtesy www.global-view.com

Balance of Trade

The trade balance portrays the net difference (over a period of time) between the imports and exports of a nation. When the value of imports becomes more than that of exports, the trade balance shows a *deficit* (this is, for the most part, considered unfavorable). For example, if Euros are sold for other domestic national currencies, such as U.S. dollars, to pay for imports, the value of the currency will depreciate due to the flow of dollars outside the country. By contrast, if trade figures show an increase in exports, money will flow into the country

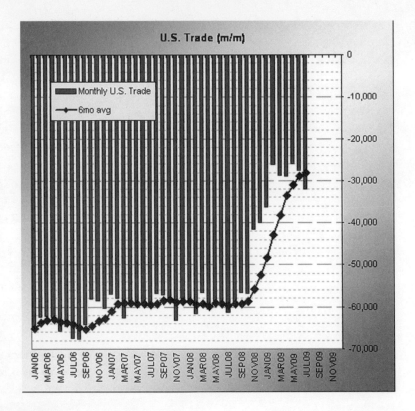

FIGURE 10.2   U.S. Balance of Trade
Courtesy www.global-view.com

and increase the value of the currency. In some ways, however, a deficit is not necessarily a bad thing. A deficit is only negative if the deficit is greater than market expectations and therefore will trigger a negative price movement. See Figure 10.2.

Purchasing Power Parity

Purchasing power parity (PPP) is a theory that states that exchange rates between currencies are in equilibrium when their purchasing power is the same in each of the two countries. This means that the exchange rate between two countries should equal the ratio of the two countries' price levels of a fixed basket of goods and services. When a country's domestic price level is increasing (i.e., a country experiences inflation), that country's exchange rate must depreciate in order to return to PPP.

The basis for PPP is the "law of one price." In the absence of transportation and other transaction costs, competitive markets will equalize the price of an identical good in two countries when the prices are expressed in the same currency. For example, a particular TV set that sells for 500 U.S. Dollars (USD) in Seattle should cost 750 Canadian Dollars (CAD) in Vancouver when the exchange rate between Canada and the United States is 1.50 USD/CAD. If the price of the TV in Vancouver costs only 700 CAD, however, consumers in Seattle would prefer buying the TV set in Vancouver. If this process (called *arbitrage*) is carried out on a large scale, the U.S. consumers buying Canadian goods will bid up the value of the Canadian Dollar, thus making Canadian goods more costly to them. This process continues until the goods again have the same price. There are three caveats with this law of one price: (1) as mentioned earlier, transportation costs, barriers to trade, and other transaction costs can be significant; (2) there must be competitive markets for the goods and services in both countries; (3) the law of one price only applies to tradable goods—immobile goods such as houses and many services that are local are not traded between countries.

Economists use two versions of purchasing power parity: absolute PPP and relative PPP. Absolute PPP was described in the previous paragraph; it refers to the equalization of price levels across countries. Put formally, the exchange rate between Canada and the United States ECAD/USD is equal to the price level in Canada PCAN divided by the price level in the United States PUSA. Assume that the price level ratio PCAD/PUSD implies a PPP exchange rate of 1.3 CAD per 1 USD. If today's exchange rate ECAD/USD is 1.5 CAD per 1 USD, PPP theory implies that the CAD will appreciate (get stronger) against the USD, and the USD will in turn depreciate (get weaker) against the CAD.

Relative PPP refers to rates of changes of price levels, that is, inflation rates. This proposition states that the rate of appreciation of a currency is equal to the difference in inflation rates between the foreign and the home country. For example, if Canada has an inflation rate of 1 percent and the United States has an inflation rate of 3 percent, the U.S. Dollar will depreciate against the Canadian Dollar by 2 percent per year. This proposition holds well empirically, especially when the inflation differences are large.

> The simplest way to calculate purchasing power parity between two
> countries is to compare the price of a "standard" good that is, in fact,
> identical across countries. Every year the *Economist* magazine pub-
> lishes a lighthearted version of PPP: Its "Hamburger Index" lists the
> price of a McDonald's hamburger in various countries around the
> world. More sophisticated versions of PPP look at a large number of
> goods and services. One of the key problems in computing a

comprehensive PPP is that people in different countries consume different sets of goods and services, making it difficult to compare the purchasing power between countries.

Gross Domestic Product

The *gross domestic product* (GDP) is the total market value of all goods and services produced either by domestic or foreign companies within a country's borders. GDP indicates the pace at which a country's economy is growing (or shrinking) and is considered the broadest indicator of economic output and growth.

GDPs of different countries can be compared by converting their value in national currency according to either exchange rates prevailing on international currency markets or the purchasing power parity (PPP) of each currency relative to a selected standard (usually the U.S. Dollar).

The relative ranking of countries may differ dramatically depending on which approach is used: Using official exchange rates can routinely understate the relative effective domestic purchasing power of the average producer or consumer within a less-developed economy by 50 percent to 60 percent, owing to the weakness of local currencies on world markets.

However, comparison based on official exchange rates can offer a better indication of a country's purchasing power on the international market for goods and services.

Intervention

Another important fundamental influence on FOREX currency prices is called *intervention.* This occurs when an official regulatory agency or a financial institution with one government directly coerces the exchange rate of its currency, usually by reevaluation, devaluation, or by the manipulation of imports and exports in some way.

Such actions may cause broad and erratic changes in the exchange rate with foreign currencies. However, it is from such anomalies that the FOREX trader may profit, if the proper stop-loss safeguards are in place.

Other Economic Indicators

The range of economic indicators and the standing reports generated from them are extensive. Here are a few others that impact currency prices.

Industrial Production

Industrial production (IP) is a chain-weighted measure of the change in the production of the nation's factories, mines, and utilities, as well as a measure of their industrial capacity and how many available resources among factories, utilities, and mines are being used (commonly known as capacity utilization). The manufacturing sector accounts for one-quarter of the economy. The capacity utilization rate provides an estimate of how much factory capacity is in use.

Purchasing Managers Index

The National Association of Purchasing Managers (NAPM), now called the Institute for Supply Management, releases a monthly composite index of national manufacturing conditions, constructed from data on new orders, production, supplier delivery times, backlogs, inventories, prices, employment, export orders, and import orders. It is divided into manufacturing and nonmanufacturing subindices.

Producer Price Index

The producer price index (PPI) is a measure of price changes in the manufacturing sector. It measures average changes in selling prices received by domestic producers in the manufacturing, mining, agriculture, and electric utility industries for their output. The PPIs most often used for economic analysis are those for finished goods, intermediate goods, and crude goods.

Consumer Price Index

The *consumer price index* (CPI) is a measure of the average price level paid by urban consumers (80 percent of the population) for a fixed basket of goods and services. It reports price changes in more than 200 categories. The CPI also includes various user fees and taxes directly associated with the prices of specific goods and services.

Durable Goods

The durable goods orders indicator measures new orders placed with domestic manufacturers for immediate and future delivery of factory hard goods. A durable good is defined as a good that lasts an extended period of time (three years or more) during which its services are extended.

Employment Index

Payroll employment is a measure of the number of jobs in more than 500 industries in all 50 states and 255 metropolitan areas. The employment estimates are based on a survey of larger businesses and count the number of paid employees working part-time or full-time in the nation's business and government establishments. Currently, the Non-Farm Payroll Report (NFP), issued the first Friday of each month, is closely watched by traders of the USD. News traders much anticipate this report because the prereport consensus of the number is typically incorrect—resulting in short-term fireworks for the USD currency pairs.

Retail Sales

The retail sales report is a measure of the total receipts of retail stores from samples representing all sizes and kinds of business in retail trade throughout the nation. It is the timeliest indicator of broad consumer spending patterns and is adjusted for normal seasonal variation, holidays, and trading-day differences. Retail sales include durable and nondurable merchandise sold, and services and excise taxes incidental to the sale of merchandise. Excluded are sales taxes collected directly from the customer.

Housing Starts

The housing starts report measures the number of residential units on which construction is begun each month. A start in construction is defined as the beginning of excavation of the foundation for the building and is comprised primarily of residential housing. Housing is interest rate–sensitive and is one of the first sectors to react to changes in interest rates. Significant reaction of starts/permits to changing interest rates signals that interest rates are nearing a trough or a peak. To analyze the data, focus on the percentage change in levels from the previous month. The report is released around the middle of the following month.

Forecasting

Fundamental analysis refers to the study of the core underlying elements that influence the economy of a particular entity. It is a method of study that attempts to predict price action and market trends by analyzing economic indicators, government policy, and societal factors (to name just a few elements) within a business cycle framework. If you think of the financial markets as a big clock, the fundamentals are the gears and springs that move the hands around the face. Anyone walking down the street can look at this clock and tell you what time it is now, but the fundamentalist can tell you how it came to be this time and, more importantly, what time (or more precisely, what price) it will be in the future.

There is a tendency to pigeonhole traders into two distinct schools of market analysis—fundamental and technical. Indeed, the first question posed to you after you tell someone that you are a trader is generally "Are you a technician or a fundamentalist?" The reality is that it has become increasingly difficult to be a purist of either persuasion. Fundamentalists need to keep an eye on the various signals derived from the price action on charts, while few technicians can afford to completely ignore impending economic data, critical political decisions, or the myriad of societal issues that influence prices.

Bearing in mind that the financial underpinnings of any country, trading bloc, or multinational industry take into account many factors, including social, political, and economic influences, staying on top of an extremely fluid fundamental picture can be challenging. At the same time, you find that your knowledge and understanding of a dynamic global market increases immeasurably as you delve further and further into the complexities and subtleties of the fundamentals of the markets.

Fundamental analysis is an effective way to forecast economic conditions, but not necessarily exact market prices. For example, when analyzing an economist's forecast of the upcoming GDP or employment report, you begin to get a fairly clear picture of the general health of the economy and the forces at work behind it. However, you need to come up with a precise method as to how best to translate this information into entry and exit points for a particular trading strategy.

A trader who studies the markets using fundamental analysis generally creates models to formulate a trading strategy. These models typically utilize a host of empirical data and attempt to forecast market behavior and estimate future values or prices by using past values of core economic indicators. These forecasts are then used to derive specific trades that best exploit this information.

Forecasting models are as numerous and varied as the traders and market buffs that create them. Two people can look at the same data and come up with two completely different conclusions about how the market will be influenced by it. Therefore it is important that before casting yourself into a particular mold regarding any aspect of market analysis, you study the fundamentals and see how they best fit your trading style and expectations.

Do not succumb to "paralysis by analysis." Given the multitude of factors that fall under the heading of "The Fundamentals," there is a distinct danger of information overload. Sometimes traders fall into this trap and are unable to pull the trigger on a trade. This is one of the reasons why many traders turn to *technical analysis*. To some, technical analysis is seen as a way to transform all of the fundamental factors that influence the markets into one simple tool: prices. However, trading a particular market without knowing a great deal about the exact nature of its underlying elements is like fishing without bait. You might get lucky and snare a few on occasion, but it's not the best approach over the long haul.

For FOREX traders, the fundamentals are everything that makes a country tick. From interest rates and central bank policy to natural disasters, the fundamentals are a dynamic mix of distinct plans, erratic behaviors, and unforeseen events. Therefore, it is easier to get a handle on the most influential contributors to this diverse mix than it is to formulate a comprehensive list of all the fundamentals.

Economic indicators are snippets of financial and economic data published by various agencies of the government or private sector. These statistics, which are made public on a regularly scheduled basis, help market observers monitor the pulse of the economy. Therefore, they are religiously followed by almost everyone in the financial markets. With so many people poised to react to the same information, economic indicators in general have tremendous potential to generate volume and to move prices in the markets. While on the surface it might seem that an advanced degree in economics would come in handy to analyze and then trade on the glut of information contained in these economic indicators, a few simple guidelines are all that is necessary to track, organize, and make trading decisions based on the data.

Know exactly when each economic indicator is due to be released. Keep a calendar on your desk or trading station that contains the date and time when each statistic will be made public. You can find these calendars on the New York Federal Reserve Bank web site using this link: www.ny.frb.org. Then search for "economic indicators." The same information is also available from many other sources on the Web or from the broker you use to execute your trades. Chapter 13, "The FOREX Marketplace," lists several web sites that monitor news releases.

Keeping track of the calendar of economic indicators will also help you make sense out of otherwise unanticipated price action in the market. Consider this scenario: It's Monday morning and the U.S. Dollar has been in a tailspin for three weeks. As such, it is safe to assume that many traders are holding large short USD positions. However, the employment data for the United States is due to be released on Friday. It is likely that with this key piece of economic information soon to be made public, the USD could experience a short-term rally leading up to the data on Friday as traders pare down their short positions. The point here is that economic indicators can affect prices directly (following their release to the public) or indirectly (as traders massage their positions in anticipation of the data).

Understand which particular aspect of the economy is being revealed in the data. For example, you should know which indicators measure the growth of the economy (GDP) versus those that measure inflation (PPI, CPI) or employment (nonfarm payrolls). After you follow the data for a while, you will become very familiar with the nuances of each economic indicator and which part of the economy it measures.

Not all economic indicators are created equal. Well, they might have been created with equal importance but along the way, some have acquired much greater potential to move the markets than others. Market participants will place higher regard on one statistic versus another depending on the state of the economy.

Know which indicators the markets are keying on. For example, if prices (inflation) are not a crucial issue for a particular country, the markets will probably not as keenly anticipate or react to inflation data. However, if economic growth is a vexing problem, changes in employment data or GDP will be eagerly anticipated and could precipitate tremendous volatility following its release.

The data itself is not as important as whether it falls within market expectations. Besides knowing when all the data will hit the wires, it is vitally important that you know what economists and other market pundits are forecasting for each indicator. For example, knowing the economic consequences of an unexpected monthly rise of 0.3 percent in the producer price index (PPI) is not nearly as vital to your short-term trading decisions as it is to know that this month the market was looking for PPI to fall by 0.1 percent. As mentioned, you should know that PPI measures prices and that an unexpected rise could be a sign of inflation. But analyzing the longer-term ramifications of this unexpected monthly rise in prices can wait until after you have taken advantage of the trading opportunities presented by the data. Once again, market expectations for all economic releases are published on various sources on the Web and you should post these expectations on your calendar along with the release date of the indicator.

Do not get caught up in the headlines, however. Part of getting a handle on what the market is forecasting for various economic indicators is knowing the key aspects of each indicator. While your macroeconomics professor might have drilled the significance of the unemployment rate into your head, even junior traders can tell you that the headline figure is for amateurs and that the most closely watched detail in the payroll data is the nonfarm payrolls figure. Other economic indicators are similar because the headline figure is not nearly as closely watched as the finer points of the data. PPI, for example, measures changes in producer prices. But the statistic most closely watched by the markets is PPI, minus food and energy price changes. Traders know that the food and energy component of the data is much too volatile and subject to revisions on a month-to-month basis to provide an accurate reading on the changes in producer prices.

Speaking of revisions, do not be too quick to pull that trigger should a particular economic indicator fall outside of market expectations. Contained in each new economic indicator released to the public are revisions to previously released data. For example, if durable goods should rise by 0.5 percent in the current month, while the market is anticipating them to fall, the unexpected rise could be the result of a downward revision to the prior month. Look at revisions to older data because in this case, the previous month's durable goods figure might have been originally reported as a rise of 0.5 percent but now, along with the new figures, it is being revised to indicate a rise of only 0.1 percent. Therefore, the unexpected rise in the current month is likely the result of a downward revision to the previous month's data.

TIP: It is not uncommon for prices to surge one way immediately after a news announcement—only to quickly turn and head in the opposite direction. Give the markets time to talk before you decide what they are saying about the news.

Do not forget that there are two sides to a trade in the foreign exchange market. So, while you might have a handle on the complete package of economic indicators published in the United States or Europe, most other countries also publish similar economic data. The important thing to remember here is that not all countries are as efficient as the G8 in releasing this information. Once again, if you are going to trade the currency of a particular country, you need to find out the particulars about that country's economic indicators. As mentioned earlier, not all of these indicators carry the same weight in the markets and not all of them are as accurate as others. Do your homework so you will not be caught off guard.

When it comes to focusing exclusively on the impact that economic indicators have on price action in a particular market, the foreign exchange markets are the most challenging. Therefore, they have the greatest potential for profits of any market. Obviously, factors other than economic indicators move prices and as such make other markets more or less potentially profitable. But since a currency is a proxy for the country it represents, the economic health of that country is priced into the currency. One important way to measure the health of an economy is through economic indicators. The challenge comes in diligently keeping track of the nuts and bolts of each country's particular economic information package. Here are a few general comments about economic indicators and some of the more closely watched data.

Most economic indicators can be divided into leading and lagging indicators. Leading indicators are economic factors that change before the economy starts to follow a particular pattern or trend. Leading indicators are used to predict changes in the economy. Lagging indicators are economic factors that change after the economy has already begun to follow a particular pattern or trend.

The problem with fundamental analysis is that it is difficult to convert the "qualitative" information into a specific price prediction. With FOREX leverage being what it is, it is seldom enough to know that a report is "bullish" for a currency without being able to attach specific values.

Econometric analysis attempts to quantify the often qualitative fundamental factors into a mathematical model. These models can become enormously complex. The problems with econometric analysis are twofold: It is difficult to objectively quantify qualitative information such as a news announcement. The interactions and specific weights of each factor are constantly in flux and the relationships between them are almost certainly nonlinear. Relationships that hold today are invalid tomorrow.

Summary

Fundamental analysis is a very deep well. It is important to understand the basic fundamentals that drive currency prices, even though most traders use technical analysis to make specific day-to-day trading decisions.

Fundamentals can be extremely powerful and useful to the trader. But they have a much steeper learning curve to use effectively than do technicals.

Even if you opt for a technical analysis trading approach, as most traders do, *do not* completely ignore the fundamentals. Use a new service to do a daily take on what is happening. Remember: Be aware of pending reports and statistical releases. They often will cause a violent market reaction one way or the other. The impact of fundamental information is more important than the information itself.

Chapter 11

Technical Analysis

Overview

The most popular and successful method of making decisions and analyzing FOREX markets is technical analysis. Technical analysis is used by large and small traders alike. The difference between technical and fundamental analyses is that technical analysis ignores fundamental factors and is applied only to the price action of the market. Although fundamental data can often provide only a long-term forecast of exchange rate movements, technical analysis has become the primary tool to successfully analyze and trade shorter-term price movements, as well as to set profit targets and stop-loss safeguards because of its ability to generate price-specific information and forecasts.

Historically, technical analysis in the futures markets has focused on the six price fields available during any given period of time: open, high, low, close, volume, and open interest. Since the FOREX market has no central exchange, it is difficult to estimate the latter two fields, volume and open interest. In this chapter, we limit our analysis to the first four price fields.

Technical analysis consists primarily of a variety of technical studies, each of which can be interpreted to predict market direction or to generate buy and sell signals. Many technical studies share one common important tool: a price-time chart that emphasizes selected characteristics in the price motion of the underlying security. One great advantage of technical analysis is its "visualness." A picture is worth a thousand words.

Bar Charts

Bar charts are the most widely used type of chart in security market technical analysis and date back to the last decade of the nineteenth century. They are popular because they are easy to construct and understand. These charts are constructed by representing intraday, daily, weekly, or monthly activity as a vertical bar. Opening and closing prices are represented by horizontal marks to the left and right of the vertical bar respectively. Spotting both patterns and the trend of a market, two of the essentials of chart reading, is often easiest using bar charts. Bar charts present the data individually, without linking prices to neighboring prices. Each set of price fields is a single "island."

Each vertical bar has the components shown in Figure 11.1.

Figure 11.2 shows a daily bar chart for the EUR/USD currency pair for the month of June 2003. The vertical scale on the right represents the cost of one Euro in terms of U.S. Dollars. The horizontal legend at the bottom of the chart represents the day of week.

A common method of classifying the vertical bars is to show the relationships between the opening and closing prices within a single time interval as either bull or bear bars, as seen in Figure 11.3.

Graphically, an open/high/low/close (OHLC) bar chart is defined using the following algorithm:

OHLC Bar Chart Algorithm

- Step 1—One vertical rectangle whose upper boundary represents the high for the day and whose lower boundary represents the low for the given time period.
- Step 2—One horizontal rectangle to the left of the high-low rectangle whose central value represents the opening price for the given period.
- Step 3—One horizontal rectangle to the right of the high-low rectangle whose central value represents the closing price for the given period.

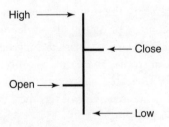

FIGURE 11.1 Anatomy of Single Vertical Bar

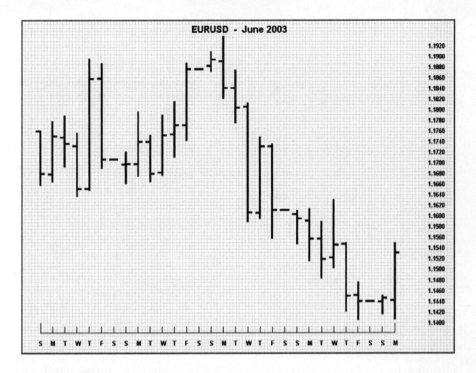

FIGURE 11.2 Vertical Bar Chart

One interesting variation to the standard OHLC bar chart was developed by author/trader Burton Pugh is the 1930s. His model involved connecting the previous set of quotes to the current set of quotes, which generates a continuous line representation of price movements. There are four basic formations between two adjacent vertical bars in Burton's system. (See Figure 11.4.)

These are often called swing charts. To see how they can be used by breaking them into four types, see Pugh Charts in Chapter 12, "A Trader's Toolbox."

Bar chart interpretation is one of the most fascinating and well-studied topics in the realm of technical analysis. Recurring bar chart formations have been labeled, categorized, and analyzed in detail. Common formations like tops,

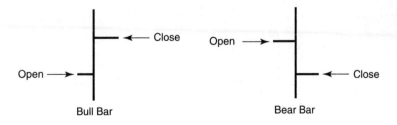

FIGURE 11.3 Anatomy of Bull and Bear Bars

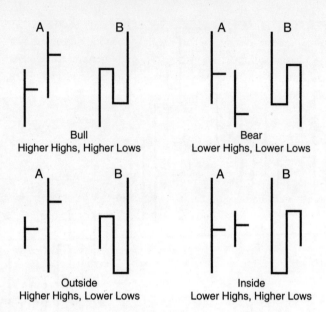

FIGURE 11.4   Continuous Line Bar Chart

bottoms, head-and-shoulders, inverted head-and-shoulders, lines of support and resistance, reversals, and so forth, are examined in the following sections.

Trendlines

A trend can be up, down, or lateral and is represented by drawing a straight line above the daily highs in a downward trend and a straight line below the daily lows in an upward trend. See Figure 11.5.

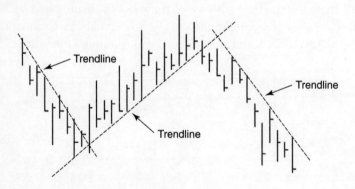

FIGURE 11.5   Bar Chart with Trendlines

A common trading technique involves the intersection of the trendline with the most recent prices. If the trendline for a downward trend crosses through the most recent prices, a buy signal is generated. Conversely, if the trendline for an upward trend passes through the most recent prices, then a sell signal is generated.

Support and Resistance

Support levels indicate the price at which most traders feel that prices will move higher. There is sufficient demand for a security to cause a halt in a downward trend and turn the trend up. You can spot support levels on the bar charts by looking for a sequence of daily lows that fluctuate only slightly along a horizontal line. When a support level is penetrated (the price drops below the support level) it often becomes a resistance level; this is because traders want to limit their losses and will sell later, when prices approach the former level.

Like support levels, resistance levels are horizontal lines on the bar chart. They mark the upper level for trading, or a price at which sellers typically outnumber buyers. When resistance levels are broken, the price moves above the resistance level, and often does so decisively. See Figure 11.6.

Many traders find lines of support and resistance useful in determining the placement of *stop-loss* and *take-profit* limit orders.

Recognizing Chart Patterns

Proper identification of an ongoing trend can be a tremendous asset to the trader. However, the trader must also learn to recognize recurring chart patterns that disrupt the continuity of trendlines. Broadly speaking, these chart patterns can be categorized as reversal patterns and continuation patterns.

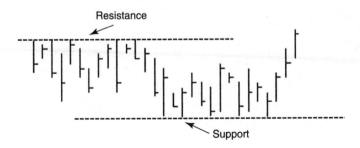

FIGURE 11.6   Bar Chart with Support and Resistance Lines

Reversal Patterns

Reversal patterns are important because they inform the trader that a market entry point is unfolding or that it may be time to liquidate an open position. Figures 11.7 through 11.10 illustrate the most common reversal patterns.

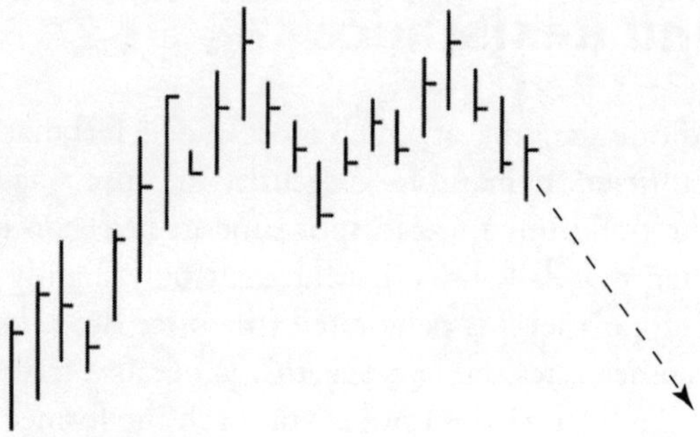

FIGURE 11.7   Double Top

FIGURE 11.8   Double Bottom

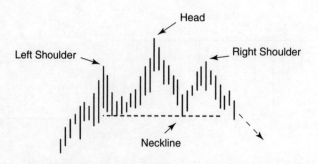

FIGURE 11.9   Head-and-Shoulders Top

FIGURE 11.10   Head-and-Shoulders Bottom

Continuation Patterns

A continuation pattern implies that while a visible trend was in progress, it was temporarily interrupted, and then continued in the direction of the original trend. The most common continuation patterns are shown in Figures 11.11 through 11.15.

The proper identification of a continuation pattern may prevent the trader from prematurely liquidating an open position that still has profit potential.

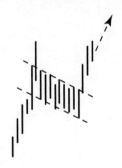

FIGURE 11.11   Flag or Pennant

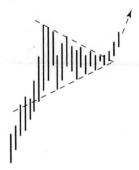

FIGURE 11.12   Symmetrical Triangle

FIGURE 11.13   Ascending Triangle

FIGURE 11.14   Descending Triangle

FIGURE 11.15   Rectangle

These are some of the most common classical bar chart formations. Do they work? Sometimes. They worked more often in years gone by when fewer traders knew about them. Nowadays, everyone knows what a head and shoulders looks like. The result? Traders will begin to anticipate the second shoulder and sell before it forms. The result—often, no head and shoulders forms—just one shoulder and a head. This is how the market discounts information. Methods that work well initially become less and less effective over the years.

Candlestick Charts

These charts have found great popularity with currency traders. *Candlestick charting* is usually credited to the Japanese rice trader Munehisa Homma in the early eighteenth century, though many references indicate that this method of technical analysis probably existed as early as the 1600s. Steven Nison of Merrill Lynch is credited with popularizing candlestick charting in Western markets and has become recognized as the leading expert on their interpretation. See Figure 11.16.

The candlestick is the graphic representation of the price bar: the open, high, low, and closing price of the period. The algorithm to construct a candlestick chart follows.

The elements of a candlestick bar are shown in Figure 11.17.

FIGURE 11.16   Candlestick Chart

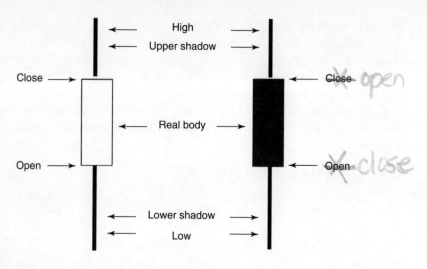

FIGURE 11.17   Anatomy of Candlestick Bar

The nomenclature used to identify individual or consecutive combinations of candlesticks is rich in imagery: Hammer, hanging man, dark cloud cover, morning star, three black crows, three mountains, three advanced white soldiers, and spinning tops are only a few of the candlestick patterns that have been categorized and used in technical analysis.

Candlestick Chart Algorithm
• Step 1—The candlestick is made up of a body and two shadows.
• Step 2—The body is depicted as a vertical column bounded by the opening price and the closing price.
• Step 3—The shadows are just vertical lines—a line above the body to the high of the day (the upper shadow) and a line below the body to the low of the day (the lower shadow).
• Step 4—It is customary for the body to be empty if the close was higher than the open (a bull day) and filled if the close was lower than the open (a bear day).

A thorough description of how to interpret candlestick charts is given in Steven Nison's books: *Japanese Candlestick Charting Techniques* (Hall, 1991) and *Beyond Candlesticks: More Japanese Charting Techniques Revealed* (John Wiley & Sons, 1994). A summary of the different candlestick patterns can also be found at www.hotcandle.com/candle.htm.

Point and Figure Charts

The modern *point and figure* (P&F) chart was created in the late nineteenth century and is roughly 15 years older than the standard OHLC bar chart. This technique, also called the three-box reversal method, is probably the oldest Western method of charting prices still around today.

Its roots date back into trading lore, as it has been intimated that this method was successfully used by the legendary trader James R. Keene during the merger of U.S. Steel in 1901. Mr. Keene was employed by Andrew Carnegie to distribute the company shares, as Carnegie refused to take stock as payment for his equity interest in the company. Keene, using point and figure charting and tape readings, managed to promote the stock and get rid of Carnegie's sizeable stake without causing the price to crash. This simple method of charting has stood the test of time and requires less time to construct and maintain than the traditional bar chart. See Figure 11.18.

The point and figure method derives its name from the fact that price is recorded using figures (Xs and Os) to represent a point, hence the name "Point and Figure." Charles Dow, the original founder of the *Wall Street Journal* and the inventor of stock indexes, was rumored to be a point and figure user. Indeed, the practice of point and figure charting is alive and well today on the floor of all futures exchanges. The method's simplicity in identifying price trends and support and resistance levels, as well as its ease of upkeep, has allowed it to endure the test of time, even in the age of web pages, personal computers, and the information explosion.

The elements of the point and figure anatomy are shown later in Figure 11.19.

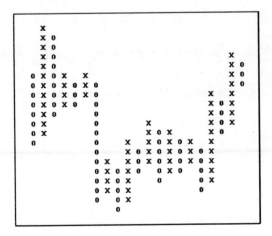

FIGURE 11.18 Point and Figure Chart

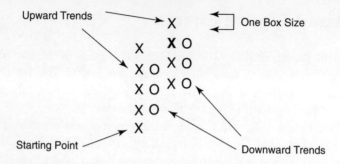

FIGURE 11.19   Anatomy of Point and Figure Columns

Two user-defined variables are required to plot a point and figure chart, the first of which is called the box size. This is the minimum grid increment that the price must move in order to satisfy the plotting of a new X and O. The selection of the box size variable is usually based upon a multiple of the minimum tick size determined by the commodity exchange. If the box size is too small, then the point and figure chart will not filter out white noise, while too large a filter will not present enough detail in the chart to make it useful. I recommend initializing the box size for a FOREX P&F chart with the value of one or two pips in the underlying currency pair.

The second user-defined parameter necessary to plot a point and figure chart is called the reversal amount. If the price moves in the same direction as the existing trend, then only one box size is required to plot the continuation of the trend. However, in order to filter out small fluctuations in price movements (or lateral congestion), a reversal in trend cannot be plotted until it satisfies the reversal amount constraint. Typically, this value is set at three box sizes, though any value between one and seven is a plausible candidate. The daily limit imposed by most commodity exchanges can also influence the trader's selection of the reversal amount variable.

The algorithm to construct a point and figure chart follows:

Point and Figure Algorithm

- Upward trends are represented as a vertical column of *X*s, while downward trends are displayed as an adjacent column of *O*s.

- New figures (Xs or Os) cannot be added to the current column unless the increase (or decrease) in price satisfies the minimum box size requirement.

- A reversal cannot be plotted in the subsequent column until the price has changed by the reversal amount times the box size.

Point and figure charts display the underlying supply and demand of prices. A column of Xs shows that demand is exceeding supply (a rally); a column of Os shows that supply is exceeding demand (a decline); and a series of short columns shows that supply and demand are relatively equal. There are several advantages to using P&F charts instead of the more traditional bar or candlestick charts.

Advantages of P&F Charts

P&F charts automatically:
- Eliminate the insignificant price movements that often make bar charts appear "noisy."
- Remove the often-misleading effects of time from the analysis process (whipsawing).
- Make trendline recognition a "no-brainer."
- Make recognizing support/ resistance levels much easier.

Nearly all of the pattern formations discussed earlier have analogous patterns that appear when using a standard OHLC bar chart. Adjusting the two variables, box size and reversal amount, may cause these patterns to become more recognizable.

P&F charts also:
- Are a viable online analytical tool in real time. They require only a sheet of paper and pencil.
- Help you stay focused on the important long-term price developments.

The author uses a point and figure routine in which the reversal is not a number of boxes but a percentage of the previous column. This accommodates his Goodman Wave Theory method described in Chapter 12, "A Trader's Toolbox."

For a more detailed examination of this charting technique, we recommend *Point & Figure Charting* by Thomas J. Dorsey (John Wiley & Sons, 2001).

Charting Caveat—Prediction versus Description

Chart patterns always look impressive and convincing after the fact. The question is: Can they be predicted or are they simply descriptive? One simple method I learned from my mentor Charles B. Goodman for studying this idea is to take an old chart with an already well-formed chart pattern. Cover it with a sheet of blank, opaque paper. Move the paper slowly left-to-right to simulate real-time trading. Would you be able to predict the chart pattern in advance? You can easily see the patterns that work—seeing the ones that did not work is more difficult.

The author has written a program, Charlie's CAT, to automate this procedure with computer charts.

Indicators and Oscillators

Beyond charting are various market indicators—calculations using the primary information of open, high, low, or close. Indicators can also be charted or graphed. Buy and sell signals and complete systems can be generated from a battery of indicators. The most popular indicators are: relative strength, moving averages, oscillators or momentum analysis (actually a superset of relative strength), and Bollinger bands.

TIP: Traders are fascinated by indicators. Numbers bring a sense of certainty. Be sure you know what an indicator is actually doing, measuring before using it.

Relative Strength Indicator

The relative strength indicator (RSI) shows whether a currency is overbought or oversold. Overbought indicates an upward market trend, because the financial operators are buying a currency in the hope of further rate increases. Sooner or later saturation will occur because the financial operators have already created a long position. They show restraint in making additional purchases and try to make a profit. The profits made can quickly lead to a change in the trend or at least a consolidation.

Oversold indicates that the market is showing downward trend conditions, because the operators are selling a currency in the hope of further rate falls. Over time saturation will occur because the financial operators have created short positions. They then limit their sales and try to compensate for the short positions with profits. This can rapidly lead to a change in the trend.

You cannot determine directly whether the market is overbought or oversold. This would suppose that you knew all of the foreign exchange positions of all the financial operators. However, experience shows that only speculative buying, which leads to an overbought situation, makes rapid rate rallies possible.

The RSI is a numerical indication of price fluctuations over a given period; it is expressed as a percentage.

RSI = sum of price rises/sum of all price fluctuations

To illustrate this, we have selected the daily closes (multiplied by 10,000) for the EUR/USD currency pair when it first appeared on the FOREX market in January 2002. The running time frame in this example is nine days. See Table 11.1.

An RSI between 30 percent and 70 percent is considered neutral. Below 25 percent indicates an oversold market; over 75 percent indicates an overbought market. The RSI should never be considered alone but in conjunction with other indicators and charts. Moreover, its interpretation depends largely on the period studied. The example in Table 11.1 is nine days. An RSI over 25 days would show, given a steady evolution of rates, fewer fluctuations. The advantage

		TABLE 11.1 Calculating RSI				
Date	Close	Daily Chg	Ups	Downs	Total	Percent
1/01/02	8894					
1/02/02	9037	+43				
1/03/02	8985	−51				
1/04/02	8944	−41				
1/07/02	8935	−9				
1/08/02	8935	0				
1/09/02	8914	−21				
1/10/02	8914	0				
1/11/02	8925	+11	54	122	176	30.7
1/14/02	8943	+18	72	122	194	37.1
1/15/02	8828	−15	29	137	166	17.5
1/16/02	8821	−7	29	93	122	23.8
1/17/02	8814	−7	29	59	88	33.0
1/18/02	8846	+32	61	50	111	55.0
1/21/02	8836	−10	61	60	121	50.4
1/22/02	8860	+24	85	39	124	68.5
1/23/02	8783	+23	108	39	147	73.5
1/24/02	8782	−1	97	40	137	70.8
1/25/02	8650	−132	79	171	250	31.6
1/28/02	8623	−27	79	183	262	30.2
1/29/02	8656	+33	112	176	288	39.0
1/30/02	8610	−46	112	215	327	34.3
1/31/02	8584	−26	80	232	312	25.6

of obtaining more rapid signals for selling and buying (by using a smaller number of days) is counterbalanced by a greater risk of receiving the unconfirmed signals.

Momentum Analysis

Like the RSI, momentum measures the rate of change in trends over a given period. Unlike the RSI, which measures all the rate changes and fluctuations within a given period, momentum allows you to analyze only the rate variations between the start and end of the period studied.

The larger n is, the more the daily fluctuations tend to disappear. When momentum is above zero or its curve is rising, it indicates an uptrend. A signal to buy is given as soon as the momentum exceeds zero, and when it drops below zero, triggers the signal to sell.

$$\text{Momentum} = \text{price on day } (X) - \text{price on day } (X - n)$$

where $n =$ number of days in the period studied.

The following example in Table 11.2 of momentum analysis uses the EUR/USD currency pair as the underlying security.

Examination of the nine-day momentum shows a clear downward trend. Momentum analysis should not be used as the sole criterion for market entry and exit timing, but in conjunction with other indicators and chart signals.

Moving Averages

The moving average (MA) is another instrument used to study trends and generate market entry and exit signals. It is the arithmetic average of closing prices over a given period. The longer the period studied, the weaker the magnitude of the moving average curve. The number of closes in the given period is called the moving average index.

Market signals are generated by calculating the residual value:

$$\text{Residual} = \text{Price}(X) - \text{MA}(X)$$

When the residual crosses into the positive area, a buy signal is generated. When the residual drops below zero, a sell signal is generated.

A significant refinement to this residual method (also called moving average convergence divergence, or MACD for short) is the use of two moving averages. When the MA with the shorter MA index (called the oscillating MA index) crosses above the MA with the longer MA index (called the basis MA index), a sell signal is generated.

TABLE 11.2 Calculating Momentum

Date	Close	9-Day Momentum
1/01/02	8894	
1/02/02	9037	
1/03/02	8985	
1/04/02	8944	
1/07/02	8935	
1/08/02	8935	
1/09/02	8914	
1/10/02	8914	
1/11/02	8925	
1/14/02	8943	+49
1/15/02	8828	−209
1/16/02	8821	−164
1/17/02	8814	−130
1/18/02	8846	−99
1/21/02	8836	−99
1/22/02	8860	−54
1/23/02	8783	−131
1/24/02	8782	−143
1/25/02	8650	−293
1/28/02	8623	−205
1/29/02	8656	−165
1/30/02	8610	−204
1/31/02	8584	−262

$$\text{Residual} = \text{Basis MA(X)} - \text{Oscillating MA(X)}$$

Again we use the EUR/USD currency pair to illustrate the moving average method (see Table 11.3).

The reliability of the moving average residual method depends heavily on the MA indices chosen. Depending on market conditions, it is the shorter periods or longer periods that give the best results. When an ideal combination of moving averages is used, the results are comparatively good. The disadvantage is that the signals to buy and sell are indicated relatively late, after the maximum and minimum rates have been reached.

TABLE 11.3 Calculating Moving Average Residuals				
Date	Close	3-Day MA	5-Day MA	Residual
1/01/02	8894			
1/02/02	9037			
1/03/02	8985	8972		
1/04/02	8944	8989		
1/07/02	8935	8955	8959	4
1/08/02	8935	8938	8967	29
1/09/02	8914	8928	8943	15
1/10/02	8914	8921	8928	7
1/11/02	8925	8918	8925	7
1/14/02	8943	8927	8926	−1
1/15/02	8828	8899	8905	6
1/16/02	8821	8864	8886	22
1/17/02	8814	8821	8866	45
1/18/02	8846	8827	8850	23
1/21/02	8836	8832	8829	−3
1/22/02	8860	8847	8835	−12
1/23/02	8783	8826	8828	2
1/24/02	8782	8808	8821	13
1/25/02	8650	8738	8782	44
1/28/02	8623	8685	8740	55
1/29/02	8656	8643	8699	56
1/30/02	8610	8630	8664	34
1/31/02	8584	8617	8625	8

The residual method can be optimized by simple experimentation or by a software program. Keep in mind that when a large sample of daily closes is used, the indices will need to be adjusted as market conditions change.

TIP: For a simple trading method—at least to get started with understanding indicators—the new trader could do worse than a moving average and an oscillator. The moving average works best in trending markets; the oscillator, in trading or sideways markets. Try to come up with a limited set of rules to generate buy and sell signals. Use the moving average to identify the trend and the oscillator to avoid being whipsawed by sideways price movements.

Bollinger Bands

This indicator was developed by John Bollinger and is explained in detail in his opus called *Bollinger on Bollinger Bands.* The technique involves overlaying three bands (lines) on top of an OHLC bar chart (or a candlestick chart) of the underlying security.

The central band is a simple arithmetic moving average of the daily closes using a trader-selected moving average index. The upper and lower bands are the running standard deviation above and below the central moving average. Since the standard deviation is a measure of volatility, the bands are self-adjusting, widening during volatile markets and contracting during calmer periods. Bollinger recommends 10 days for short-term trading, 20 days for intermediate-term trading, and 50 days for longer-term trading. These values typically apply to stocks and bonds, thus shorter time periods will be preferred by commodity traders. See Figure 11.20.

Bollinger bands require two trader-selected input variables: the number of days in the moving average index and the number of standard deviations to plot above and below the moving average. More than 95 percent of all daily closes fall within three standard deviations from the mean of the time series. Typical values for the second parameter range from 1.5 to 2.5 standard deviations.

As with moving average envelopes, the basic interpretation of Bollinger bands is that prices tend to stay within the upper and lower band. The distinctive characteristic of Bollinger bands is that the spacing between the bands varies based on the volatility of the prices. During periods of extreme price changes

FIGURE 11.20 Bollinger Bands

(that is, high volatility), the bands widen to become more forgiving. During periods of stagnant pricing (that is, low volatility), the bands narrow to contain prices.

Bollinger notes the following characteristics of Bollinger bands:

- Sharp price changes tend to occur after the bands tighten, as volatility lessens.
- When prices move outside the bands, a continuation of the current trend is implied.
- Bottoms and tops made outside the bands followed by bottoms and tops made inside the bands call for reversals in the trend.
- A move that originates at one band tends to go all the way to the other band. This observation is useful when projecting price targets.

Bollinger bands do not generate buy and sell signals alone. They should be used with another indicator, usually the relative strength indicator. This is because when price touches one of the bands, it could indicate one of two things: a continuation of the trend or a reaction the other way. So Bollinger bands used by themselves do not provide all of what technicians need to know, which is when to buy and sell. MACD can be used in conjunction with Bollinger bands and RSI.

Indicator Caveat—Curve-Fit Data

Most indicators curve-fit data. You must define one or more price or time variables to calculate the indicator. In a moving average you must select how many time units to average. The indicator is said to be "curve-fit" to that data. The pre-Socratic philosopher Heraclitus said it best: "You cannot step twice into the same river"; and so it is with the FOREX markets. An instance variable that worked perfectly in one trading session can fail miserably in the next as the market environment changes. Opinions vary widely on this caveat. Indicators are immensely popular in FOREX. Co-author of the first edition Jim Bickford was a champion of them, whereas I believe they have limited value. At the least an indicator should be constructed in such a fashion that the instance variables are adjusted for the changes in market environment. Indicators that work well in trending markets (high directional movement and low volatility) fail in trading markets (low directional movement and high volatility) and vice versa. If you use a battery of indicators, be sure they are evenly divided between trading markets and trending markets for balance. For an excellent discussion of the classic trading versus trending concept, see *Forex Patterns and Probabilities* by Ed Ponsi (John Wiley & Sons, 2007).

Wave and Swing Analysis

Wave and swing analysis is one of those nebulous terms that means different things to different people. It is often associated with swing trading, which also harbors a variety of connotations (the swing trader usually keeps a trade open longer than the typical session or day trader).

Within the framework of this book, I define wave or swing analysis as the study of the distance between local peaks and troughs in the closing prices for the purpose of identifying recurring patterns and correlations. The swing chart, like its older sibling the point and figure chart, requires the use of a massaging algorithm that filters out lateral congestion (*whipsawing*) during periods of low volatility. For this purpose, a minimum box size must be selected. Within currency trading, this is almost always a single pip in the quote (second) currency of the currency pair. Additionally, a minimum reversal quantity must be selected. This is simply the number of pips (box sizes) required before a retracement can be drawn in the opposite direction (the continuation of an existing trend requires only one box size to plot the next point).

Unlike the P&F chart, the swing chart does not necessarily distort the time element. That is, swing charts are frequently overlaid directly on top of a vertical bar chart since both use the same numerical scaling for the *x*- and the *y*-axis. (See Figure 11.21.)

In Figure 11.21, it is clear that a swing chart is a sequence of alternating straight lines, called waves, which connect each peak with its succeeding trough and vice versa.

FIGURE 11.21 Bar Chart with Swing Analysis Overlay

The swing analyst is particularly interested in retracement percentages. Market behavior is such that when a major trend does break out, there is a sequence of impulse waves in the direction of the trend with interceding retracement waves (also called corrective waves). The ratio of the corrective wave divided by the preceding impulse wave is referred to as the percentage of retracement. Famous analysts such as William D. Gann and Ralph N. Elliott have dedicated their lives to interpreting these ratios and estimating the length of the next wave in the time series.

Gann believed that market waves moved in patterns based on, among other things, the Fibonacci number series, which emphasizes the use of so-called magic numbers such as 38.2 percent, 50 percent, and 61.8 percent. Actually, there is no magic involved at all; they are simply proportions derived from the Golden Mean or Divine Ratio. This is a complete study unto itself and has many fascinating possibilities. Visit www.groups.dcs.st-and.ac.uk/~history/Mathematicians/Fibonacci.html for more details on Fibonacci and his work.

In his analysis of stocks in the 1920s and 1930s, Elliott was able to identify and categorize nine levels of cycles (that is, a sequence of successive waves) over the same time period for a single bar chart. This entailed increasing the minimum reversal threshold in the filtering algorithm, which creates fewer but longer waves with each new iteration. He believed each major impulse wave was composed of five smaller waves while major corrective waves were composed of only three smaller waves. I refer interested readers to the web site www.elliottwave.com for more details on Elliott and his theories.

Cycle Analysis

Every market is composed of traders at different levels slugging it out. Scalpers, day traders, and position traders are all attempting to profit from price changes. Each group has a different time focus or horizon. Cycle theory believes these groups behave in cyclical fashion and that some composite of their behavior would parallel the market. If that composite were identified, the cyclical parameters could be run past today's price into tomorrow's, resulting in a forecast. I experimented with a cycle tool, the Expert Cycle System, not to predict the market but to examine the ways to find such a composite. (See Figure 11.22.)

Trading Systems

This chapter serves as a road map into the realm of technical analysis. It is a wondrous realm indeed, but it is easy to get lost there. Time series analysis is a complex and ever-changing discipline. Advanced studies include deviation

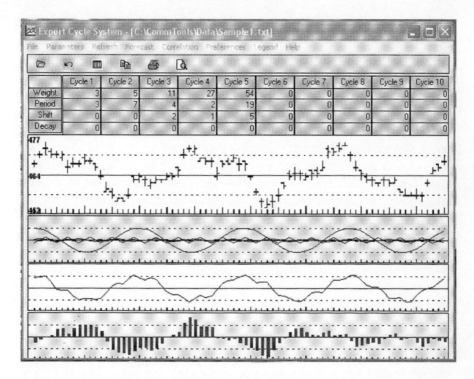

FIGURE 11.22 The Expert Cycle System

analysis, retracement studies, statistical regressions, Fibonacci progressions, Fourier transforms, and the Box-Jenkins method, to name just a few. A separate realm is the attempt to transfer methods from other disciplines to market analysis such as data mining.

Many traders have developed more comprehensive systems for trading using technical analysis. FOREX traders may also wish to consider the technical analysis of Charles B. Goodman, including the Goodman Swing Count System (see Chapter 12, "A Trader's Toolbox") and the Goodman Cycle Count System—collectively Goodman Wave Theory. Joe DiNapoli's DiNapoli Levels are popular and the basis of the educational course of Derek Ching's HawaiiForex (www.HawaiiForex.com). Charles Drummond's Point & Line Method has many ardent followers. Elliott Wave Theory is the granddaddy of them all and remains popular with FOREX traders.

The Technician's Creed

All market fundamentals are depicted in the actual market data. So the actual market fundamentals need not be studied in detail.

The technician believes prices have memory—that past prices do influence future prices. If you get in a market you have to get out. History repeats itself, and therefore markets move in fairly predictable, or at least quantifiable, patterns. These patterns, generated by price movement, are the raw buy and sell signals. The goal in technical analysis is to uncover the signals exhibited in a current market by examining past market signals.

Prices move in trends. Technicians typically do not believe that price fluctuations are random and unpredictable. Prices can move in one of three directions: up, down, or sideways. Once a trend in any of these directions is established, it usually will continue for some period. Trends occur at all price levels: tick, 5-minute, 1-hour, 1-day, weekly. What is a trend at the 1-minute level is obviously just a small blip on the radar on a weekly chart. The various price levels are interconnected in intricate and fascinating ways.

Never make a trading decision based solely on a single indicator or chart pattern. The eclectic approach of comparing several indicators and charts at the same time is the best strategy. Try to move from the most general conditions of a market to the most specific. Sift your technical tools finer and finer until they result in a trade.

As in all other aspects of trading, be disciplined when using technical analysis. Too often, a trader fails to sell or buy into a market even after it has reached a price that his technical studies have identified as an entry or exit point. This is money management and psychology, not technical analysis, and both are *very* important.

The basic types of technical analysis tools are charts, moving averages, oscillators, and momentum analysis. Chapter 12, "A Trader's Toolbox," puts forth a suggested program for developing your own technical analysis arsenal. Your analysis of the markets is only one of three components to successful trading—money management and psychology are the others.

Summary

The number of technical analysis charts, indicators, methods, and systems can fill a small library. The subject is fascinating but be objective and remember that your ultimate goal is to make money. Keep your technical analysis arsenal to a minimum. Remember that the most popular methods, such as bar chart formations and support and resistance, are used by many traders. The market gradually discounts chart patterns and indicator signals when used by many traders over a long period of time. Also, most traders do not succeed—draw your own conclusions.

Your analysis of the markets is only *one* component of your trading system. In fact, two other components are more important, in the opinion of the author: money management and psychology (discussed in detail in later chapters). Most traders who fail (and most traders do fail) tend to spend all their energies on developing a trading system at the expense of money management and trading psychology. *Do not be like them!*

A Trader's Toolbox

Fundamentals almost certainly drive the long-term trends of currencies, but trading is a short-term affair. Most traders do not even hold a position from one eight-hour session to another. "If U.S. interest rates go up, then the USD will rise"—this is true in some cases, false in others. There are so many other factors determining currency prices that an accurate observation one time may even be incorrect the next. Correlations, between them, almost certainly nonlinear, come and go without notice. But even if one knew a statement to be correct, how does that help a trader in the short term? Leverage is the name of the game, and no one wants a $10,000 loss while waiting for a fundamental factor to work.

Ergo, I strongly recommend that the new trader develop a simple technical analysis toolbox to get started trading currencies. You may add to the toolbox later or make adjustments. It is important to keep your tools balanced. Do not have four tools effective in trading markets and only one that works in trending markets. This implies that you know what an indicator, charting technique, or other technical tool really does. But begin your FOREX career by keeping it simple.

General Principles

As you select technical analysis tools keep in mind:

- Most tools can be classified as designed for either trading (sideways) or trending markets. Thus, the majority of traders use similar tools although they may assemble them in somewhat unique toolboxes. The majority almost always loses.

- Be certain you know what a technical tool is doing, what it is measuring, before adding it to your toolbox.

- Seek synergy. Does your tool add to and/or complement your other selections?

- Avoid overkill. Keep it simple!

What does an indicator really measure? Do you really need it in your toolbox, or can you glean the information from a chart? Consider Figure 12.1. This shows prices depicted as a bar chart on the top and a relative strength (RS) indicator (see Chapter 11, "Technical Analysis") on the bottom. Functionally Relative Strength measures the slope of a line (trend); it is a form of the slop-intercept formula you learned in Algebra I − y = mx + b. Does the Relative Strength indicator below add anything that you cannot see on the bar chart? To some extent, it depends what you want and need.

TIP: To avoid offending RS aficionados, the author must mention that this indicator sometimes helps spot tops and bottoms when a new high (or low) in prices is not matched by a new high (or low) in the RS indicator.

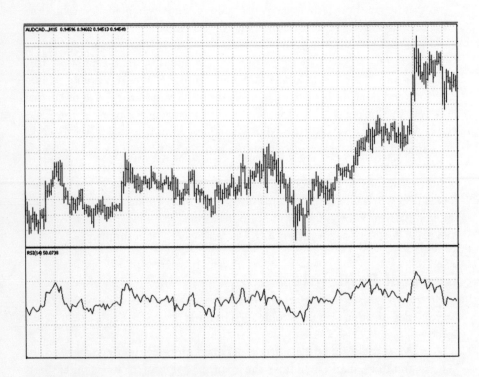

FIGURE 12.1 Charts or Indicators?

Source: TradeviewForex, www.tradeviewforex.com and www.metaquotes.net

It is quite often possible to eliminate indicators because you can more easily see the same information on a chart. This is the thesis of Charles Goodman's Market Environment (ME) charting technique. See Chapter 18, "Improving Your Trading Skills," for more on ME. If you get as much bang for your buck as you can, two or three indicators will be enough to get started.

A KIS Toolbox

This toolbox is only an example of how to select a few basic tools for trading. Survey the field—it is huge—and pick wisely.

I recommend a toolbox consisting of:

- A chart interpretation technique.
- At the most three indicators.
- A noncomplementary check tool; one that is substantially different from your primary trading tools. If you use indicators to trade, a simple bar chart would be a noncomplementary tool. An advisory service may also be used here.
- An easy-to-use heuristic for analyzing a market with your tools. The trading heuristic is discussed in more detail in Chapter 15, "The Plan! The Plan!"

A Chart Interpretation Technique

The Goodman Swing Count System (GSCS) was developed by commodity trader Charles B. Goodman and used by him until his death in 1984. Michael D. Archer, whom he mentored, further developed the system. GSCS is a method for interpreting charts. You may use bar, swing, or point and figure; bar charts are the easiest and most common. A unique charting technique Mr. Goodman used, Box Charts, has not yet been programmed into software.

Like all chart interpretation techniques, it is not applicable to all charts all the time. Not every chart forms a pennant or a head and shoulders, and not every chart forms a Goodman Wave. But the variety in FOREX is rich enough that you will find many trading opportunities across all time frames.

The Goodman Swing Count System is one of two components to *Goodman Wave Theory*. The other component is the Goodman Cycle Count System (GCCS). GSCS analysis may become involved, but you can learn enough quickly to put it into action finding trade candidates. What follows is only a brief introduction to Goodman Wave Theory and GSCS. For a deeper look see *15 Essential FOREX Trades* by John Bland, Jay Meisler, and Michael Archer (John Wiley & Sons, 2009), or *The Goodman Codex* by Michael Duane Archer (B.R. Jostan and Company, 2009). More information is on the author's web site, www.goodmanworks.com.

GSCS Rules

There are eight rules to GSCS. The five below are the most basic of them.

The 50 Percent Rule

This rule is almost as old as the market itself. It states simply that at the 50 percent retracement of a trend, prices find at least a temporary equilibrium.

The logic is that in the aggregate all the traders who participated in the initial trend are at a break-even point. More specifically: Half the buyers have losses, half have profits; half the sellers have losses, half have profits.

As seen in Figure 12.2, the price value of trend or swing B is 50 percent of A. Swing A is called a Primary Swing. Swing B is called a Secondary Swing.

The Measure Move Rule

This could be considered a corollary of the 50 Percent Rule. Should prices start to trend in the direction of the initial trend from the 50 percent price point, the buyers will hold onto their positions, and the sellers will be forced to liquidate.

The end result is that a second Primary Swing will form of equal value to the initial swing.

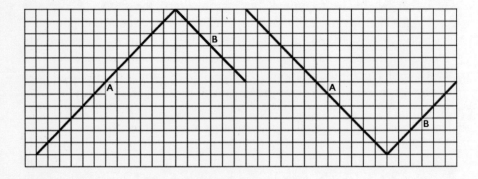

FIGURE 12.2   The 50 Percent Trade Rule

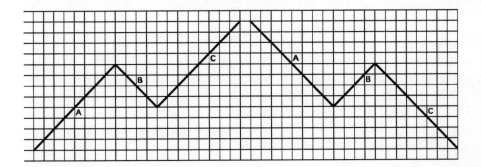

FIGURE 12.3 Basic Goodman Matrix

Charles Goodman called this A-B-C formation a "matrix" and considered it the basic market formation. It is a subset of the Pugh Bull or Bear formations, discussed below.

As seen in Figure 12.3, the price value of trend or swing C is the same as A and twice B.

The Wave Propagation Rule

One of Goodman's most useful discoveries was that prices often form or build as a series of propagating matrices or measured moves. Each matrix becomes a swing in the propagation of successively larger matrices.

This is a distinct difference and, in my opinion, improvement over Elliott Wave Theory.

As seen in Figure 12.4, the price value of D, the return swing, is 50 percent of A-B-C. The matrix A-B-C is now considered itself as a single trend in GSCS theory.

Trend E is anticipated to be of the net price value of A-B-C. The complete formation of A-B-C-D-E is a Goodman Wave. Though it may look similar to an Elliott Wave, the Return Swing and how it is calculated makes an enormous difference.

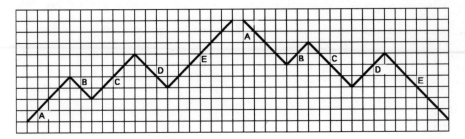

FIGURE 12.4 The Goodman Wave

The 3-C Rule

This was the most astonishing discovery Mr. Goodman made about the markets. It states that if the 50 percent objective is not perfectly met, the over or under of the measurement will be made on the measured move, the second Primary Swing.

In Figure 12.5 the 50 percent measurement missed by one chart unit (the value of B is three instead of four units) and is made up by the full measured move measurement in the third swing.

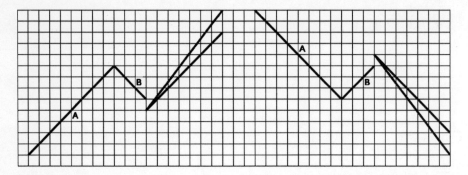

FIGURE 12.5 The GSCS 3-C Rule

FIGURE 12.6 3-C Over/Under Measurement

Source: TradeviewForex www.tradeviewforex.com and www.metaquotes.net

TIP: The 3-C Rule states that whatever price value is missed on the 50 percent move will be made up on the measured move. Calculations are done in this way: (1) Calculate the value missed (either over or under the 50 percent move); (2) begin counting from the 50 percent price point in the direction of trend A; (3) calculate the final price point as if the 50 percent move had been in effect; and (4) add or subtract the value in Step 1 to find the anticipated adjusted price points for trend C. The two objectives, Over and Under, may be marked with parentheses. It is not uncommon for prices to first go to the Under measurement, hesitate, then go on to the Over measurement. See Figure 12.6.

The 3-C stands for carryover, compensation, and cancellation.

Curiously, the 3-C Rule is often effective even when the B measurement is dramatically off the 50 percent point.

There are a number of other GSCS rules and principles but these two trade setups will suffice for getting started: the Double Intersection and the Return.

The Double Intersection Rule

This is the most useful chart formation I have ever used. It occurs when the measured move of a swing or matrix intersects at the 50 percent point of the next larger matrix in a wave propagation. If one 50 percent move represents equilibrium, two represents even stronger equilibrium. Prices often react sharply from these double intersections.

TIP: Although this is not functionally accurate, it is useful to think of traders at different price levels or matrices. Like irrational numbers, they may not in truth exist, but they are useful for analysis.

In the Double Intersection in Figure 12.7, the traders in swing A have the same equilibrium point as the traders in matrix 1-2-3. The 50 percent move of A-B intersects the end point of the 1-2-3 matrix.

At this point a trader would use a timing tool to enter the market in the direction of the Primary Swing A anticipating a second Primary Swing C to

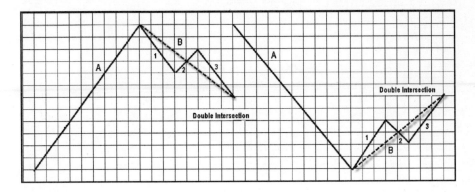

FIGURE 12.7 The Double Intersection Trade Setup

occur. I use the Dagger (See Chapter 18, "Improving Your Trading Skills") but moving averages and other indicators will work, also.

There are several Double Intersection templates using the various combinations of the 50 Percent Rule and Measured Move Rule at different points of a matrix.

Trading the Return

Refer again to the Wave Propagation in Figure 12.4.

When most traders see the D trend or swing on a chart they think in terms of Elliott Wave Theory where D is simply related to C. In GSCS, D is in fact the Return or Propagation Wave, representing a 50 percent return of the entire A-B-C matrix. It almost always has a longer price duration than A, B, or C, and price reversals may be powerful. Such behavior is tradable. (See Figure 12.8.)

TIP: Watch for charts where trend D digs into the marked spot intersecting B and C. This spot often offers strong support and resistance, and can be a good point to watch to enter for a trend E in the direction of A and C.

Here is a return setup where the first component was a matrix and the second component was a swing. See Figure 12.9.

Once a Return point is identified, use an entry signal tool to enter with the major trend or Wave direction.

Goodman Wave Theory is the topic on the author's web site, www. goodmanworks.com.

TIP: Always try to enter a market with the major trend and minor trend—and against the intermediate trend. Buy strength, sell weakness. You want the long-term trend in your favor (the major trend) and the short-term momentum (minor trend). But you want to enter after a meaningful correction (the intermediate trend).

I have discovered that GSCS complements two other trading ideas well: Nofri's Congestion Phase and Pugh Formations.

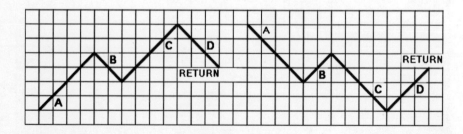

FIGURE 12.8   The Return Swing Setup

FIGURE 12.9 Return Setup—Matrix and Swing

Source: TradeviewForex www.tradeviewforex.com and www.metaquotes.net

The Nofri Congestion Phase Method

This simple but useful idea was presented by Eugene Nofri in *Success in Commodities* (Success Publishing, 1975). It is out of print but sometimes available on www.eBay.com or www.abebooks.com. Nofri was a floor trader in the corn market, but like most technical trading ideas this one is applicable to FOREX.

There are 32 total formations, but the simplest one is to watch for two trading units when price goes up or down followed by two trading units when prices go down or up but remain inside the range formed by the first two units.

The prediction is that the fifth price unit will be in the direction of the first two units (see Figure 12.10).

This can be used as an entry signal or as a short-term trading method.

Pugh Swing Chart Formations

This is a simple but effective charting method. The formations were identified by Burton Pugh, a famous grain trader of the 1930s and 1940s. There are only four basic chart formations: Bull, Bear, Inside, and Outside. Highs and lows are always referenced to the previous data unit. (See Figure 12.11.) The four types

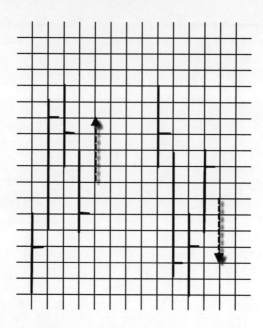

FIGURE 12.10 Basic Nofri Formation

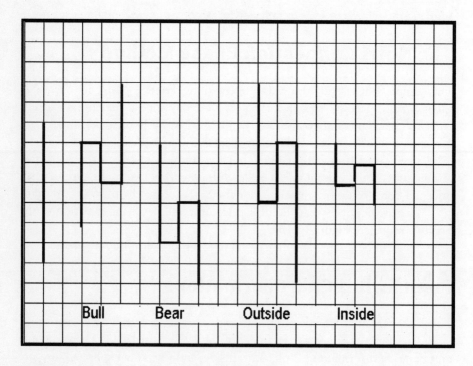

FIGURE 12.11 Pugh Chart Formations

cover every possible price action over a set time frame. Combinations of Pugh formations create not only all the classical chart patterns but interesting and unique ones as well.

A Pugh formation is always in reference to the preceding formation's high and low.

  A. Bull Formation
      Higher high and higher low from preceding formation
  B. Bear Formation
      Lower low and lower high from preceding formation
  C. Outside Formation
      Higher high and lower low from preceding formation
  D. Inside Formation
      Lower high and higher low from preceding formation

Trends tend to be series of Bull Formations (uptrend) and Bear Formations (downtrend). Consolidations tend to be combinations of Inside and Outside formations.

The famous Head and Shoulders Top and Bottom is actually two sequential Bull (or Bear) Formations followed by a Bear (or Bull) Formation.

In fact all conventional bar chart formations shown in Chapter 11, "Technical Analysis," can be reduced to a Pugh series.

I keep a running notation of Pugh formations and look for patterns in the series.

You may use 1, 2, 3, 4 for the four formations. I use "1" for a Bull, "0" for a Bear, "11" for an Outside, and "00" for an Inside. A vertical line "|" is used to separate them. You might also use brackets "[ ]."

A notation might look like this:

1|10|10|00|11|1|01|10

Use "bathtub analysis" described in Chapter 18, "Improving Your Trading Skills," to study charts using Pugh formations and series—and to find new ones, as well.

A Moving Average and Oscillator Battery

A battery is a combination of indicators. When the indicators in a battery are combined to generate buy and sell trade signals via a set of rules, it is referred to as an expert advisor. A battery or an expert advisor could be used as a primary trading method or as a check on the primary method. All trading platforms offer moving averages and oscillators. See Chapter 11, "Technical Analysis," details on moving averages and oscillators.

A moving average typically works when a market is trending in one dition or another. An oscillator is most effective when a market is moving sideways. Look for points where:

- A market is above the moving average line but the oscillator is falling sharply or below the zero line. This can indicate that a market is still in an uptrend but in a buying range because it has lost some downward velocity, at least temporarily.

- A market is below the moving average line but the oscillator is rising sharply or above the zero line. This may indicate that a market is still in a downtrend but in a selling range because it has lost some of the downward velocity, at least temporarily. (See Figure 12.12.)

TIP: Remember, trends and trading ranges are relative to the price scale you are using. A trend on an hourly chart is probably made up of a number of five-minute mini-trends and trading areas. Use scales for your moving averages

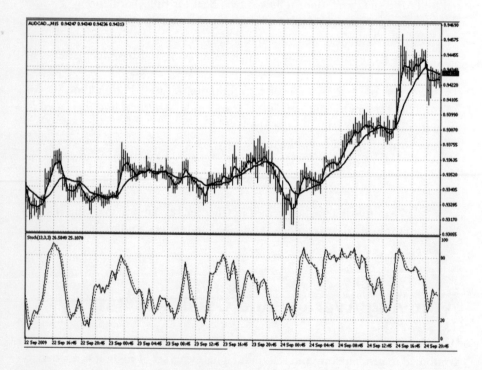

FIGURE 12.12   A Simple Indicator Battery
Source: TradeviewForex, www.tradeviewforex.com

and oscillators in harmony with the scale of the price chart you are watching. Do not use a 10-day moving average on a 10-minute chart; you will see essentially nothing but a straight line. The smaller the parameters you pick the more signals you will generate. The trade-off is this: You will get in earlier on good trades but you will also get in on more bad ones. More sophisticated tools attempt to filter out at least some of the bad trades with additional indicators or trading rules.

It is possible to computerize and automate an indicator battery with a set of rules determining when they generate a buy or sell signal. Most of the platforms mentioned in Chapter 14, "Retail FX Platforms," have this capability. Such programs are called Expert Advisors or EAs.

Contrary Opinion

At the old Peavey commodity office, around 1975, I befriended a trader who successfully traded using nothing but a Moving Average-Oscillator tool in conjunction with contrary opinion. Contrary opinion states that if a large majority of traders thinks a market will rise, it will fall. If a large majority thinks it will fall, it will rise. The reasoning is that if everyone thinks a market will go up, they have already bought, and there is no more buying power to maintain the trend.

R. Earl Hadady wrote a book on contrary opinion. Again, it was for the futures markets, but it would be a good read for any FOREX trader. Take a look at *Contrary Opinion* (Hadady Publications, 1983).

Contrary opinion theory, while well developed and quantified in futures, is less so in FOREX. Jay Meisler's www.global-view.com does a weekly trader poll. Archer's www.goodmanworks.com will soon offer a FOREX contrary opinion tool.

More on this subject in the section "Going Against the Crowd" in Chapter 18, "Improving Your Trading Skills." Trolling the major FOREX forums once a week will give you a good idea of trader sentiment on the major currency pairs.

Volume and Open Interest

These are two exceptionally useful technical analysis tools. Although available to the futures trader, they are not currently available to the FOREX trader. Without a central clearinghouse it is impossible to collect this information directly although it may be calculated indirectly by reverse-engineering from other data and statistics.

Heuristics

Every chess player worth his salt uses a heuristic with every turn to move. A heuristic is typically a set of ordered questions that must be answered before making a move. A heuristic can be simple or complex, resulting in a critical path flow chart. The new FOREX trader would be advised to develop a simple heuristic for every contemplated trade.

The more involved your trading method, the longer will be your heuristic. I recommend simplicity and clarity in all aspects of trading.

Your final heuristic should include both money management and psychology parameters.

For the previously mentioned KIS trading program a bare-bones trading method heuristic might look like this:

- Is there a GSCS formation worth considering?
- If yes, which one?
- What are the Pugh formations and series forecast?
- Is there a Nofri formation?
- Do all of these occur in the same time and price zone?
- Does the Moving Average-Oscillator battery confirm the trade or anticipated price direction?

Begin with your primary tool and work through the others. Optimally each tool will identify a trade or potential trade at the same price and time level.

TIP: You want to go from general to specific. Find "something interesting" on a chart then drill down with your toolset and see how well it is qualified to be a trade candidate. The heuristic to find a trade candidate should ideally be a subroutine in your overall trading heuristics.

Be patient; there are many opportunities and it pays to wait for top-notch trading candidates. It is far better to under trade and miss a winner here and there than to over trade and accumulate losers.

Summary

"Technical analysis is a sea in which a gnat may drink and an elephant may bathe" to paraphrase an old chess proverb. No matter how involved your trading method is, remember the markets can only go up, down, or sideways. And sideways does not count unless you are trading options. Complications do not make winners—being correct about the trend does.

For a more comprehensive discussion of developing both a toolbox and a trading program, see *Getting Started in Forex Trading Strategies* (John Wiley & Sons, 2007) by Michael D. Archer.

There are many worthy books on technical analysis. Enough, I am sure, to fill a small library. See Appendix F, "Resources," for some books I have found of value.

Of the three components to trading, trading techniques get the most publicity—perhaps because they are easier to communicate. Traders have hundreds of tools to trade although most are variations of a few general types. The composition of toolboxes also varies enormously from trader to trader. But almost all successful traders share the same psychological attributes and basic money-management rules.

The FOREX Marketplace

The rapid expansion of retail FOREX trading has spawned a large online marketplace of products and services. Sorting through this vast labyrinth of information is a daunting task; services come and go rapidly, changes and upgrades are frequent, and the sheer volume is constantly increasing. Most of the material can be divided into these categories:

- Portals and forums
- Broker-Dealer Reviews
- Charting and technical services
- FOREX education
- News and calendars
- Live data and APIs
- Historical data
- System development tools
- FOREX managed accounts
- Advisory services
- Online reference guides
- Spread and binary betting
- Periodicals—in print and online
- Books

Broker-dealers partner with third-party vendors though not as often as at one time. More and more brokers are providing a full suite of services under their own name and/or in their own trading platform. The exception is the growth in the number of brokers offering one of the primary third-party trading platforms—typically integrated with the broker's data feed and order process. See Chapter 14, "Retail FX Platforms," for more on this development. The selection and reviews in this chapter are intended as a sampler of what is available. The inclusion of a web site should not be considered a recommendation of it, and the exclusion of another should not be considered disapproval. Space is limited. My editor works on a one-martini-lunch budget, and I am reminded of it constantly. Reviews of all the services now offered would require a complete book—a large one. I have generally omitted categories not pertinent to beginners whose charter is to be self-directed traders, such as signal services, so-called Expert Advisors, and automated order-entry tools. The emphasis is on web sites with content for traders who intend to do their own thing, although we have included a section on money management for those who wish to explore the option of having a professional trader work currency markets for them.

I have endeavored to exclude web sites with annoying pop-ups, but always beware; a reliable pop-up blocker is recommended when cruising the Internet. Many of these web sites have advertisements; some of them are quite obtrusive and distractive. Welcome to Capitalism 101.

TIP: The web sites in Appendix F, "Resources," are intended to offer the new trader a self-guided tour of the FOREX landscape.

Organizing Your Bookmarks

There are several good programs for organizing your web site links, all more robust than the native Favorites in Internet Explorer.

> **Bookmark Buddy, www.bookmarkbuddy.net** Most FOREX web sites offer content on more than one of the subjects listed earlier. I have found Bookmark Buddy to be superior for cross-referencing this information with its Category/Sub-Category/Bookmark arrangement.
>
> **LinkStash, www.rosecitysoftware.com** A new flavor, the social book
>
> **LinkStash, http://www.xrayz.co.uk/linkstash/** Very customizable, cross-platform compatible. A new flavor, the social bookmark, assumes that someone else can surf the Web better than you, a thousand surfers are better than one, and that somehow they know exactly what you are seeking. www.del-icio-us.com is just one of a dozen of them now.

Portals and Forums

These sites offer link lists (directories) as well as FOREX services, products, learning articles, and tools. Most sites also provide reviews of broker-dealers.

Forums allow traders to communicate on a variety of issues and have become enormously popular.

As anyone who has spent time on the Internet realizes, there is enormous cross-pollination of links. If you find one or two good directories or link lists on a subject, they will lead you to many others. The key is keeping everything organized so you are not constantly backtracking or cruising down dead-end cyber alleys.

Forum Dos and Don'ts

Do carefully read the forum rules before subscribing. Read your posting over once or twice before submitting. Do not say something on a forum you would not say face-to-face. Before posting, check your facts, and be sure you can substantiate the information.

Do not waste your time engaging in polemics with professional forum trawlers who have nothing better to do. Forums can be useful, but do not get hooked on them; they are addictive. I take one hour each week to scan the forums.

> www.global-view.com This is the granddaddy of FOREX portals and forums, and is loaded with excellent content; a recent web site redo makes navigation easier. If you are new to FOREX this web site is a one-stop-shop. John Bland's and Jay Meisler's site also offers excellent links as well as educational, resource, and advisory tools. Unlike most others where new traders reign, many of the industry's movers and shakers frequent the Global Viewpoint Inc. (GVI) forums. John and Jay, like many forum operators, are sticklers about their rules and etiquette. (See Figure 13.1.)

TIP: There are two or three professional traders on the Global-View forum whose advice is very, very accurate. They do not post often and do so

Global-View Trading Tools

Live FX Rates	Daily Chart Points	Economic Calendar
Live Forex Charts	Forex Database	Chart Gallery
Live USDX Chart	Daily Forex Forecasts	Market Tracker
Live Market Quotes	Interest Rate Forecasts	QUICKLINKS

FIGURE 13.1 The Global View Web Site
Source: Global Viewpoint, Inc., www.global-view.com

unobtrusively. Co-founder John Bland is one of the most astute fundamentalists in the business and Jay Meisler's contacts reads like a who's-who of FOREX.

www.goforex.net Created by Steve Moxham from New Zealand, this is a fine resource, with a new design, and it is slick and well organized. The Articles repository is superior and the Links directory is representative. It is becoming commercialized—from the viewer's side at least, the downside of success—but that is the name of the game in portals. Author Archer was booted from the Ask-an-Expert e-column for his nonmainstream ideas but still checks in from time to time. GoForex is a must-see beginner's reference. Several excellent FOREX calculation tools are on this web site.

www.fxstreet.com An early participant, this web site just keeps getting better although the advertisements are a minor annoyance.

www.forexfactory.com A wide variety of forums to suit traders of all levels of experience.

www.piptrader.com Strength is reviews but an informative portal, also.

www.trade2win.com Lots going on here, but commercial.

See Figure 13.2 for the Most Popular list of FOREX Forums and Portals

Broker-Dealer Reviews

Most of the portals and forums offer broker-dealer reviews.

www.forexpeacearmy.com The most frequented reviews of brokers, signal services, money managers, and educational services. The moderator keeps a sharp eye for shills.

www.goforex.net Reliable reviews. Moderator Steve Moxham also works hard to keep things honest.

Global-View	**www.global-view.com**
GoForex	**www.goforex.net**
FXStreet	**www.fxstreet.com**
Forex Factory	**www.forexfactory.com**
Forex Forums	**www.forexforums.com**

FIGURE 13.2   The Most Popular FOREX Portals and Forums

TIP: Be sure to read the caveats regarding broker-dealer reviews in Chapter 7, "A Guide to FOREX Brokers."

Charting and Technical Services

These services generally are combined into a single entity especially if they are live, but not always. They can be expensive and are difficult to justify if you are, for example, trading a mini-account with $1,000.

A significant issue is how your charts will integrate into your trading platform. If you are using a live chart service, the data stream may be different from the data stream on which you enter orders with your broker-dealer. It is best if you can integrate your charting service into your trading platform or at least your broker-dealer's data stream. In Chapter 7, "A Guide to FOREX Brokers," we note the broker-dealers who offer integrated third-party charts and technical tools.

For most traders, the charting and technical tools offered with the broker-dealers trading platform are sufficient. Next best is a third-party vendor whose service is integrated into the broker's platform or at least reads the broker's data feed. Do not be overwhelmed. As a new trader, Keep It Simple is your touchstone to success.

Chart services are live, daily (end-of-day, EOD), or historical. Some services offer a combination of chart types. Most live services and daily services offer historical charts. Daily data is not of much use to the FOREX trader. We suggest that the new trader try to be happy with his or her broker-dealer's charts and technical services, at least initially.

> **www.Intellichart.com** Superior charting service with a strong set of tools and parameter settings. The service is named FXtrek and integrates with several broker-dealer platforms. Customer service—a weak area in FOREX—is lightning fast at IntelliChart (see Figure 13.3). A simple scripting language for testing new trading tools is in development.

> **www.esignal.com** This service has been around for many years. Its early life was difficult but it is a reliable service today. It caters to stock and commodity traders but offers a wealth of charts and technical tools; a FOREX data stream is available. Their Formula Script 2 (EFS2) for development of technical indicators and methods is weaker than TradeStation's EasyLanguage. The web site is difficult to follow, and we found sales support poor. It is also one of the independent trading platforms reviewed in Chapter 14, "Retail FX Platforms."

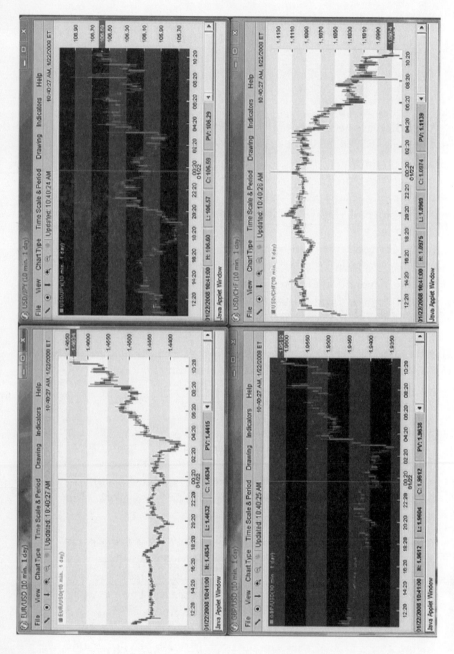

FIGURE 13.3 The FXTrek Charts
Source: Intellicharts, Inc., www.FXtrek.com

www.4xcharts.com A division of Trading Intl, www.tradingintl. com. Popular charts for currency traders.

www.tradestation.com Like eSignal, a difficult early life but solid now. Strength is to stocks and commodities, but they offer both trading and a FOREX data feed (through Gain Capital). For system developers, their EasyLanguage script is well developed and documented. Support is excellent. It is also one of the independent trading platforms reviewed in this chapter.

www.dailyfx.com Online charts in a Java environment.

www.barchart.com Offers stock, commodity, and FOREX charts. EOD and historical. The web site is confusing, but the charting services are good, and customer support is decent.

www.newsimpact.com A fascinating and useful web site. SpikeCharts are used to analyze news events; not dissimilar to the author's Shockwave concept, but more thoroughly researched and implemented.

FOREX Education

Most of the larger retail broker-dealers offer some level of educational experience for beginners, ranging from articles, tutorials, and live and on-demand webcasts. Supplement any training or mentoring you do with no more than a mini-account. Experience is the ultimate teacher. The emphasis here is on complete courses, teaching you all aspects of FOREX trading without any specific trading methodology although the demarcation between those that do and those that do not is not always well-defined.

www.babypips.com A truly excellent beginner's resource. Well maintained and organized. The School of Pipsology is an excellent quick-course in the basics of FOREX. (See Figure 13.4.)

www.markettraders.com MTI offers a comprehensive course but also attempts to direct students to their brokerage partner.

www.hawaiiFOREX.com This Introducing Broker offers an integrated educational tract along with their FOREX trading services through GFTFOREX. Derek Ching strives to find the best instructional programs and does substantial due diligence before offering a new service. His current program is based on the technical analysis work of Joe DiNapoli. Perhaps your accountant will approve expenses for a trip to Hawaii for one of his excellent seminars. Aloha!

www.FOREXtradingandeducation.com Tutorials, coaching, and mentoring.

www.FOREXtrainingworks.com The author offers instruction on the Goodman trading methods on www.goodmanworks.com.

It is possible you can find one of these that complement your own trading methods and act as a check on your own work.

School of Pipsology

Forex education is crucial for beginners.

BabyPips.com's **School of Pipsology** is designed to help you acquire the skills, knowledge, and abilities to become a successful trader in the foreign exchange market. Our definition of a successful trader is having the ability to do three things:

1. **Make pips**
2. **Keep pips**
3. **Repeat**

If you can repeatedly do these three things, then you're on your way! But it's no cakewalk.

Remember when you attended grade school? No? Well, according to our memories, here's how it worked.

You start schooling at the age of five and enter Kindergarten. The next year you enter 1st Grade. If you pass, the next year you enter 2nd Grade, and so on, all the way up to the 12th Grade. Depending on what grade you're in, you'd attend one of three *schools*:

1. **Elementary school** (Kindergarten - 5th grade)
2. **Middle school** (6th grade - 8th grade)
3. **High school** (9th grade - 12th grade)

This is how our lessons are broken apart, so you can relive the past and also be able to learn and study forex trading techniques at your own pace – but our high school goes beyond the 12th grade!

FIGURE 13.4   The Babypips Web Site
Source: Babypips.com LLC, www.babypips.com

News and Calendars

Most broker-dealers offer news and announcement services and it is enough for most traders. My take on the news is this: Do not try to trade the news, but watch how the market reacts to it for trend indications. Remember that the initial price impact of news is often dramatic, but it may take several hours to be fully absorbed. It is not uncommon for prices to react sharply in one direction initially, then gradually trend in the opposite direction for much of the trading session.

Your daily trade plan should always note relevant news and announcements for the pairs you trade. If you must trade the news, use one of the news trading tools available. Perhaps the best is Felix Homogratus' www.secretnewsweapon.com.

The author's favorite:

www. global-view.com A well-organized and useful news web site. Frequently updated. Jump over to the forums before a news release to learn traders' takes on it. (See Figure 13.5.)

www.forexeconomiccalendar.com You can sign up for their e-mail newsletter of major economic events and indicators for the week.

www.econoday.com An awesome subscription service for serious traders. They offer a few basic services at http://basic.econoday.com. If you trade on fundamentals, here is the depth of information you require.

www.tradethenews.com Offers a News Squawk (audio) service through your computer speakers. Close your eyes, and it's 1970, again—a time when squawk boxes were the leading-edge technology!

Live Data and APIs

Live data streams typically come bundled with some other service such as live charting. If you receive the data stream or feed by itself it is called an Application Program Interface (API). API data streams are used if you plan on developing your own trading system(s).

APIs also drive web-based tools, or applets.

Similar to a charting service, your API should closely match the feed from your broker-dealer, otherwise your trading signals will not match the prices offered to you on your trading platform. The best solution is to get the API from your broker-dealer for system development. Many brokers now offer their API to developers at little or no cost if you have a live FOREX account. It makes little sense to develop a trading system or method with an outside API nowadays.

FX Monthly Calendar updated weekly - - FX Schedule

05/10/09	07:58		EZ	Sep SVC PMI	**Cons:** 50.6	**Last:** 49.9
05/10/09	08:30		UK	Sep Svc PMI	**Cons:** 53.9	**Last:** 53.2
05/10/09	09:00		EZ	Aug Retail Sls yy	**Cons:** −2.6%	**Last:** −1.8%
05/10/09	09:00		EZ	Aug Retail Sls mm	**Cons:** −0.5%	**Last:** −0.2%
05/10/09	14:00		US	Sep SVC PMI	**Cons:** 50.0	**Last:** 48.4
05/10/09	17:00		US	10-yr TIPS	**Cons:** n/a	**Last:** n/a
06/10/09	00:00			**TUESDAY**	**Cons:**	**Last:**
06/10/09	00:30		AU	Aug Trade A$bln	**Cons:** n/a	**Last:** −1.55b
06/10/09	03:30		AU	RBA RBA (3.00%)	**Cons:** unch	**Last:** unch
06/10/09	07:15		CH	Sep CPI yy	**Cons:** n/a	**Last:** −0.8%
06/10/09	07:15		CH	Sep CPI mm	**Cons:** n/a	**Last:** +0.1%
06/10/09	08:30		UK	Aug Mfg Out mm	**Cons:** +0.3%	**Last:** +0.9%
06/10/09	08:30		UK	Aug Ind Out mm	**Cons:** n/a	**Last:** n/a
06/10/09	08:30		UK	Aug Mfg Out yy	**Cons:** −9.3%	**Last:** −10.1%
06/10/09	08:30		UK	Aug Ind Out yy	**Cons:** n/a	**Last:** n/a
06/10/09	14:00		CA	Sep Ivey PMI	**Cons:** n/a	**Last:** 55.7
06/10/09	17:00		US	TRY 3-yr	**Cons:** n/a	**Last:** n/a
06/10/09	20:30		US	API Energy	**Cons:** n/a	**Last:** n/a
07/10/09	00:00			**WEDNESDAY**	**Cons:**	**Last:**

FIGURE 13.5   The Global-View Forex Economic Calendar
Source: Global Viewpoint, Inc., www.global-view.com

Do not get involved with this unless you are an experienced programmer. Integrating data I/Os and caching algorithms are not for the squeamish. The integrated trading platforms in Chapter 14, "Retail FX Platforms," have gone a long way toward making this particular process obsolete.

www.gaincapital.com

www.mbtrading.com

www.pfgbest.com

www.dbfx.com

www.dukascopy.com

www.oanda.com

The newest generation of integrated third-party platforms all have robust programming languages or scripts. The author has been able to write almost all of his programs in NinjaTrader's NinjaScript. APIs now serve only the most specialized advanced needs.

Historical Data

If you are developing a trading system, begin with historical data available by CD or download. It is much less expensive than an API. You also at least postpone the programming headaches of an API. Most charting and testing platforms also offer historical data. A strong correlation with your broker's data feed is not as important for systems testing—if you use a sample including a wide range of market environments.

www.disktrading.com Clean data, price is right, and customer service is excellent. Formatted for all the major platforms including NinjaTrader and Metatrader. See Figure 13.6.

www.snapdragon.co.uk Exceptionally clean historical data but not cheap. Offers other excellent services to the FOREX trader and developer. Founder Adam Hartley is knowledgeable and helpful. A new product offering integrates TradeStation with Oanda.

www.esignal.com

www.dukascopy.com; www.cqg.com Here, also, the integrated trading platforms now offer extensive historical data as well as back-testing and simulated trading capabilities.

System Development Tools

Somewhere over the rainbow is the perfect trading system; I hope you find it!

Some of these systems are also integrated trading platforms, reviewed in Chapter 14, "Retail FX Platforms." With so much integration of features and

```
"Date","Time","Close"
1040817 4 1.2355
1040817 4 1.2356
1040817 7 1.2355
1040817 7 1.2356
1040817 7 1.2355
1040817 7 1.2356
1040817 7 1.2355
1040817 8 1.2356
1040817 9 1.2355
1040817 9 1.2356
1040817 10 1.2355
1040817 10 1.2356
1040817 11 1.2356
1040817 11 1.2355
1040817 11 1.2356
1040817 12 1.2355
1040817 15 1.2356
1040817 19 1.2358
1040817 20 1.2357
1040817 20 1.2358
1040817 20 1.2357
1040817 20 1.2358
1040817 21 1.2357
1040817 26 1.2358
1040817 27 1.2356
1040817 30 1.2355
1040817 30 1.2357
1040817 31 1.2355
1040817 31 1.2356
1040817 32 1.2355
1040817 33 1.2356
1040817 34 1.2355
1040817 34 1.2355
1040817 35 1.2354
1040817 35 1.2355
```

FIGURE 13.6 Disktrading Historical Data
Source: www.disktrading.com

capabilities—charting, indicators, order-entry, system development—the line of demarcation has become quite thin.

www.ninjatrader.com NinjaTrader is a free application for advanced charting, market analytics, automated strategy development, and trade simulation. Some traders already consider it to be the Cadillac of system development tools, because it does everything and does it all well. Traders can use live data from Gain Capital, TradeStation, and eSignal as well as many other broker-dealers and data vendors. It includes a surprisingly robust strategy wizard for basic strategy development and uses NinjaScript, a C#-based scripting language for advanced work. Support is awesome. (See Figure 13.7.)

"NinjaTrader charts visualize all your orders and positions in addition to standard market data. All your working orders,

FIGURE 13.7 NinjaTrader
Source: NinjaTrader, LLC, www.ninjatrader.com

positions, and executions are plotted on the chart with bars and intelligently marked labels. With NinjaTrader Charts, you can instantly see how far or close your stops and targets are relative to key support and resistance levels." From www.ninjatrader.com.

www.metaquotes.com MetaTrader. Popular and integrated with many broker-dealer platforms. A common comment on the forums: "I like MetaTrader, but the broker is awful." The MetaTrader platform is also reviewed in Chapter 14, "Retail FOREX Platforms." The company appears to be having some growing pains or a mid-life crisis with the rollout of their new MT5 platform and MQL5 language.

www.FOREXtester.com FOREXTester's software simulates actual market conditions with historical data for strategy testing; think of it as a flight simulator for FOREX traders! It has a great deal of potential because it integrates with a full-featured Pascal-like programming language, Delphi 7, and also C++. Support is variable. (See Figure 13.8.)

FOREXTester allows traders to reproduce historical currency rate fluctuations with the regulated speed of price updating. Thus, a trader can make trading decisions on history, manually test trading ideas, and monitor trading results in the form of trading statistics and equity line. All in all, a useful product. But this class of tools is losing ground to those that offer live broker connectivity.

www.tradestation.com TradeStation's EasyLanguage is well developed. There is a significant amount of documentation and literature, as well as third-party programmers. You may wish to have someone write a trading method for you from your own basic idea and design. (See Figure 13. 9.)

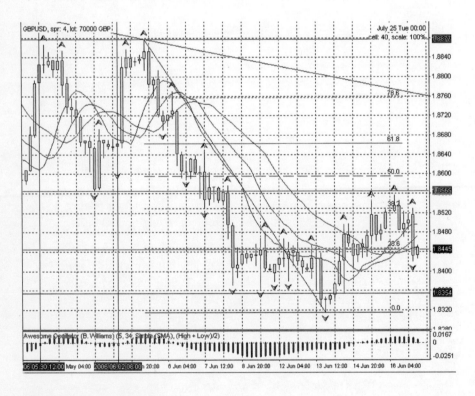

FIGURE 13.8 ForexTester

Source: ForexTester Software, www.forextester.com

```
Condition1 = Low < Low of 1 bar ago;
Condition2 = Close < Close of 1 bar ago;
If Condition1 and Condition2 then Buy;
```

FIGURE 13.9   TradeStation EasyLanguage
Source: TradeStation Securities, www.tradestation.com

www.esignal.com The eSignal scripting language is called EFS2. eSignal has more than 100 third-party vendors supporting it.

www.gordago.com An easy-to-use visual systems-building system although the toolset is not extremely robust. Good for the nonprogrammer who simply desires to manipulate indicator batteries.

www.wealth-lab.com Advertises for stock traders, but we assume it can be used for currency trading. Lots of documentation and help online but the web site appears somewhat chaotic. Probably worth digging deeper, however.

   TIP: When testing any trading system—yours or someone else's—be sure to test it over a wide range of market environments. See Chapter 18, "Improving Your Trading Skills." Most systems' back tests fail in real time because the test data is not representative of a wide and evenly distributed range of market environments.

FOREX Managed Accounts

The premise of this book is that you desire to make your own FOREX trading decisions. It is also possible to have your account managed by a professional money manager.

   Be leery of managed accounts promising too much. Fifty percent a year—consistently—is big money. $10,000 invested is more than $75,000 in five years at 50 percent, $320,000 at 100 percent. Look for consistency in performance more than how much a manager made in his or her best year. Generally, the more the manager aims to make, the more risk involved. A 20 percent annual return with low risk is better than 100 percent with high risk. I recently received a solicitation for a manager promising 15 percent a month! Compounded, you own the world in about six years.

   Carefully analyze a manager's performance, and look for market environments that may be an Achilles' heel. See Chapter 16, "Money Management

Simplified," for more on market environments. Be sure that costs are subtracted from gross performance. Costs may also give you an idea of how frequently the manager trades. Inquire if the manager is participating in the broker's pip spread income. Such an arrangement might encourage a manager to trade frequently.

Managed accounts can be individual or aggregated in a fund. Fund participation typically begins at $5,000 and individual managed accounts at $25,000.

Most of the major broker-dealers offer management services. They have already completed a thorough due diligence, but do not let that stop you from doing your own.

TIP: Invest with a money manager or a fund after one or two down months. Catch them at the bottom of their equity cycle—not the top.

Two Approaches to Performance Analysis

Performance analysis asks this core question: "How much can I make for how much risk"; basically, this is the risk/reward ratio of a money manager.

The conventional approach to performance analysis has become extremely complex, involving numerous mathematical and statistical methods and ratios. The most common is the Sharpe Ratio.

Sharpe Ratio   This popular performance ratio was developed by Nobel laureate William F. Sharpe. The Sharpe Ratio typically is calculated by subtracting a risk-free investment rate, such as the 10-year U.S. Treasury bond, from the rate of return for an investment or portfolio, then dividing the result by the standard deviation of the investment or portfolio return. The Sortino Ratio attempts to smooth the occasional spike in the Sharpe Ratio but is otherwise similar.

More pedestrian approaches to analyzing risk: (1) How frequently does the manager trade; (2) what was his maximum drawdown (loss of equity from a peak); (3) what is the average amount of account equity exposed to trading margin; (4) what is the average ratio of winning trade to losing trade in both dollars and aggregate numbers; (5) how long is his or her track record?

ME   Author Archer uses Market Environments (ME) to analyze performance.

ME divides all markets into functions of *directional movement* (DM) and *volatility* (V). If each function is rated on a scale of 1 to 10 from very low to very high, it gives a matrix of 100 market environments from (1,1) to (10,10). (See Table 13.1.) Look for money managers who have done well in a broad spectrum of MEs instead of just a scattered few. Performance—good

Table 13.1 A 10 × 10 DP/V ME Matrix									
1	2	3	4	5	6	7	8	9	10
1	1	1	1	1	1	1	1	1	1
1	2	3	4	5	6	7	8	9	10
2	2	2	2	2	2	2	2	2	2
1	2	3	4	5	6	7	8	9	10
3	3	3	3	3	3	3	3	3	3
3	3	3	3	3	3	3	3	3	3
4	4	4	4	4	4	4	4	4	4
1	2	3	4	5	6	7	8	9	10
5	5	5	5	5	5	5	5	5	5
1	2	3	4	5	6	7	8	9	10
6	6	6	6	6	6	6	6	6	6
1	2	3	4	5	6	7	8	9	10
7	7	7	7	7	7	7	7	7	7
1	2	3	4	5	6	7	8	9	10
8	8	8	8	8	8	8	8	8	8
1	2	3	4	5	6	7	8	9	10
9	9	9	9	9	9	9	9	9	9
1	2	3	4	5	6	7	8	9	10
10	10	10	10	10	10	10	10	10	10

or bad—that occurs in a mostly contiguous area of the matrix (clusters) can tell you much about the manager's trading methods. A short track record with a broad ME sample may be better than a long track record with hot and cold ME clusters. See Chapter 18, "Improving Your Trading Skills," for more on ME applications to trading.

Peter Panholzer

One of the most respected names in the managed FOREX business is Peter Panholzer. Already in 1979 Peter Panholzer ran what is today believed to be the first-ever systematically managed currency program offered to the general public at large, the Magnum Program at ContiCommodity, with over 300 accounts, indeed a very early example of currency alpha as a separate independent asset class. (See Figure 13.10.)

DynexCorp

Dynamic Currency Alpha

FIGURE 13.10   DynexCorp
Source: DynexCorp, Ltd, www.dynexcorp.com

     Mr. Panholzer, Partner of DynexCorp, offers our readers a brief summary of the latest managed money trend, Investable FX Indices. FXSelect utilizes a pool of managers and rotates them in and out of action based on proprietary performance algorithms:

After 30 years of toiling to achieve episodic profits in currency trading, my whole outlook on life (and stress) has changed since I am involved in what I deem the best—and unmatched—risk-adjusted returns currently available in the FX field.

     DynexCorp was invited by Deutsche Bank London AG, alongside with Mercer Consulting and Parker Global Strategies, to be index architects for Deutsche Bank's FXSelect platform.

Highlights:

- Index developed and managed by DynexCorp, by invitation of Deutsche Bank
- Investable Custom FX Index designed and managed by DynexCorp using the pioneering Deutsche Bank FXSelect Platform
- This index is superior to any single FX manager performance, and also superior to simple equally weighted allocation – the index dynamically represents the best 5 to 15 of 70 currency alpha managers at any point in time

- High Sharpe Ratio, Low Volatility
- Daily Liquidity
- Stop-Loss monitored and guaranteed by Deutsche Bank

Why investable FX index?
Single currency manager performances are notoriously EPISODIC. The message to investors is: Don't hire single currency managers.

This is our FXSelect edge:

1. Our quantitative and qualitative selection algorithm: As veteran FX manager we are familiar with many traders and their styles; our quantitative model very quickly determines "exclusions."

2. We use only "real" daily data achieved on the FXSelect platform: Historic data supplied "on a reported basis" are not as reliable as the "real" daily data achieved on the FXSelect platform.

3. We can switch managers on any day and at no cost: When investing in conventional multi-manager currency funds, consider that the manager selection process is costly and the manager selection length is quite inflexible.

—Peter Panholzer

A number of companies track individual and fund FOREX account performance.

- www.parkerglobal.com
- www.managedfutures.com
- www.mainfo.org

Advisory Services

Almost every magazine and newsletter today is either online or available online. Gone forever are the glory days of the hardcopy *Harry Schultz Letter, Dines Letter, Holt Advisory,* and *Myer's Energy and Finance.*

FOREX Market letters and signal services are reviewed on www.forexpeacearmy.com

WDFX

www.wdfx.co.uk

Trust me on this. I do not normally recommend Signal services. But Mark at WDFX Forex is good. He's a longer term trader in a world of scalpers. They also offer a Trading Room forum and an Expert Advisor.

An excellent supplement to your own trading tools. Of course, past performance is never a guarantee of future results, but WDFX has some solid FX benchmarks indicating some long-term staying power.

Currency Bulletin

www.currencybulletin.com An interesting FOREX newsletter/advisory with a long track record in FOREX. The author uses this service as a check on his own long-term chart analysis.

GoodmanWorks

www.goodmanworks.com The author publishes the GoodmanWorks Blog 6–8 times each week. It focuses on the Goodman trading methods—Goodman Wave Theory and Market Environments, offering instruction as well as trading ideas. The web site also updates this book, answers readers questions, and digs deeper on topics in this book with the Getting Started Blog.

EuroTrader

www.eurusdtrader.com Jimmy Young's advisory service has attracted a loyal following. One focus is trading vis-à-vis the frequent news releases in the FOREX arena.

If you plan to be a self-directed trader, consider using two advisory services: one of them to complement your own analysis and one of them "out-of-the-box" to give you a fresh perspective. I use two services to confirm my own work but rarely follow the trade recommendations unless they also match up with my own thinking.

Online Reference Guides

www.investopedia.com Superior reference on technical analysis, charting, and other aspects of trading. New articles are published almost daily. Material is geared to the new and inexperienced trader and leading-edge ideas are discouraged.

Spread and Binary Betting

Spread Betting It has been said that retail FOREX market makers are essentially bookmakers. You might wish to consider spread or binary betting on currencies. Be sure to check the legality where you reside.

Most of these offer binary options on currencies in a variety of flavors.

www.deltaindex.com One of the oldest spread betting web sites.

www.fxbt.com This web site offers binary options in a number of markets, including FOREX. You take a yes or no side to a financial question such as "Will the EUR/USD go over 1.3700?" Or you can speculate on the likelihood of a hurricane. Government-regulated and open only to U.S. citizens.

www.nadax.com Trade the political, financial, and weather events that make up at least part of the fundamental picture for currencies.

www.igindex.co.uk Offers a dealing platform and charts.

Periodicals—In Print and Online

www.forexjournal.com *Forex Journal* is the sister publication to *Trader's Journal.* Editor Dickson Yap does an excellent job with both. Unlike many editors in this space he is not afraid of new ideas. Content is varied and stimulating. See Figure 13.11.

www.currencytradermag.com Excellent content although it tends to mainstream ideas for the most part.

www.e-FOREX.net By subscription, pricey but excellent if you are serious about the inner workings of the FOREX industry.

FIGURE 13.11 Forex Journal

Euro Money Magazine

www.euromoney.com

Futures Magazine

www.futuresmag.com Just a shell of its former glory days when Darrell Jobman was editor.

FX – Week Magazine

www.fxweek.com

Technical Analysis of Stocks and Commodities

www.traders.com A 25-year treasure trove of technical analysis. If you can afford it, buy their complete articles volumes, available in hard copy or dvd.

Books

www.traderspress.com I would be remiss if I did not accord special mention to Ed Dobson's Traders Press, www.traderspress.com, which has been around for decades. They carry a number of FOREX-specific books as well as hundreds of newly published and reprinted books on technical analysis. One of the author's all-time favorite market books is Mr. Dobson's *The Trading Rule That Can Make You Rich* (Traders Press, 1979).

For specific titles and out-of-print books, see www.abebooks.com, www.amazon.com, www.bn.com, www.alibris.com, and the ubiquitous www.ebay.com.

Summary

As I stated at the beginning of the chapter, this is but a small sampling of what is available to the currency market participant. Armed with these links and a reliable bookmark manager, you should be able to navigate to almost anything in the burgeoning FOREX marketplace. Begin with some idea of what you want and need, but be open to new and out-of-the-box ideas, also.

14

Retail FX Platforms

Many FOREX brokers use their own proprietary platform, but the trend is to use one of a number of standard cross-broker platforms that have become popular. This is a potential win-win-win situation. The broker wins by not having to invest large amounts of money in constant development, the platform vendor can concentrate on upgrading their service with new features and more stability, and the trader just sits back and makes money trading.

Platform vendors make every effort to get as many brokers to offer their platform as possible, not just because it means more business. When traders shop platforms they want to know that if Broker ABC does not pan out for them they can go to Broker XYZ and use the platform they have become accustomed to trading. Here I am discussing the front-end trading terminal. There is the back-end server software and setup, which is required (in most cases) for the broker to have installed to run the client terminals.

TIP: You may need to dig deep on a broker's web site to find which trading platforms it supports. Sometimes the Search function will help. The vendors also usually list the brokers who currently use their platforms.

The reviews below are ordered on a mix of popularity, broker support, and feature-richness, based on my research. Many brokers use multiple platforms and some offer one of these exclusively. Of course, popularity should not be your only criteria. You want to be comfortable with both your broker and your trading platform. Table 14.1 lists the candidates.

TABLE 14.1 Retail FOREX Platforms	
NinjaTrader	www.ninjatrader.com
eSignal	www.esignal.com
ProTrader	www.protrader.com
MetaTrader	www.metaquotes.net
TradeStation	www.tradestation.com
StrategyRunner	www.strategyrunner.com
FXCM	www.fxcm.com

Professional FX Platforms

There are a number of trading platforms designed for the professional trader, which are beyond the scope of this work but merit a mention. (See Table 14.2.) Several retail FOREX brokers now offer the Currenex platform to their clients.

Trading Platform Features

A trading platform is defined by the features it offers to users. Brokers look for what the platform offers to them on the server side. For each platform we review the following:

Connectivity to the broker's data feed.

Integrated order entry and management.

Without these two features a platform is not fully integrated with the broker-dealer.

Charts and indicators
Almost every retail FX trader uses charts and indicators. The sheer number and permutations of these available—especially indicators— is simply staggering.

TABLE 14.2 Professional FOREX Platform	
Currenex	www.currenex.com
FlexFX	www.flextrade.com
FXall	www.fxall.com
HotspotFX	www.hotspotfx.com
ProTraderPlus	www.fxbridge.com

Depth of market (DOM)
This shows standing orders in the market and the amount bid or asked at prices near the last price. It is useful information for placing orders—especially large ones that might eat several bids or asks in execution.

Scripting or programming language
Advanced traders often wish to program their own indicators and trading systems or EAs. These can vary in ease of use and capabilities. Generally, the easier they are to use, the less robust.

Testing and historical data
Traders want to test their ideas and their programs on the same platform on which they will ultimately live trade them. Simulated trading, a form of back-testing, is all the rage.

API connectivity
Advanced traders may wish to create a program too complex for the trading platform's scripting language, in which case they will need to tap into the broker's data feed, then port the program in some fashion to the trading platform. As the capabilities of these platforms advance, I predict this need will all but disappear in the next few years. NinjaScript version 7 is in many respects superior to API.

Automated trading
The ability to automatically execute the trades generated by a trading system or EA is becoming more and more popular. But it is not for the novice.

In the past stability has been an issue for currency trading platforms. But all of those listed here may be considered stable and reliable with two caveats—some tend to take more computer resources than others and all have at least a few small bugs. In combination with a live data feed these are enormously complex programs requiring a sophisticated server-client arrangement.

The author has used the MetaTrader platform for years but is migrating to NinjaTrader. I am something of a service fanatic. NinjaTrader's support is excellent whereas multiple e-mails to Metaquotes went unanswered. NinjaTrader's feature set and scripting language is better than MQL4 or MQL5—at least for my needs.

I have worked with all of the platforms listed and they all are stable and feature-rich. Some are definitely better than others but much of the decision on which one you choose is based on personal needs and personal tastes. All of them have many loyal and adoring fans. The new trader can definitely live without Depth of Market, Scripting Language, API Connectivity, and Automated Trading.

NinjaTrader

NinjaTrader is currently on version 6.5. A major upgrade, version 7.0 was expected in the first quarter of 2010—it has been anxiously awaited by NinjaTrader aficionados. The author was in the beta group and came away very impressed.

NinjaTrader is more customizable than MetaTrader. The flip side of the coin is that it is more difficult to set up and learn. Pre-built configurations or a modular approach would help the neophyte ease into this truly awesome platform. NinjaTrader does offer many live and on-demand webcasts to assist traders with all aspects of application. Support from the vendor is stellar. Their user forum is lively and offers much advice on using the platform and developing systems and methods with NinjaScript.

NinjaTrader has some excellent features. Two the author appreciates are Market Replay and Strategy Analyzer. For U.S. traders who miss the ability to hedge positions, Ninja allows all orders to be entered into its system—and only sent for execution as price targets and other parameters are met in real time.

The NinjaScript language is a C# subset with add-on functions and objects for system development.

Navigation is a little tricky as the charts in a Workspace cannot be docked. Also, if you have very high resolution monitors you may need to make font size adjustments to allow all text to fit in some NinjaTrader windows. Version 7 is much less a resource hog than previous versions and—it appears—the list of frustrating little bugs is down substantially.

The number of NinjaTrader users is growing quickly and more broker support in FOREX is likely to follow.

Report Card: Broker Support: B, Features: A+, Stability: B, Vendor Support: A+, Ergonomics and Ease of Use: B, Third-Party Support: B+. See Figure 14.1.

MetaTrader

The current leader of the pack. Dozens of foreign and domestic brokers offer MetaTrader as either their primary platform of as one of the platforms in their stable. I have no numbers but MetaTrader through the life of their MetaTrader-4 (MT4) has garnished a substantial percentage of the business. While MetaTrader has its own forum and there are three other popular MetaTrader forums, the company itself does not offer direct support to end-users. They

FIGURE 14.1　NinjaTrader www.ninjatrader.com

seem a tad cocky and are obviously enjoying their well-earned success in the marketplace. But there is a Yin and a Yang to everything.

As this book goes to press MetaTrader-5 (MT5) with its new object-oriented scripting language (MQL5) was just released to the public beta testing; unfortunately too late for a full review. It was scheduled for release in the summer 2009 but the fast-hitting new NFA rules for anti-hedging and First In First Out (FIFO, see Chapter 4, "Regulation: Past, Present, and Future") sent them back to the drawing board to make the platform compliant for U.S. domiciled brokers.

It is likely the older MetaTrader-4 will remain online with some foreign brokers for a period of time. As noted in Chapter 4, "Regulation: Past, Present, and Future," many traders found their methods and money management upset by NFA Compliance Rule 2-43. MetaTrader-5 is a completely new build and from the forums it seems to be quite buggy at the time of this writing although it is not yet available to brokers and is still in beta testing. Indicators and expert advisors for MT4 will not work as-is—upward compatibility is limited; only the simplest of indicators will not need to be rebuilt. The client terminal of MT5 has a dazzling array of graphic features, new indicators, and 21 time frames for charts. The new scripting language, MQL5, is closer to a full object-oriented

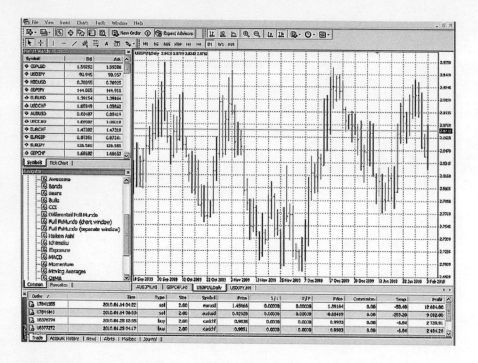

FIGURE 14.2   MetaTrader-4 www.metaquotes.net

language such as C++. Programs in MT5 are said to run 5 to 10 times faster than in MQL4. As a consequence Metatrader-5 can support substantially more complex indicators and expert advisors.

MT5 can be used for stocks, futures, and FOREX as long as the broker server is set up to accommodate them. The order palette and order management system has been modified extensively.

Report Card: Broker Support: A, Features: B+, Stability: A, Vendor Support: C, Ergonomics and Ease of Use: B, Third-Party Support: A+. See Figure 14.2.

eSignal

eSignal has been in this space for almost 20 years; they have had the time to get things right. The platform is feature-rich, well thought out, and well designed. Service, a weak link in the past, has become truly excellent in the past year. Installation and setup is similar to NinjaTrader—it is a bit tricky—but the platform is a pleasure to use. eSignal's scripting language, EFS2, while easy-to-use, appears to be weaker than MQL4, NinjaScript, or ProTrader's onboard scripting tool.

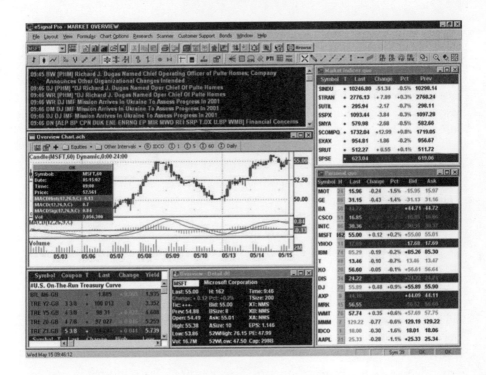

FIGURE 14.3 eSignal www.esignal.com

eSignal has more than 100 third-party programmers and companies that build indicators for the platform or can create custom platforms to your own specifications. The company has a solid cadre of brokers who have integrated the platform at various levels including PFGBest, MBTrading, Oanda, FXCM, and Gain Capital.

Automated trading is not currently a feature but eSignal has set 2010 for the year to offer it on the platform.

A serious contender as is, a stronger scripting language could move it even higher.

Report Card: Broker Support: B, Features: B+, Stability: B+, Vendor Support: B+, Ergonomics and Ease of Use: A, Third-Party Support: B. See Figure 14.3.

ProTrader

ProTrader is the new kid on the block. ProTrader is attempting to muscle-in on MetaTrader and NinjaTrader territory. It is unique because it is paired with a powerful back-end solution for the broker—a definite plus in getting it accepted in the industry! ProTrader.net requires a broker to have the ProTrader server setup. ProTrader seems to have been designed from the broker side out to the user side, just the opposite of MetaTrader's design flow from the user side.

ProTrader MultiStation can, according to ProTrader, connect from anywhere on the planet with an Internet connection to any broker. They claim to currently have 20 broker-dealers aboard. A new broker can be set up in just a few days. It can handle stocks and commodity futures as well as FOREX. I found ProTrade support excellent.

ProTrader has given much emphasis to the broker side of things during development. But the user has not been forgotten. In addition to its own scripting language, ProTrader supports MetaTraders MQL language and TradeStation's EasyLanguage. Porting of external language programs will be possible in the future, as well. Neat!

Its feature palette is currently not as strong as NinjaTrader, MetaTrader, or eSignal—but it is making fast progress. The author found the charts disappointing and found the demo a little difficult to install, but once up, it ran fine.

ProTrader really wants to do it all and that is no small task. The downside: Usability and stability have suffered, but improvements seem to be made on a regular basis. The vendor offers excellent support to both brokers and traders.

Report Card: Broker Support: C+, Features: B, Stability: B, Vendor Support: A+, Ergonomics and Ease of Use: B+, Third-Party Support: C.

TIP: Watch this company. If they do what they say they can do—and keep their high-level service model—it will be a game-changer. See Figure 14.4.

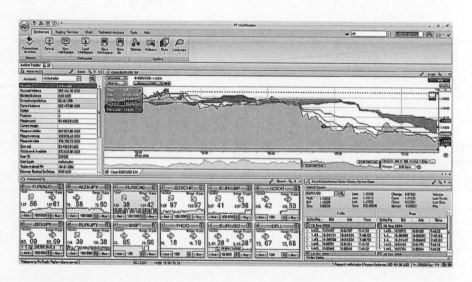

FIGURE 14.4 ProTrader www.protrader.com

TradeStation

TradeStation is the second oldest platform in this category, and is now on version 8. It began as a stocks-only platform, added commodity futures and finally FOREX about five years ago. Its primary weakness is that the trader must use the TradeStation brokerage services and the company has only a single source FX feed. The scripting language, EasyLanguage, I would rate third to NinjaScript and MQL4 but it is the easiest to learn for those who wish to get a feel for building their own indicators and trading systems. The TradeStation MATRIX may be the best of the Depth of Market tools in the class. The historical database is extensive. The platform design and layout is intuitive and comfortable, but the single broker aspect is an issue for many FOREX traders.

> **TradeStation did not reply to multiple requests for information. The above review is based on a demo platform and information culled from their web site.**

Report Card: Broker Support: N/A, Features: A, Stability: A, Vendor Support: B–, Ergonomics and Ease of Use: A, Third-Party Support: B+.

StrategyRunner

StrategyRunner started off strong but seems as if it is in a holding pattern right now. Competition is tough, as you can imagine. But they do have both futures and FX brokers continuing to support it. If one of the front-runners slips, it could still move back into the pack.

> **StrategyRunner did not reply to multiple requests for information. The above review here is based on a demo platform and information culled from their web site.**

Report Card: Broker Support: C, Features: B, Stability: B–, Vendor Support: C–, Ergonomics and Ease of Use: B, Third-Party Support: C–.

FXCM

FX Trading Platform is FXCM's in-house platform. It is included because you can see quite a few introducing brokers (IBs) and FXCM partners using the platform and back-end technology. If you like FXCM as a broker, this could be your trading platform. If not, move along. No scripting language.

> **FXCM did not reply to multiple requests for information. My review is based on a demo platform and information culled from**

their web site. Whether you trade with FXCM or one of their many IBs, you will be tied to the full FXCM back-end. In that regard I recommend carefully reading the reviews for this broker.

Report Card: Broker Support: B–, Features: B+, Stability: B+, Vendor Support: B–, Ergonomics and Ease of Use: B+, Third-Party Support: N/A.

TIP: Know your trading platform inside and out before live trading. Navigating a trading platform and such mechanical tasks as order placement and management must be second nature. FOREX trading is fast-paced. You want to spend your time analyzing markets, not trying to remember how to open a chart window.

OpenQuant

This platform appears to be somewhere between an API and professional platform on one side and a retail platform on the other. The author found the web site, www.openquant.com, interesting. But the project appears to be somewhat dormant and an e-mail inquiry took a full month to be answered.

Kid in a Candy Store

All of these platforms are great fun to explore. But keep focused on your current requirements and where you anticipate you will be in one or two years. Switching platforms is certainly possible—I have done it twice in ten years. But that is not fun. Beginning with a well thought out list of your needs and a thorough due diligence of several candidates, a trading platform selection should last you for a long time.

Summary

Which integrated trading platform (if any) you select depends on many personal preferences and your individual want-list. What features do you need, is obviously the first question. But do not be swayed simply by the feature set; other factors merit serious consideration.

Much of the selection process is a subjective matter. Does it have enough brokers supporting it? Be sure one or more of the brokers you selected in Chapter 7 actively support the platform of your choice. As in the case of brokers,

I recommend you e-mail the trading platform vendor once or twice with any questions to get a line on the quality of support. Finally, do the brokers who use the platform support it wholeheartedly or is it just sort of "there"? Where vendor support is poor that is a critical issue. Some vendors—NinjaTrader—support their platform directly; others—MetaTrader—rely on the broker to support the platform to the user.

Part 4

The Complete FOREX Trader

Chapter 15

The Plan! The Plan!

FOREX trading is a fast-paced enterprise. You need to make decisions quickly, react instinctively, and not drop any of the multiple balls in the air. Leverage is one of the primary reasons traders are attracted to currency trading. It also magnifies mistakes.

Every trader will want to come to the table with a plan encompassing all aspects of his or her trading program. It does not need to be complicated. In fact it should not be complicated so it does not distract or take up too much time. But it must be well laid out, all encompassing—and effective. And, you must abide by it consistently.

In this chapter I detail a basic, simple FOREX trading plan and some examples of how it works for me in real-time trading. You certainly want to modify it and customize it to your own needs, skills, experience, and techniques.

I am assuming that you have selected a broker, created a KIS toolbox for making trading decisions, and are comfortable with the broker's trading platform. You can certainly practice your plan with a demo account to see how it feels, get the bugs out, and make adjustments. The most common plan error—next to having no plan at all—is making it too complicated and involved.

TIP: The Plan—Keep It Simple! It is of no value if you do not use it consistently.

Parts of the Plan

The Plan may be separated into three steps:

1. Pretrade Planning
2. Trade Session Planning
3. Post-Trade Planning

The FX markets run 24 hours nonstop from Sunday afternoon to Saturday afternoon, the continental USA time zones. Unless you are using an automated trading program you cannot possibly trade full time. The market as such is a process but traders are only able to work it in discrete time segments. A big part of planning is to compensate for this difference; keep a view on the constant flow of prices even though you might only trade four or five hours a day—and perhaps not even every day.

The three steps, therefore, should form a loop. Your pretrade planning should get you back in the groove of the markets quickly to execute the trade session planning. Your post-trade planning should note ideas and information you pick up and use for the next pretrade period. The touchstone for success here: When you arrive at your computer to trade, how fast can you get back into the groove?

Plan Materials

Here is a list of materials you will need to implement the plan. Again, feel free to add, subtract, or modify them accordingly. See Table 15.1.

You can keep all of this information in longhand or on a computer. I much prefer keeping them on computer files—Word documents and Excel

Table 15.1 Trade Plan Materials

Mission-Critical Information Sheet

Trading Tables (from Chapter 6)

30 Trade Campaign Worksheet

Log Charts

Biofeedback Chart

Trade Heuristic Worksheet

Continuation Charts

Performance Evaluation

spreadsheet. Whatever works best for you is the way to go. That said, I make hard copies of much of it for study and ready reference.

TIP: All of these are in the Getting Started section of www .goodmanworks.com.

Mission-Critical Information Sheet

This should be information at your fingertips during every trading session. Most of it pertains to your broker and your account. See Figure 15.1.

Biofeedback Form

I know, this sounds really silly and so 1960s. But it works. Be honest about your evaluations. When, at the end of 30 trades, you map the emotions you came to trade with and the results thereof, you will be surprised! See Figure 15.2.

The Snowflake Method

Before studying the Trade Heuristic Worksheet I want to mention the Snowflake Method, which is a key component of my own heuristic.

The concept of the Snowflake is to gradually hone in on a trade. Go from the most general features of a chart and your trading method to the most specific. Fill in with outlines until you see a clear picture. Look at the following small online Java applet of the Koch Snowflake:

http://math.rice.edu/~lanius/frac/koch/koch.html.

Trade Heuristic Worksheet

The Trade Heuristic is used for Step 2, Trade Session Planning. This is your reference for however you find a prospective trade. Its primary purpose is to make sure you do not skip important parts of finding a trade and following through on it. Go from general to specific, gradually qualifying trades as they meet your trading method benchmarks. A heuristic is a series of questions or operations you must work through to find a trade. I call finding a trade the "FAT" process. See Figure 15.3 for the full heuristic outline.

Below is a brief discussion of the heuristic. You may wish to read the remainder of this chapter first, and then come back to my explanations.

MISSION-CRITICAL INFORMATION					
Broker 1		**Broker 2**		**Broker 3**	
Website		Website		Website	
ID		ID		ID	
Password		Password		Password	
Account #		Account #		Account #	
Contact		Contact		Contact	
Order Backup		Order Backup		Order Backup	
Support Email		Support Email		Support Email	
Support Telephone		Support Telephone		Support Telephone	
Minimum Lot Size/Increment		Minimum Lot Size/Increment		Minimum Lot Size/Inrement	
Account Balance		Account Balance		Account Balance	
Risk-Reward Ratio					
Fix Dollar Take Profit (T/P)					
Fix Dollar Stop Loss (S/L)					
Lot Size Traded					
Pip Value ($$$/Lot Size Traded)					
Open Positions and Orders in the Market					

FIGURE 15.1 Mission-Critical Information

Biofeedback Form

	−5	−4	−3	−2	−1	0	1	2	3	4	5
Session Date											
Session Time											
Beginning of Session											
End of Session											
Comment											
Session Date											
Session Time											
Beginning of Session											
End of Session											
Comment											
Session Date											
Session Time											
Beginning of Session											
End of Session											
Comment											
Session Date											
Session Time											
Beginning of Session											
End of Session											
Comment											
Session Date											
Session Time											
Beginning of Session											
End of Session											
Comment											

FIGURE 15.2 Biofeedback Form

TRADE HEURISTIC WORKSHEET AND CHECKLIST

Presession
    Mission-Critical Information
    Fill in Biofeedback Form
    Enter Green Session Lines
    Note Pending News and Announcements
    Review Continuation Charts from Previous Session

Session
    Review all Charts on Trend Time Frame
    Review all Charts on Watch Time Frame
    Candidates - FAT Form
        Chart Formation
        Indicator Battery
        Confirming Tools
        Complementary Tools
        Money Management Parameters
        Reality Check
        Go to Entry Time-Frame Chart
        Entry Signal
        Place Order, S/L and T/P
        Monitor on Watch Time Frame

Postsession
    Annotate Continuation Charts
    Fill in 30 Campaign Worksheet
    Annotate Log Charts and Attach to Campaign Worksheet
    Fill in Biofeedback Form
    Enter Red Session Lines

FIGURE 15.3   Trade Heuristic Worksheet

My primary trading approach is Goodman Wave Theory and Market Environments. My primary time is spent projecting waves and waiting to see if they develop as I anticipated. I basically arrange the charts from least promising to most promising, in accordance with the snowflake idea. I have a number of Trade Setup templates that I am looking for to find a candidate; the closer I get to seeing one of them, the more promising the chart is for me.

Your trading method will no doubt differ from mine. But the idea should be the same. Gradually zero in from interesting charts to promising charts to candidate charts. The goal is to Find A Trade (FAT).

Presession Planning

Sit down; gather your materials. Open your trading platform. Do the Biofeedback Form. I draw green Session Lines on all my charts right away, denoting when I started that session. This is all about finding a groove. See Figure 15.4.

www.tradeviewforex.com and www.metaquotes.com

In this example the Beginning Session Lines are thick vertical lines; the Ending Session Lines are thin verticals. I actually use green and red for session

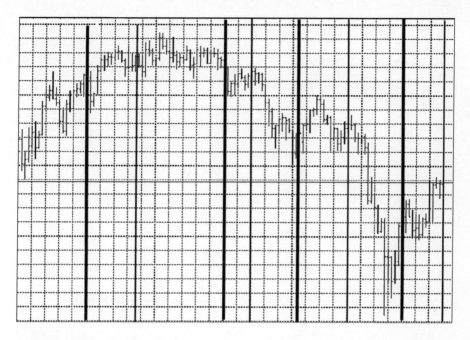

FIGURE 15.4 Session Lines
Source: TradeviewForex www.tradeviewforex.com and www.metaquotes.net

lines with the same thickness. These lines help you quickly see what has transpired since you last traded.

Finally, note any pending news, announcements, or economic indicator statistics that will come out while you are trading—for the pairs you have in your Watch, Candidates, and Open list. You may get this information from any of the calendars I mention in Chapter 13, "The FOREX Marketplace." My favorites are the Global-View calendar, www.global-view.com, and the Forex Economic Calendar, www.forexeconomiccalendar.com.

Scan a few charts as a finger exercise. Now review your continuation charts and see what the markets have done since you were away—the areas from the last red Session Lines to the green one you just entered. Did you miss any important moves? What hasn't changed and what has changed? All of this, of course, is asked based on your trading method.

Session Planning

Identify Trade Candidates

    The Hopper

    Watch

    Candidates

I keep charts in three NinjaTrader Workspaces or MetaTrader Profiles. Hopper charts are typically 1-Day charts, which look interesting. I project price points for them into the future and wait to see if those points get hit or approached. Watch charts are 1-Hour charts. These are pairs, which for one reason or the other, have looked good enough to move to a higher status. My normal chart view is 1-Hour. When and if a Watch chart completes a Goodman template, I move it to the 15-Minute Candidate chart, periodically check the market against my FAT form, and wait for a specific buy or sell signal.

Determine Money Management Parameters: Stop-Loss (S/L) and Take-Profit (T/P).

While I am waiting for my candidates to generate a buy or sell signal I make a quick risk-reward calculation. Where does my stop go; my take-profit? If they are not at least 3:1 in favor of take-profit, the trade is going to need to be exceptionally good for me to take it, even if I get an entry signal. Conversely, if the ratio is very high (5:1 or better) I might take the trade even if it has a few warts.

Reality Check

Close your eyes; meditate on something else a minute or two. Then look at the chart one last time. Did you miss something? Did you see something that is not there? Wishful thinking involved?

Enter the Trade

I use the Dagger entry principle to enter markets. See Chapter 18, "Improving Your Trading Skills," for details. Once my trade is confirmed (or often with the buy or sell order) I also enter a stop-loss (S/L) and take-profit (T/P).

Monitor the Trade

What I am mostly looking for here is a price point where I can raise my S/L to break even or close. Then, I sit on my hands. Once a stop has been placed I never move it back down or back up. Instead of watching over the trade—I made my decision and now I must live with it—I spend my time looking for more candidate trades.

Exit the Trade

Either my Stop-Loss (S/L) or Take-Profit (T/P) is elected.

TIP: Spend you time finding solid trade candidates. Once you enter the trade place your S/L and T/P and sit on your hands. If your S/L is not hit you are simply waiting for prices to move in your direction enough to move the stop-loss to breakeven. A successful trade should be thought of as two steps, breaking even and then making money. In between there is not much to do but wait. Use your time to explore other candidates.

Worksheet and Log Chart

Once the trade is over, I do a Log Chart and enter the details into my 30 Trade Campaign worksheet and attach the log chart showing the trade and perhaps a note to refresh my memory when I do a performance review. See Figure 15.5.

Needless to say, I have glossed over many details. For example, using a trailing stop and taking a profit early if I get a windfall. When I enter a trade I draw an imaginary line from my entry to where I think my T/P may be hit estimating how long the trade will take. If at any time prices greatly move away from the line on the direction of my T/P, I will take a windfall profit. See Figure 15.6. The area roughly between the two lines is the windfall area. I am more likely to take a windfall early in a trade (50 percent of my expected gain in 10 percent of the time) rather than late in a trade (80 percent of my expected gain in 60 percent of the time).

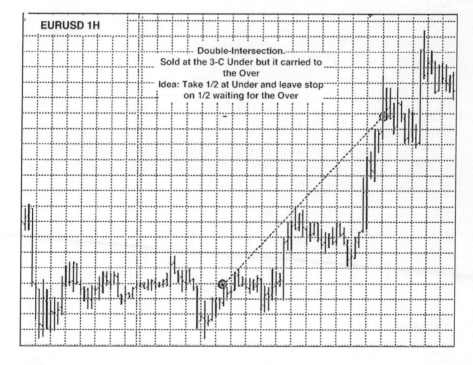

FIGURE 15.5 Log Chart
Source: TradeviewForex www.tradeviewforex.com and www.metaquotes.net

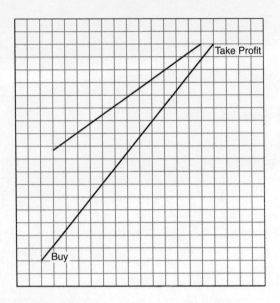

FIGURE 15.6   Windfall Profit

Postsession Planning

At the end of the trading session, I place vertical red Session Lines on all my Hopper, Watch, and Candidate charts. When I come back next time, I know exactly where I left. In conjunction with the Continuation charts, I can find my groove in five minutes. If I do not feel comfortable after 30 minutes I may well just pass the session.

Last, I annotate my Continuation charts and once more fill in the Biofeedback chart. The session is over. I confess I take my work home with me, but that is a personal decision to make for each trader.

30 Trade Campaign Worksheet

This is where you log your trades and supplemental material. Log whatever information is available, as soon as it is available. This, obviously, is a continuously updated document. But at the end of every 10 trades you will use it for diagnostics, self-evaluation.

I like to print hard copies and attach charts showing each of my trades. I call it a Log Chart. You may want to add a few brief annotations to that chart.

30 TRADE CAMPAIGN WORKSHEET										
Compaign #										
Lot Size	Date	Pair	Position	In	S/L	T/P	Out	P/L Pips	P/L $$$	Template
A1										
Comment										
A2										
Comment										
A3										
Comment										
A4										
Comment										
A5										
Comment										
A6										
Comment										
A7										
Comment										
A8										
Comment										
A9										
Comment										
A10										
Comment										
Evaluation										

FIGURE 15.7   30 Trade Campaign Worksheet

Those might include your entry and exit, where you raised or lowered stops (if you did), and perhaps a brief text note to help you recall the trade days or weeks later. Figure 15.7 is my 30 Trade Worksheet. It is downloadable in the Getting Started section of www.goodmanworks.com.

Continuation Charts

This is a method I developed for my own trading—to bridge the gap between the continuous process market and discrete trading sessions. It is also your loop from the end of one session to the beginning of the next. It will allow you to smoothly catch up on markets where you left off. Before I used it, I found I spent 15 to 30 minutes of each new session just catching up and getting back in the groove. See Figure 15.8 for an example of such a chart. Again, how you annotate it is going to be based on your own trading method and tools you use to trade. Mine had tended to get a bit complex. Start with just some basic

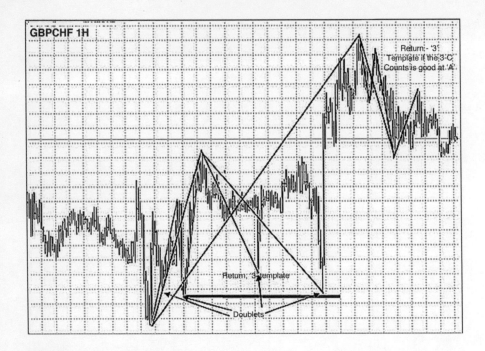

FIGURE 15.8 A Continuation Chart
Source: TradeviewForex www.tradeviewforex.com and www.metaquotes.net

annotations to jog your memory. You may wish to add the Log information at the end of each trade to the continuation chart.

I have also developed an extensive syntax for my annotations, based on the Goodman trading methods. Yours do not need to be so complete, but be consistent about their use. See Figure 15.9.

The primary idea is to have a set of symbols to annotate a chart quickly and consistently.

TIP: If you trade small time-frame charts—anything less than 1-hour—and you are away for more than a few hours between sessions, too much price activity will have disappeared when you next trade. If so, either compress your continuation chart, making the space between bars smaller, or go to the next higher time frame for your continuation chart.

SnagIt

The scheme here is to annotate the markets you are following at the end of each session. When you next trade, referring to those visual notes will, if done properly, get you back in the trading groove quickly and efficiently.

Matrices are colored Black, Red, Green, and Purple – from largest to smallest.

TE = 50% Point, Total Equilibrium
ATE = Adjusted Total Equilibrium on Carryovers
O = Over measurement, U = Under measurement. Brackets [ ]
R = Return (Swing or Point)
DI = Double Intersection
TI = Triple Intersection
X = Goodman Knot, XX = Double Knot
B = Breakaway
3C = 3–C Rule
SK – Stick
TTT – Spread Triples

Matrix by Swings
P1 = Primary Swing One   P1A, P1B, P1C
S1 = Secondary Swing   S1A, S1B, S1C
P2 = Primary Swing Two   P2A, P2B, P2C

Matrix by Points or Swings - from largest to smallest
1-2-3-(4), A-B-C-(D), W-X-Y-(Z)

Points of a Swing
P1 = Beginning Point
P2 = 50% Point / TE
P3 = End Point
P4 = Primary Measured Move Point ('P1' is a Primary Swing)
P5 = Secondary Measured Move Point ('P1' is a Secondary Swing)

FIGURE 15.9 The Goodman Syntax for GSCS

I use a tool from TechSmith, www.techsmith.com, named SnagIt for my annotations. It is somewhat feature-rich but you can learn the basics in one or two hours and be up-to-speed. If you prefer, you can print the charts and annotate them by hand. In fact, even though I annotate with SnagIt I still print my charts and refer to them between sessions. Sometimes you will see something important between sessions because your mind is fresher, so you do not miss the forest for the trees. See Figure 15.10.

Performance Diagnostics

For this part of the Plan you can refer to the 30 Trade Campaign Worksheet and Log charts.

Do not try to draw grandiose conclusions from the results of a single trade—good or bad. The human mind loves to generalize, even if it has a small sample of data. Avoid the temptation. With the Campaign Trade Method

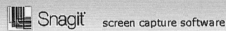

Product Tour

Capture anything you see on the screen. Edit
and combine those captures. Share them via
your favorite applications. Organize and find them
again later. The more you use Snagit, the more
ways you'll find to use it!

FIGURE 15.10   SnagIt
Courtesy of TechSmith, Inc. www.techsmith.com

(CTM) 30 Trade idea, you analyze your performance every 10 trades. At the end
of 30 trades, you dig deep.

The CTM is designed to break your grubstake into 30 trades, all of which
can be losers, though I sincerely hope that is not the case!

I have mentored quite a few traders over the years. I know of many who
threw in the towel too early, without bothering to look for areas where they
could improve performance.

Figure 15.11 are the questions you should ask and the items to look for
after every 10 trades and again, in more detail, after a full campaign of 30 trades.

TIP: Small, evolutionary adjustments may make a big difference to the
bottom line.

Record Keeping

Beyond the 30 Trade Campaign Worksheet there are a number of records you
should keep. Please remember your Uncle Sam or Uncle Vladimir or Uncle
Chang has opted in as your partner in the event of your success. While your
broker will send you everything you need for taxes, you should from time to
time print the account summary from your trading platform. Records of
deposits and withdrawals should also be made into hard copies. Ditto all
account forms and correspondence with your broker. *When in doubt—print it.*

Expenses incurred as a result of trading may be tax deductible. But please
do not take my word for it; ask your accountant. In any case, keep copies of
your expenses right down to the paper clips that keep your log charts attached to
your campaign worksheet!

Trade Statistics

Number of Winners
Number of Losers
Ratio of Winners to Losers
Biggest Profit
Biggest Loss
Average Profit
Average Loss
Profit Threshold

Trade Profile

What did I do right in the Biggest Profit? How can I do it more often?
What did I do wrong in the Biggest Loss? How can I avoid it next time?

What pairs did I do best?
What pairs did I do worst?

Market Environments
Did I do better in high Directional Movement or low Directional Movement markets?
Did I do better in high Volatility markets or low Volatility markets?
Did I do better in Thin or Thick Markets?

How did I rate vis-à-vis the Common Errors of New Traders?
How can I keep my errors from occurring in the future?

How carefully did I follow my Trade Plan?
Can I make corrections or changes to my Trade Plan?

Summary

_____
_____
_____
_____

Take Action

_____
_____
_____
_____

FIGURE 15.11　Performance Evaluation Checklist

When Things Go Wrong

The 30 Trade Campaign Worksheet is designed to provide a built-in diagnostic tool. But there is a difference between a single or a few problems and a case of just everything seeming to go against you. Errors seem to snowball—and in FOREX a snowball can become an avalanche quickly. Try to catch yourself before things get too out of control. The tendency is to trade more; the smart thing to do is to trade less—or not at all until you can sort things out rationally.

Here is a list of common errors new traders make. Peruse your 30 trades using this list. You may find one or two or three errors—all easily correctable—that will turn things around for you.

- *Trading without a stop-loss order:* Neglecting to set a stop-loss order, placed in the market and not a mental stop, is asking for financial disaster. Did you suffer a large loss because of not entering a stop-loss order on a trade?

- *Trading without a take-profit objective:* These, too, should be in the market once you have entered a trade and had it confirmed by your broker. Did a healthy profit deteriorate because you wanted more?

- *Trading too many pairs at one time:* I recommend only a single trade at any one time for the novice; three at the most. Did you have too many balls in the air, and one or more of them fell through?

- *Trading in high volatility markets:* Were the pairs traded in high volatility markets? The novice should stay with low and midrange volatility pairs.

- *Trading the news:* Did you attempt to trade the news? Or did you incur a large loss because of a news event while you had an open position? Keep your FOREX calendar handy, and try to be flat and out of the market at least until the post-news shockwave has set in for an hour or two.

- *Trading exotic and obscure pairs:* Were you tempted to trade exotic pairs? The liquidity in these markets is poor and fills on orders can be dreadful.

- *Pyramiding:* Did you add to a losing position in hopes of breaking even on a bounce? This is a common new trader error and can result in a large loss. Pyramiding a winning trade is risky business; pyramiding a losing trade spells disaster.

- *Trade plan:* Did you stick with your predetermined trade plan—or vary from it? Did you follow your trading method, attitude, and money management heuristics for each and every trade?

- *Whipsawing:* Were you whipsawed? This means being caught in a volatile sideways market and constantly reversing your position attempting to catch the trend that never comes. This happens to everyone and is part of the game. If we do not catch our entry after two tries, we move on or go to the sidelines. You should never quickly reverse a position. That implies you have suddenly reversed all of your planning and trade analysis.

- *Overconfidence:* After a couple of winning trades, it is easy to catch the *King Kong Syndrome*—the warm feeling that everything you touch will turn to gold. It will not. Each trade is a clean slate. The market does not know if you are hot or cold.

- *False expectations:* Currency trading offers no guarantees. Do not become discouraged by losses but do not expect to make a fortune overnight. "Take care of the dimes, and the dollars will take care of themselves."

- *Being prepared:* Did you come to the trading session fully prepared with your FOREX calendar and trade plan in hand? Or did you just sit down and decide to make a couple of trades? Currency trading is serious business and requires a serious attitude all of the time.

- *Clouded judgment:* Are you as objective as you can be, keeping fear and greed at bay? The leverage in FOREX is substantial, and losing focus even momentarily can be harmful.

- *Money management:* Did you follow your money management parameters closely? It is easy to stray from one's plan slightly and soon find you are far down the wrong road, unable to turn back easily.

- *Emotional upheaval:* Did you trade at a time when for whatever reasons you were emotionally agitated or worried about something? Bringing sadness or elation to the market will skew your judgment in almost every case. Never trade when under emotional duress or stress.

TIP: The market environments (ME) methodology also provides an inherent performance evaluation technique. Review the log charts of your 30 trades. Note the approximate directional movement and volatility of each. A rating between 1 and 4 is enough. Now look at the results of each trade. Are there patterns? Most traders do well in certain ME clusters, worse in others.

Did you have one or two large losses or large winners? Can you see a way to change your trading method or money management to eliminate the former, find more of the latter? Did you do well in certain pairs; poorly in certain pairs?

If these fail to achieve results, you may need to consider saying "uncle" to FOREX trading. Never trade with money you cannot afford to lose. If you wish to try again, wait until such time as you can attain a new grubstake. You can keep studying; demo accounts cost nothing.

We all bring different skills and abilities to the table of life. We cannot all excel at trading; some just seem to have the knack for it, some do not.

Summary

Even a bad plan is better than no plan at all. At least a bad plan can be improved, made into a good plan. Keep it simple. Do not commit yourself to doing things you will not do consistently. I have seen traders with such long and involved plans and heuristics I must wonder when they find the time to actually trade!

Do not be discouraged if your first 10—or even 30 trades—fail to match your expectations. The FOREX race often goes to the steady, not the swift. Stay the course. If you conclude it is necessary to make adjustments—to your trading method or money management—consider them carefully before making the changes. What are *all* the implications?

Never make revolutionary changes to your plan or any component—at least not in the course of a single campaign. The market is a process; you simply want to ease into the groove. Evolutionary changes are the ticket.

I mentioned several different types of charts in this chapter. Hopper, Watch, and Candidates are charts on your trading platform; the demarcation is by time frame. A Continuation chart is one you make at the end of each trading session to assist you in getting up to speed quickly for the next session. A Log chart is made after each completed trade to attach to your campaign worksheet. You may combine the continuation and log charts into a single chart to simplify things.

All the forms in this chapter are in the Getting Started section of www.goodmanworks.com.

There are four specific heuristics: (1) The heuristic to find a trade (FAT); (2) the money management heuristic; (3) the attitude heuristic; and (4) the diagnostic heuristc. They are interwoven in one general heuristic, which is your Plan of presession, session, and postsession duties. A workable trading plan and supplemental materials and processes is truly half the battle.

Money Management Simplified

F or the new trader, money management is the art and science of breaking even. That does not sound very exciting, does it? Not what you expected from the FOREX markets? I am reminded of the person who purchased a one-dollar lottery scratch ticket and won one dollar. "I already had a dollar; if I wanted it I would have kept it!" But the logic here is quite sound. Most new FOREX traders are shown the door quickly. You must break even on a position before it begins making money for you. The longer you are in the game the more you will learn and the better your chance for long-term success.

Always think of a trade as a two-step affair: Breaking even *and then* making a profit. Next to "Sit on your hands" this is the best advice I can offer a new trader.

Breaking Even—The Belgian Dentist

No, you do not enter a trade just to exit 30 seconds later. Breaking even is about managing your money and staying in the game. It is about thinking in terms of capital preservation and waiting for good trades to present themselves. My mentor, Charles B. Goodman, said it over and over: "You'll make most of your money sitting on your hands. If you lose your grubstake, the game is over."

Think of making a trade in two steps:

Step 1. Get to a point where you can bring your stop to breakeven.

Step 2. Sit on your hands, let the market do the talking, and see if your take-profit objective is elected before your stop-loss. Long price moves in FOREX are common. If you do not believe me just review the one-day charts. Such moves take time to develop and you must be in the market to reap the gains. You cannot make a 200-pip profit if you pounce every time 30 pips is offered to you.

Be conservative with your lot size, the number of trades you make, your trading method. Mr. Goodman preached the Belgian Dentist approach to money management. In Europe a Belgian Dentist is a term for an ultraconservative investor. "Even a Belgian Dentist would buy this stock!"

Expectations

Your trading method will tell you when you have a good trade candidate. Your money management program will tell you if you should take the trade. No trade, no matter how good it looks, should be taken if your preset money management parameters cannot be met. Money management is also vital to placing stop-loss orders to minimize risk and take-profit orders to capture gains.

Do not expect to hit 80 percent winning trades with a 10:1 ratio of stop-loss to take-profit. Do not expect to make millions trading a $500 account. Do expect to progress in fits-and-starts; three steps forward, one backward. Every trend has corrections; sometimes steep.

Trader Profiles

You need to set money management parameters and live with them and by them. To do this you must first determine your trader profile—Guerilla, Scalper, Day Trader, Position Trader.

Although traders are in actuality on a continuum from short-term traders to long-term traders, all of them fall into three or at most four distinct classes with specific money management needs.

The Guerilla

The guerilla trader seldom stays in a position for more than a few minutes. Taking 10 to 20 pips from a trade is considered a good deal. Guerillas often trade the news and need low pip-spread even to survive. When you make

20 trades a session, the pip costs add up quickly. I do not recommend that the new trader attempt the guerilla style of trading.

The Scalper

One level up from the guerilla is the scalper. A scalper may extend his or her profit horizons to perhaps 30 or even 50 pips in a volatile market. A scalper might trade a pair once or perhaps twice a session. Being a scalper is a reasonable space for the new trader. But, again, costs can be significant. The counterbalancing idea is that you cannot (usually!) lose too much money only being in the market or exposed for 30 minutes to an hour.

The Day Trader

The day trader seeks profits in the 50- to100-pip range. Such a trader must often sit between multiple sessions or seek markets with high directional movement. By seeking larger profits a day trader can afford to make quite a few losing trades, if none of them is large. The day trader only needs a few good trades a week to make the program effective. By staying longer in the market day traders are exposed to more unforeseen circumstances and market-jarring news events or announcements. I am a day trader. It is a good profile for new traders, also.

The Position Trader

Few retail FOREX traders can afford the heat of staying over not only several sessions but several days in a market. Yes, you can make a killing as the EUR/USD goes from 1.2500 to 1.3500 in two weeks. You can also lose it all in a single trade. The exposure is enormous over such periods of time. If you perceive a longer-term trend, you can catch most of it—or perhaps even more by trading the intermediate swings—as a day trader. This is certainly not a profile for the new trader.

I have met several new traders who are sure they want to capture only long-term profits and ride out the corrections along the way. Until you've seen a market move against you 200 or 300 pips and erode half or more of your profit it is impossible to say whether you will or will not be able to follow this strategy. Easy to say, difficult to do!

Now we can examine the primary money management parameters and build out each for the two suggested trader profiles. (See Table 16.1.) These factors are dependent variables. In many instances, one depends on the other. Once you have done a few dozen FOREX calculations, the relationship of these factors will be second nature to you. Practice. Do not be afraid to heat up your demo account or use an online FOREX calculator such as the ones at www.forexcalc.com or www.oanada.com. Refer to Chapter 6, "Trading Tables."

TABLE 16.1 Money Management Parameters	
Trader	Profit Objective
Guerilla	10–20 Pips
Scalper	20–50 Pips
Day Trader	50–200 Pips
Position Trader	200 + Pips

TIP: Most brokers, especially market makers, do not like short-term traders and they may initiate safeguards on their trading platforms to discourage them.

Capital Allocation—Aggregate   What is the maximum amount of your total margin capital that you should allocate at any one time? Brokers may require different margins for the same number of units of different pairs—and they change them often, as well. I recommend that the new trader never have more than one position going at a time. You will have a lot of unused margin but a lot of cushion and staying power, also.

Typically, guerillas and scalpers may be often margined at nearly 100 percent. Day traders generally should stay under 75 percent and position traders, 50 percent. The more exposure you have and the longer you expect a trade to take, the less total margin you should have in play at any given time.

TIP: The guerilla and the scalper have this over the day trader and the position trader: The longer you are in the market, statistically, the more likely you are to be in when the market does a *reality check*—a fast and violent price move, often as the result of a news release, but not always.

Capital Allocation—Per Trade   If you never want to go over 75 percent margined, even that is high. If a trade takes an average of 25 percent, that's a maximum of three concurrent positions, more than enough simultaneous action for most of us.

Leverage   Leverage is the total value of the trade divided by the margin required. Trade Value/Margin. If a trade has a value of $10,000 and it cost you $500 to trade that pair, your margin is 20:1.

Your broker will give you multiple leverage possibilities, which can be set on your trading platform. Start at the lowest, usually 20:1 and move up by the smallest increments possible as you have success.

For these next two ratios, it is vitally important that they work together and with your trader profile in harmony.

TIP: The Profit/Loss Ratio and Winners/Losers ratio are closely related in an inverse fashion.

Profit/Loss Ratio The higher your Winner/Loser Ratio, the lower can be your Profit/Loss Ratio. If you average a $500 profit for every $100 loss you can have a Winner/Loser Ratio of less than 50 percent (more losers than winners) and still do very well.

Winners/Losers Ratio Here is the flip side. The higher your Profit/Loss Ratio, the lower can be your per-trade Winner/Loser Ratio. If you hit 80 percent of your trades, your Profit/Loss ratio can be razor thin, and you will still be successful.

The goal is to have all these work together in harmony, in a realistic structure, in accordance with your trader profile. Note how these last two are inversely proportional to one another.

Parameters for Trader Profiles

We can now set suggested money management parameters for the two recommended Trader Profiles. (See Trader Profiles below.)

Scalper Profile Parameters

Pip Gain Goal	50 pips
Per-Trade Profit/Loss	2:1
Winners/Losers Ratio	1:1

Trader Profile (1):

> **Campaign Scenario:** A scalper makes 10 trades. He wins on five and loses on five. On the winners he nets 50×5 pips = 250 pips. On the losers he nets -25×5 = 125 pips. He's okay, but he'll feel cold water if either ratio goes the wrong way for any length of time. Many scalpers would give an arm to maintain a 2:1 per trade ratio.

Day Trader Profile Parameters

Pip Gain Goal	150 pips
Per-Trade Profit/Loss	3:1
Winners/Losers Ratio	1:2

Trader Profile (2):

> **Campaign Scenario:** A day trader makes 10 trades. He wins on three and loses on seven. On the winners he makes 150 pips $\times$ 3 = 450 pips. On the losers he is -50×7 = 350 pips. Life is good, but it depends on keeping the per winners-losers ratio from falling.

The success of a trader is always a delicate and precarious thing. You can see from the above how small changes in ratios could turn either one of these traders to the negative side. Linear changes in parameters can result in exponential changes in results.

When analyzing your performance, use these ratios and observe how they might be changing over time, and how much they vary per trade. It is important to understand these basic FOREX calculations before actually trading.

The Campaign Trade Method (CTM)

This concept was developed by Bruce Gould in his enormously insightful advisory letter for commodity traders published in the 1970s. Mr. Gould's work is highly recommended to all traders in all markets. For information on his offerings go to www.brucegould.com.

In conjunction with the trader profile this method provides an ad hoc method of setting fixed-dollar amounts for stops and taking profits. Once you have some experience trading, you may wish to discontinue this approach or meld it with a method of stop-loss and take-profits inherent in your trading method.

There are three stop-loss methods: (1) The System Stop where and when a trading system also generates stops internally; (2) a Mechanical Stop; and (3) the Fixed Dollar Stop. In Figure 16.1 the A is a System Stop based on GSCS,

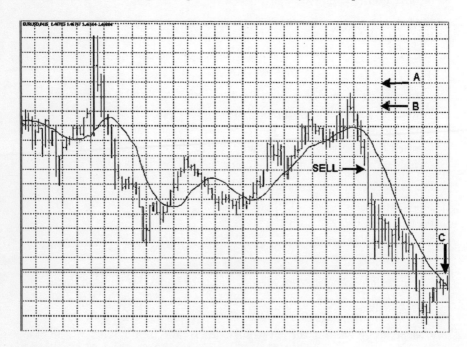

FIGURE 16.1   Stop-Loss Methods: Comparison Method
www.tradeviewfx.com and www.metaquotes.com

B is a Fixed Dollar Stop, and C is a Mechanical Stop. Here the Mechanical Stop is crossing the 13-Unit Moving Average line to the upside. The System Stop is based on the GSCS double Intersection failing. The Fixed Dollar Stop is based on a 3:1 S/L to T/P ratio.

Calculating CTM Profit and Loss

Step One. What is your trading capital or grubstake? If you are in the midsection of the bell curve, it is probably between $1,000 and $10,000. You can trade with less (in a mini- or micro-account), or you can trade with more. We are here considering not your micro- or mini-account, which should be funded with no more than $500, but your full-fledged trading account.

Let us assume your stake is $3,000. Remember, this is money you can afford to lose. Your spouse may yell at you if you lose it but at least the kids will not go hungry.

Step Two. Allocate your money into three imaginary campaign parcels. You will have three campaigns to get long-term traction in the markets. If you lose campaign #1 you can regroup and go on to campaign #2, and so forth. This gives your trading some basic structure, something almost no new traders have or even think about.

Step Three. Allocate each of your $1,000 pots into 10 trades, risking a set $100 per trade. (See Table 16.2.)

Your stop-loss is mechanically calculated in advance as a pip value equal to $100.

Step Four. Refer to the profile parameters above, and work backward. If you are a scalper and seek 3:1 profit to loss ratio, you want to make $300.

Step Five. You only now need to know how many units to buy or sell. Refer to your pip gain in the same profile. The scalper wants to make 30 pips per trade, on average. All you must do now is calculate how many units make $300 on 320 pips, and your trade money management parameters are ready to go.

Do not reset or adjust your campaign schedule until you have made 30 trades and completed all three campaigns.

TABLE 16.2	Allocating Your Account Grubstake		
	Trading Capital Day Trader		
	$3,000		
Campaign	#1	#2	#3
Trades	10	10	10
Profit Objective	$300	$300	$300
Stop-Loss	$100	$100	$100

Before you execute a trade, review these five steps. Together they constitute your money management heuristic.

The CTM is also an excellent vehicle for keeping track of your trading and
offering a method for critical review of your progress. At the end of each 10
trades review your performance objectively. What did you do right? What did
you do wrong? Which markets were successful—and which were not? How did
the winning trades differ from the losing trades? What can you do to eliminate
the worst losing trade on the next 10 trades?

Protecting Profits

No trader likes to see a tidy profit turn back into a break-even trade. What to do?

The most common technique is called a *trailing stop*. This means that in
some manner you raise (or lower) your stop-loss as the trade moves in your
favor. You may use a simple pip-dollar trailing stop. For each 25 pips (or 50 pips
or 100 pips depending on your trade profile) raise your stop a like amount or
close to it. This is mechanical, easy to execute, and may work some of the
time—not that anything in FOREX works all of the time!

I prefer to modify this by waiting for corrective moves back against my
trade. When the trend resumes and the correction appears over, then I will trail
a stop. More on this also in Chapter 18, "Improving Your Trading Skills."

You can also break your lot size into two equal parts. If you traded a
20,000 lot, work it as two 10,000 lots. Liquidate one 10,000 lot as you have
a fair profit, ride the other 10,000 lot with a trailing stop. You can also enter a
trade in two lots in similar fashion. Remember that your broker will always close
lots as First In First Out (FIFO).

There is a delicate balance between taking fair profits and letting profits
ride. It is more art and experience than science and method. The balance
depends to some extent on your trading style, trader profile, and profit threshold (see Chapter 6, "Trading Tables"). I tend to lean on the side of letting profits ride. My experience through the years is that losses cannot be avoided. Even
small ones add up—and I find that the big profits are really the money that
drops to the bottom line at the end of the year.

Stop-Loss Orders—Physical or Mental?

As indicated earlier you can either set stops using my campaign method or you
can set them in accordance with your trading method. Some trading methods
generate stop-loss prices, some do not. In the later instance I continue to advise
that you pass a trade if the stop-loss your trading method requires is excessive. If

you are trading as a scalper, do not take a trade requiring a 75-pip stop-loss. When in doubt, stay out; do not let your trading method overrule common sense.

TIP: Once entered, do not pull your stop-loss order or move it against the direction of your trade. Live with it, good, bad, or ugly. Manipulating stop-losses is for the expert, and even for experts, it is a dicey business. A trade is a process and tinkering with the process once it is in motion is a *bad* idea. As a new trader be sure that your stop order is in the market at all times. Enter it as a pure stop order so that if the price is hit, the stop is executed. A bad fill in a fast market is better than no fill at all.

If you scale into a position, perhaps entering an order for one-half your selected lot size and the second one-half later only add the second lot if the position is profitable. NEVER add to a losing position under any circumstances.

There is an ongoing discussion among traders, teachers, and researchers as to whether stops should be mental or actually placed in the market. For the new trader I believe the answer is slam-dunk territory for most traders. Put them in the market. Whatever you do—do not walk away leaving a position open, unattended, without a stop in the market. New traders have so much sensory and emotional data hitting them from all sides that adding the duty of exiting a trade per one's strategy on the fly is just asking too much.

TIP: Do not anthropomorphize about the market if your stop gets hit. Truly, the market cares not whether you win or lose. On the other hand if comparison to other broker platforms shows your stops are being regularly harvested—it may be time to switch brokers. But make sure you have multiple evidence before doing so; switching brokers can be disconcerting in and of itself. Remember that data feeds do vary because there is no central clearinghouse or exchange in FOREX and data feeds (bids and asks) come from a wide range of sources, no two brokers having the same ones. If the difference between a bar chart high between two platforms is only four or five pips it is probably not harvesting. Ten pips, maybe. More, almost certainly.

Selecting Currency Pairs to Trade

I recommend that the novice trader begin by trading the major USD and EUR currency pairs only. These pairs usually entail a lower bid-ask pip spread, which increases your profit potential while reducing your transaction costs. Although it may not matter for the small trader, they are also the most liquid of all currency pairs. If you venture forth past the majors, stay with combinations of the Euro (EUR), British Pound (GBP), Japanese Yen (JPY), Australian Dollar (AUD), and Canadian Dollar (CAD).

My inclination is to avoid the EUR/USD itself because it is frequently impacted by news.

Irrespective of currency pair, attempt to trade only markets with modest volatility and high directional movement. Scalpers and guerilla traders prefer high volatility pairs; day traders and position traders prefer markets with high directional movement.

Over long periods of time both directional movement and volatility for any given pair changes, but typically the change is gradual. After you trade a pair for a reasonable period of time, you see that each has its own unique personality. I can often identify an unlabeled pair simply by doing a market environment analysis. See Chapter 18, "Improving Your Trading Skills."

Summary

Know your FOREX calculations, especially those that impact money management decisions. Practice with them on a demo account as much and as often as you can. Play "What If" scenarios to sharpen your understanding of the relationships between not only the calculations but the basic money management ideas presented here. Once you are comfortable, factor in your trader profile.

I recommend the campaign method of money management for new traders. You can meld in parameters derived from your trading method as it develops, if you wish. But the basic campaign parameters should always trump anything else, in my humble opinion. If your trading method money management parameters are, too often, too far away from your campaign parameters, it is probably the trading method parameters that need changing. Use the 30 Trade Campaign Worksheet from Chapter 15, "The Plan! The Plan!"

The profit/loss ratio and winners/losers ratio must be in harmony and in accordance with your trader profile.

TIP: A small change in only one or two money management factors can make a big difference in overall trader performance. Keep this in mind especially when evaluating trade performance.

Add a money management heuristic to your trading method and attitude heuristics. Go through all of them before executing a trade. It will take time at first, but after 20 or 30 trades it will require but a few seconds. The bottom line: Are your Risk-Reward (S/L and T/P) and Winners-Losers ratios in line with your trading profile?

Psychology of Trading

Ten years ago you would find, if you looked, perhaps one or two books written about the psychology of trading. Today there are nearly a dozen on the market. I think this is partly a function of the fact that almost everything that can be said about trading methods has been said. I say "almost" because I am constantly peppering my editor with proposals for more books!

There is perhaps another reason. Traders are finally coming to the realization that a trading method—no matter how good—does not in itself lead to consistent success in the market.

When you were a teenager, your mother or father probably accused you at one time or another of having an attitude.

Traders have an attitude also, although probably not of the kind your parents meant. While trading methods are as varied and different as snowflakes, successful traders seem to share a set of attitude traits and money management techniques. In this chapter and Chapter 16, "Money Management Simplified," I delineate and discuss these common traits and techniques.

Much has been written about the power of positive thinking from Napoleon Hill's classic *Think and Grow Rich*, to psycho-cybernetics, to the "Seth Material" and Abraham. My own belief is that our consciousness is an active agent in the unfolding universe, not the passive onlooker of most of Western philosophy. Imagine and visualize success in some concrete form or image. You may find the universe coming to you.

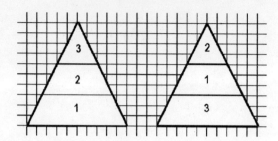

FIGURE 17.1   The Trading Pyramid

The Trading Pyramid

As I have mentioned previously, there are three components to a trading program: trading method, money management, and psychology or attitude. The vast majority of traders spend almost all of their efforts affecting a trading method. Ninety percent of market books are still trading method tomes. In fact, most successful traders will tell you, of the three components, the trading method is the least important.

You are well advised to allocate significant thought and effort to attitude and money management. (See Figure 17.1.) How much you order their relative importance determines your trading pyramid. The diagram on the left is the correct pyramid—or at least some similar shape. The diagram on the right is the incorrect pyramid—giving too much emphasis to the trading method and too little to money management and attitude.

"1" is Money Mangement, "2" is Psychology, "3" is Trading Method.

Most traders place their trading method at the base as the most important and substantial. Money management is in the middle and psychology of trading gets little attention at the top. To my way of thinking money management must be the base, then psychology, and a trading method as a finishing touch. An argument could certainly be made that psychology of trading should be the base. Top traders share more attitude characteristics than anything else.

Fear and Greed, Greed and Fear

Fear and greed are the base emotions that drive every market. They are instinctive to humans and unless you use an automated computer program to trade, your goal can only be to control them and not to eliminate them.

Since economic booms, busts, and bubbles keep recurring, year after year, century after century, it is clear evolution is not going to transfer the skills learned in one generation to another and, as Santayana warned, we seemed doomed to repeat the past. People have short memories, and fear and greed keep returning; a hedge fund bubble was followed by the dot.com bubble, in turn followed by the real estate bubble in less than a decade. A second hedge fund bubble may not be far away.

We tend to get greedy when we are making money and overstay our welcome; we tend to become fearful when we are losing and again overstay our welcome. These emotions cause us to mentally freeze and delay making critical decisions that would be in our own best, rational interest. Making a decision implies change and there is nothing more difficult for a human being.

One successful trade can cause overconfidence and lead to what I call the King Kong Syndrome—the warm, good-all-over feeling that we can do no wrong. A large losing trade can cause enormous self-doubt, leading us to make revolutionary changes in our trading program when, in fact, a little time away from the market and a few evolutionary adjustments would put us back on track.

The late Pete Rednor, office manager at Peavey and Company where I apprenticed as a commodity trader in the early 1970s, would wait for a trader to get the King Kong Syndrome. When the trader next placed an order, Pete would go to a telephone in the back office and place the identical order—but in reverse. He usually won, and when the trader lost it all and stopped trading, Pete lamented the loss of a trading system.

The key is containing the emotions of fear and greed within a relatively slight area. To do that, you must in turn be able to anticipate the onset of fear or greed, and find methods for controlling them before they impact trading decisions. Biofeedback works for some people; mediation for others. Yoga, vigorous exercise, sedentary hobbies, and reading are other psychological health remedies.

Never be afraid of the markets but always respect them. Never be hesitant to simply walk away for a few hours or a few days. The markets will not go away; they are happy to wait for you to return. Never trade when you are emotionally distraught. I had trouble dealing with missing a good trade opportunity for many years. Eventually I had the experience to see that good trades are always going to be available.

It is common for new FOREX traders to be literally mesmerized by the movement of the prices as seen on charts. The short-term charts—1-minute, 5-minute, and 15-minute—move quickly up and down and carry your emotions right along with them.

Profiling Performance

Good records of your trading will help you build profiles you can review from time to time. Often a marked change in profiles will be a leading indicator of a bout of fear or greed. Monitor your trading results on a weekly basis. Use the biofeedback form of Chapter 15, "The Plan! The Plan!" and again discussed in Chapter 16, "Money Management Simplified."

Look not only for how much money you are making—you cannot win them all—but look also to see the patterns in trade series that went well for you. Profit/Loss ratios, the currency pairs that worked the best for you, the types of markets—trading or trending—that worked well. How often did you move a stop or profit objective? Constantly jiggling stops-loss, take-profits, and your trading process are an early warning sign.

"Know Thyself," the ages-old Socratic saying, is a trader's watchword. Only you know which factors cause emotional unbalance, and which do not. As I used to tell my schoolaphobic son, "Lay low, hang loose." I know one trader who uses Camtasia from www.techsmith.com. He webcams his entire sessions and reviews them for his facial expressions and body language.

Do not try to be totally objective—it is an unattainable goal for a human and not even a worthy goal. There are good instincts hiding in the subjective and you do not want to bury them in your subconscious.

The Attitude Heuristic

In Chapter 13, "The FOREX Marketplace," I suggest a heuristic for your trading method. I like to keep a mental chart of my emotions; an attitude heuristic. Imagine a graph going from 0 in the middle to −1 at the bottom and +10 at the top (see Figure 17.2). Greed is the top half; fear, the bottom half. Sure, it is exciting to make a trade. It is even more satisfying to close out a winner. And it

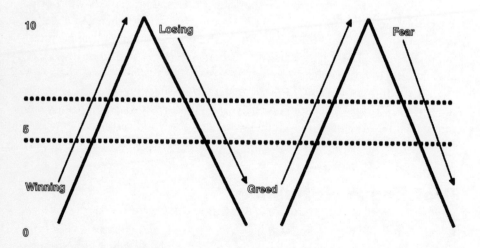

FIGURE 17.2   Charting Fear and Greed

is a disappointment to see a trade go bad. Do not expect your emotions to stay between 4 and 6; you are human. They will not. At least after tracking yourself for a few weeks you will know when you are in the danger zones, perhaps above 8 or below 2 or more importantly when you are headed toward a danger zone. Review these numbers vis-à-vis your performance. You will be surprised how much you learn and the ways you can benefit. If you can eliminate 1 out of 3 losing trades you will almost certainly be successful in the long run. The line between winning and losing can be razor thin.

TIP: Use the Biofeedback Form in Chapter 15, "The Plan! The Plan!" to chart your fear and greed.

Characteristics of Successful Traders

No one has all these characteristics all of the time. But having known literally hundreds of traders, I can assure you that most of them share most of these characteristics—most of the time.

- Successful traders tend to have control over their emotions—they never get too elated over a win or too despondent over a loss.
- Successful traders do not think of prices as "too high" or "too low." Prices are numbers; zeros are zeros whether there are three of them or seven of them. If the size of the trade makes you nervous, it is too large; scale down.
- Successful traders do not get emotionally attached to a market or a trade. They do not anthropomorphize about the markets: "They're going after stops now," or "The market is nervous," or "The market must know something I don't." Just thinking in such terms is an error. The market is not out to get you.
- Successful traders do not panic. They make evolutionary changes to their trading program, not revolutionary changes.
- Successful traders do not flinch at making a decision, pulling the trigger once everything has lined up for a trade.
- Successful traders treat trading as a business, not a hobby or game—even if it is a hobby.
- Successful traders stay physically fit.
- Successful traders do not trade when they are emotionally stressed or under duress.
- Successful traders hang up the DO NOT DISTURB sign when they are trading.

- Successful traders come prepared for all eventualities on any given trading session. They come to work with a plan that includes many contingencies and not just for what they hope will happen. In your trading program you should have predetermined responses to the following "What happens if . . ." situations: Prices open sharply higher or lower; the market is quiet; the market is volatile; the market makes new highs; the market makes new lows; the market opens higher and reverses; the market opens lower and reverses.

- Successful traders trade only with money they can afford to lose. Trading FOREX is speculation, not investment. It can be exciting, exhilarating—and addictive. Being emotionally involved with the money at risk is a formula for losing if ever there was one.

- Successful traders spend as much time on improving their attitude and money management as they do their trading method.

- Successful traders keep a low profile and do not discuss their trading with others.

- Successful traders let the market do its thing and try to take advantage. Unsuccessful traders attempt to impose their will on the markets.

- Successful traders know the rare occasion when it is wise to let their instincts override a decision.

- Successful traders consistently review their trades.

TIP: After you have completed your time on a demo account and are preparing to trade live, review this list as a self-evaluation test.

Summary

FOREX trading will greatly magnify any emotional or psychological hang-ups or concerns you bring to each trading session. Trading when not in top form is asking for financial injury in the same way driving drunk is asking for physical injury. Leverage is to FOREX what speed is to driving.

The line between winning and losing can be thin. Small changes can directly affect your bottom line—in a big way.

Dismiss the importance of attitude at your own peril. More than any other factor, it is what separates the winners from the losers in FOREX and other trading arenas.

18

Improving Your Trading Skills

ere I present a series of tactical and strategic trading ideas culled from years of trading.

Screenwriter Lew Hunter claims it is the small touches that make a movie special. It is the same for traders. The small touches you add to your trading program can make it stand out from the crowd—and I know the crowd usually loses. Small touches can also add a personal flavor to your trading, giving it a unique style. It may astound you how a small jiggle can change bottom-line performance in a big way—for better or for worse. Think about your trading program with some perspective; consider the totality of it all, but keep an eye on the details, too. Is it coherent, efficient? Do the various parts work together well, perhaps offer a little the-whole-is-greater-than-the-sum-of-its-parts synergy? Are you pleased and proud of it? Does it have *style*?

I have divided these touches into the more specific techniques and the more general skills.

Techniques

I recommend only implementing these techniques after you have your basic Trading Plan in place. Then, try each one in sequence—one at a time—to see if any of them add to the synergy of your approach.

Trending and Trading Markets

Markets have traditionally been classified as trading markets or trending markets, meaning that they move predominantly sideways or predominantly up or down. For an excellent modern look at this conventional approach I recommend Ed Ponsi's *FOREX Patterns and Possibilities: Strategies for Trending and Range-Bound Markets* (John Wiley & Sons, 2007).

This classification is useful, but it is limited and general. Markets are much more than simply trending or trading. Further, trending and trading are relative. A five-minute chart of the EUR/USD may be trading while an hourly chart may be trending. (See Figure 18.1.)

Market Environments (ME)

ME is a method for more precisely quantifying the classical idea of trading versus trending markets. It is enormously useful as a complement to your trading method, money management, back-testing, and performance analysis. It can also be used in what is called *quant* in the industry—risk, portfolio, and money manager analysis.

ME also teases out indicator-like information directly off charts without the need for calculation. Bar charts work perfectly. Market Environments was developed by Charles B. Goodman and I have done further development and research.

There are two primary MEs, two secondary MEs, and a single tertiary ME. Just using the two primaries can add meaningfully to your trading arsenal.

Directional Movement (DM) and Volatility (V)

Directional movement is the net price change from price-time point A to price-time point B. In Figure 18.2, visualize a straight line from the low price at the beginning of the first bar of each chart to the high price of the end of the last bar of each chart. The former has high directional movement, the latter has low directional movement. This is the net price change.

There are precise methods for measuring DM, but the core concept is simplicity and avoiding the calculations necessary with indicators.

$$\text{Directional Movement} = P(\text{rice})2 - P(\text{rice})1$$

With A at 0-0 divide the 90 degrees of the chart into five sections. Scale the 90 degrees to equal 100 percent and make each segment 20 percent. Label them 1 through 5.

Volatility is the gross price movement from A to B, given a specified minimum price fluctuation value. You may obtain a ratio with V/DM. Look at a

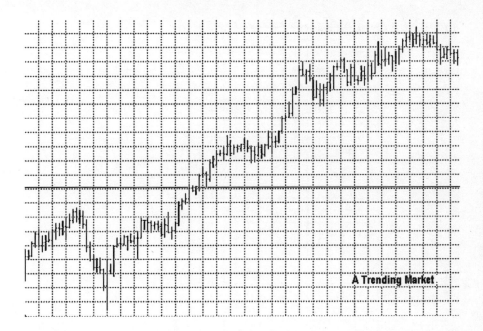

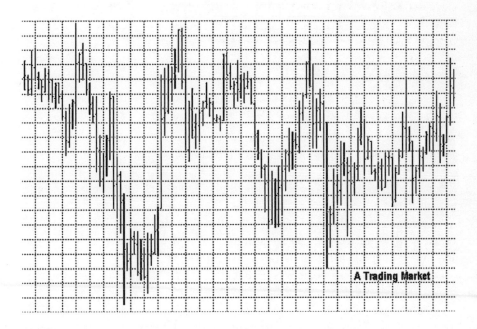

FIGURE 18.1   Trending and Trading Markets

Source: TradeviewForex, www.tradeviewforex.com, and MetaTrader, www.metaquotes.net

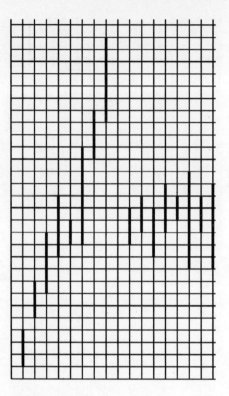

FIGURE 18.2   ME—Directional Movement (DM)

sampling of 50 or 100 charts to get an idea of volatility ranges, then divide the samples into five equal segments as with DM.

In the conventional classification volatility would be similar to trading, although a market may possess both high directional movement and high volatility over a specified time period. (See Figure 18.3.)

You can plot DM and V either on a 10 × 10 matrix (see Chapter 13, "The FOREX Marketplace") or use a continuum from 1 to 10 where 1 is lowest V and lowest DM and 10 is highest V and highest DM.

Every market can be defined as one of these 100 MEs or on a continuum in ordered pairs of (DM, V). (See Figure 18.4.)

Compare this to the ME matrix in Chapter 13, "The FOREX Marketplace." They are two different methods for visualizing the same information.

An ME cluster is a contiguous set of ME pairs, either on a continuum or a matrix.

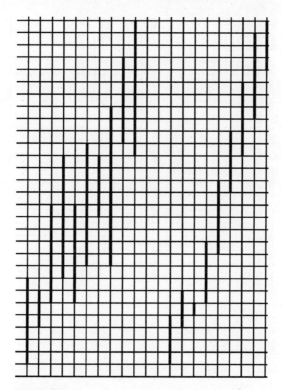

FIGURE 18.3   ME—Volatility

Price and Time Rhythm (PR and TR)

The secondary MEs are Rhythm—Price Rhythm and Time Rhythm—and Thickness.

The markets often have regular price and time rhythm. But you cannot see them if you are not looking for them and do some basic counting.

For time rhythm, measure the length of time (number of time units along the horizontal scale of a bar chart). Measure bottoms to bottoms and tops to tops; make an average of each. The closer the average is to each of the specific instances, the more regular the time rhythm.

For price rhythm do the same measurements of uptrends and downtrends. Keep a running record of both values and again, average them. (See Figure 18.5 and Figure 18.6.)

$$(1, 1), (1, 2), (1, 3), (1, 4), (1, 5) \ldots (10, 6), (10, 7), (10, 8), (10, 9), (10, 10)$$

FIGURE 18.4   ME—A Continuum of DM/V

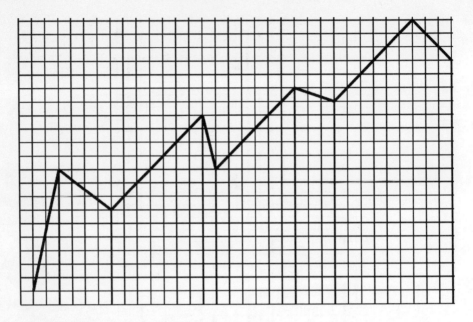

FIGURE 18.5   ME—Price Rhythm

While all four of these elements can and have been precisely defined mathematically, simply eyeballing a chart for rough estimates is often satisfactory. You will be surprised how many areas on the chart you will find where price rhythm and time rhythm intersect. These are strong support and resistance areas.

A market has regular rhythm if in averaging the peaks and valleys, the average you derive is not far from any of the specific values.

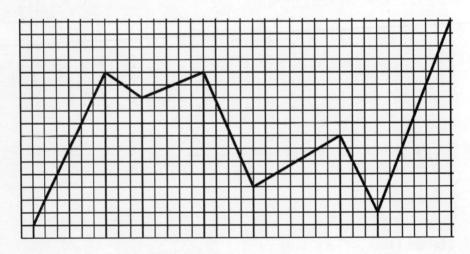

FIGURE 18.6   ME—Time Rhythm

For example, if you count price peaks and valleys as: 6, 3, 7, 4, 8, 4, 6, 3, 7, 5, 6, 2, and average the peaks (6, 7, 8, 6, 7, 6) and valleys (3, 4, 5, 3, 5, 2) you can see that this market has excellent price rhythm. But you cannot see it unless you look! Do you want to buy on a peak or on a valley?

TIP: Many indicators actually tease out various ME elements. Sometimes it is easier and just as efficient to find that information by eyeballing a chart.

Thickness (T)

Thickness is loosely defined as how much the range from high-to-low of a bar overlaps the previous bar. The more overlap, the thicker the pair or market. Thick markets by definition also possess low volatility and low directional movement. It is enough to define two ranges of thickness—thick (1) and thin (0). (See Figure 18.7.)

I have found that my trading program works exceptionally well in thick markets. Therefore I seek out such markets to watch on a regular basis. The astute observer will have noticed thickness is related closely to directional movement and volatility.

TIP: Thickness can be illusory. If the ratio between the two currencies of a pair is close to 1.00, they will be thick by necessity—but not necessarily thick in the ME sense.

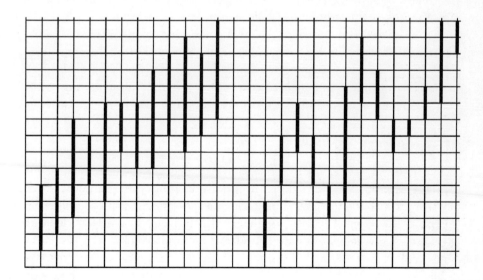

FIGURE 18.7   ME—Thickness

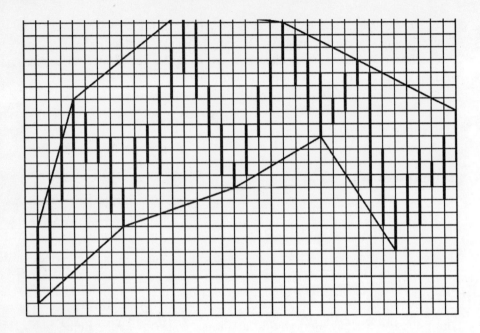

FIGURE 18.8   ME—Shape

Shape (S)

To determine shape, draw a line along the significant tops of the market. You can use the same peaks you used for price rhythm. Draw a line along the significant bottoms of the market; you can use the valleys you used for price rhythm, also. Shape is useful with the study of rhythm. (See Figure 18.8.)

The shape forms a rough channel—Mr. Goodman called it a sema-phore—in which prices have moved. Average the widths of the channel from top-bottoms to seek predictable regularities.

TIP: You might not want to enter a buy side order near the top of the channel average or enter a sell side order near the bottom of the channel average.

ME Applications

Before initiating a trade, seek to define, even if roughly, directional movement and volatility. What do you see? Do they fit in with the conclusion you reached from the analysis of your other tools? If not, why not? Is it important? In your Plan this analysis could be either near the beginning of your heuristic—to spot pairs with good general conditions—or near the end, as a confirming tool.

Look at the time rhythm and price rhythm. Is the timing of both rhythms good for a trade? If either the time rhythm average or price rhythm average is off substantially, it may be good to take a bit longer look before pulling the trigger. If both are off, perhaps consider passing the trade. If it is still on when the rhythms come into line, then you may have a winner. Is the market thick or thin?

A Market Environment Profile is the complete set of MEs for a given chart. A brief notation might look like this:

$$DM = 2.2, V = 3.1, PR = 4.4, TR = 4.0, TK = 1$$

Specific currency pairs will sometimes exhibit stable market environment profiles over relatively long periods of time. For each trade you make, keep a short notational record of the directional movement and volatility for that market. Once a month, compare your winning trades with your losing trades. Almost all traders find they do better in some primary MEs than in others.

To dig deeper, keep ME profiles for all ME elements on your trades, and look for winning ME clusters and losing ME clusters.

Mutual and hedge funds, which use multiple managers, may use this last idea to allocate funds to specific managers for specific anticipated long-term MEs; managers receiving more money to trade in markets in which they excel, less in markets in which they do poorly. An ME cluster is a contiguous grouping of ME pairs in an ME matrix. Trading systems that work well over historical data only to almost immediately flop in real time almost always had a high majority of their big winners in one or two small ME clusters.

Market environments may also be used to back-test systems and methods using historical data. Rather than looking for the usual suspects of Sharpe Ratio and so forth, look for methods that did well in a wide range of market profiles.

TIP: A short, well-constructed ME data set will be a better test than years of data concentrated in a few clusters or even a real-time test.

The Three Chart System

This is a well-known, popular, and effective tool. Each trader profile should use three FOREX charts with different time unit scales for each currency pair they trade. The middle chart is the Watch analysis chart; use it to actually find trade candidates. The largest unit chart is the Trend chart, used for keeping track of the primary trend. It provides perspective so the trader does not lose the forest for the trees spending so much time on short-term charts. The smallest scale chart is the Timing chart, used to make entries and find stop-loss and take-profit levels with precision (see Table 18.1, Trader Profile Charts on page 238).

I would not trade without the Three Chart System.

The Dagger Entry Principle

This is embarrassing in its simplicity but it is effective. More often than not, simpler is better.

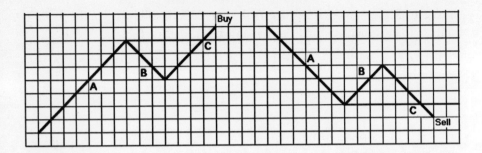

FIGURE 18.9   The Dagger Entry Principle

The principle first appeared in an article, "Conservation with a Gnome," by Michael D. Archer and R. David Van Treuren in *Denver* magazine (July 1977).

It involves three easy steps:

1. Identify the major trend within the context of your trading profile.

2. Wait for a significant correction, a secondary trend in the opposite direction of the major trend. A significant correction is typically a minimum of 25 percent.

3. Enter your trade as soon as prices resume moving in the direction of the major trend.

The Dagger presupposes that you have already identified a trade candidate from your trading program work and are watching for an entry point. (See Figure 18.9.)

Although this sounds suspiciously like the Ross Hook, it was developed by Charles B. Goodman in the 1950s, long before the good Mr. Ross's trading days. The logic of the Dagger: you want to go with the major trend, but only after a price correction—so that you will not get quickly caught in one; and you want to go with the short-term momentum and not step in front of a charging short-term bull or bear.

TIP: You can also use a variety of the Dagger to place trailing stops: Wait for the market to make a corrective move against your position—and hopefully not stop you out; wait for the market to make a new high (or low) in the direction of your trade; raise your stop to the low (on a down move) or to the high (on an up move) of the corrective swing. Do this in turn as the market makes such in-trend Daggers. It will often work three, four, or five times before a reality check takes you out of the market—but by then you should have a handsome profit.

Futures trader and writer Joe Ross has indeed formulated a variation of this and made a near science out of it. His book, *The Ross Hook*, is highly recommended.

Range Finder

This useful indicator was independently discovered by multiple commodity futures traders, but Arne Gronfelt generally gets the credit for it. I find it also useful with FX charts.

The formula enables the trader to forecast the next bar High/Low. Charts are refractive, so you can use it on anything from 1-Minute to 1-Week. To find the next bar Low, you add today's High + Low + Close, then divide the sum by 3, then multiply the total by 2, and from that figure you subtract today's High. The result is often a close approximation of the next bar's Low price. To find the next bar High, use the same initial equation but rather than the High subtract the current bar. The result is often a close approximation of the next bar's High.

$$\text{Next LOW} = (H + L + C/3) \times 2 - H$$
$$\text{Next HIGH} = (H + L + C/3) \times 2 - L$$

TIP: Use the Range Finder on all three of your trader profile charts to get a forecast at different price levels. Watch especially for where they overlap.

Correlation and Transitivity

Currency pairs are co-relational. The price of each side of the pair depends on the price of the other side of the pair. Correlation refers to how similarly (or dissimilarly) two different pairs move over a period of time.

Correlation is typically measured between 1.00 and 0.00. At 1.00 two pairs are perfectly correlated—every time one moves up the other moves up. At 0.00 the two pairs are perfectly non-correlated—every time one moves up the other moves down.

It is easy to see that certain pairs are naturally correlated, for example, the EUR/CHF and GBP/CHF. Correlations typically trade in a fairly narrow and well-defined price band, but can change more dramatically over a period of time.

Correlation can be used to analyze markets and make trading decisions. Some traders watch for trading opportunities as the band between two pairs narrows then expands. But the most common use is portfolio and risk allocation. A trader would typically not want to have three highly correlated pairs on as trades at the same time. If one of them goes bad, they will all go bad.

A real-time correlation table is available on the Oanda web site at http://fxtradeinfocenter.oanda.com/charts_data/fxcorrelations.shtml.

Transitivity is similar to correlation and the two concepts overlap. Suppose considering shorting the Japanese Yen (JPY) and are watching both the and CHF/JPY. The transitivity pair, the EUR/CHF, may give you ht into which will be the weaker of the two JPY pairs.

TABLE 18.1 Trader Profile Charts			
Guerilla	1-minute	5-minute	30-minute
Scalper	5-minute	30-minute	1-hour
Day Trader	30-minute	1-hour	4-hour
Position Trader	1-hour	12-hour	1-day

Skills

Skills are more judgmental than techniques, which can be precisely quantified. Skill take more practice, time, and experience to learn and apply effectively.

Sitting on Your Hands

Traders do not particularly enjoy sitting on their hands. It is akin to going to a casino and not throwing a few dollars into a slot machine. The underlying concept is to be patient and wait for trades that really line up for your personal trading program—trading method, attitude, and money management. FOREX provides more than 20 highly liquid currency pairs and multiple time frames. The trader is never long without an opportunity. Take your time, pick and choose, then seize the moment! "Wait," as Mr. Goodman would say, "for the sitting ducks." I would much rather miss a good trade and not win than roll snake-eyes and lose money unnecessarily.

Be an active watcher; you are sitting on your hands, not covering your eyes. Ask questions, form hypotheses, see how the market reacts, draw conclusions, take notes. You can learn from your in-progress trades without doing anything to alter them. If you feel you are getting too attached to the trade, move on—look at other charts for new opportunities.

Once you have entered a trade, you have for the moment done everything you can do. Now it is time to sit on your hands. Do not watch in-progress trades too carefully; the charts will incite you to make changes or just to do something. Take a look at a 1-Day chart. As you can see major trends are common, *but they take time to develop.* If you close a trade every time you have a few pips profit you will never make enough to cover your losing trades.

Time Filters

The author has done enormous statistical work on time filters. Some of these studies were published in the now out-of-print and privately published the "Currency Trader's Companion" series. Below is a brief overview of the subject.

These are not mission-critical ideas but can help you improve your trading skills along the way. Once again—small changes can make meaningful improvements to the bottom line.

Market Opening

Officially the FOREX market opens at 5:30 P.M. Eastern, though different brokers react differently in different time zones. Keep in mind that over the weekend all currency pairs carry an extra premium in transaction cost. A normal 3-pip bid-ask spread during normal trading hours may increase or balloon to a 10-pip or even 20-pip spread on weekends.

Once the weekend transaction costs return to normal, many pairs exhibit high volatility due to economic influences that occurred over the weekend. The effects of these influences have been pent up while traders have been away. Analyzing a set of a number of currency pairs enhances profit opportunities. Frequently a trend emerges in one direction or the other and continues until the weekend influences have been absorbed by the markets. This may entail tracking several more pairs during the early hours of Monday morning than one would normally follow. When opportunity knocks . . .

Market Closing

Many corporations like to clear out last-minute orders on Friday afternoon to avoid possible rollover charges and reduce the risk of holding substantial positions over a weekend. Three-day weekends exacerbate this phenomenon. This equates to increased volatility right before the market closes at 4:20 P.M. on Friday afternoon.

If you trade during the peak period of volatility, always be certain to liquidate your trades before the bid-ask spread jumps to its increased weekend range.

Time of Day

For the most part, the higher volatility periods revolve around banking hours in New York City. This overlaps only slightly with banking hours in London and Frankfurt. Another factor is the time zone in which your broker is located. Taking these three factors into consideration plus your own time zone, you should be able to determine periods of high volatility that increase risk and reward. See Appendix D for details on time zones and banking hours.

Day of Week

The days on which the market opens and closes have already been discussed. Other days of the week may also have special significance. For instance, new interest rates are normally published on Thursday, which causes immediate changes in USD pairs.

Keep your FOREX calendar computer-side and be aware of pending news for the currencies you trade.

Trading the News

Don't do it!

There are many news traders—those who wait for a news event and try to catch the reaction it invariably entails. I strongly recommend against trading the news for new FOREX participants. Volatility goes into overdrive and although profits can be large and fast, so can losses. Such opportunities do not fit my sitting duck or Belgian Dentist advice for new traders.

The NFA Compliance Rule 2-43 anti-hedging provision has impacted the way many news traders operate.

I have observed a phenomenon I call *shockwave*. In many instances the initial reaction to news or an announcement will be a short but sharp price move in one direction. Then occurs the shockwave: a price movement in the opposite direction of the initial reaction, quite often significantly longer in both time and price duration.

All traders should have a daily calendar of pending, scheduled announcements for the currencies they trade. My advice is not to trade these announcements. In fact, I prefer to be on the sidelines just before the announcement and until the shockwave has run its course.

Watch the market's reaction to the news. Is the reaction as anticipated, or different? Traders sometimes refer to this as "expectation." Expectation, if it is different from reality, can tell you a lot about the technical underpinnings of the market at that particular time. Did the market shrug its shoulders to bullish news? Perhaps its underpinnings are weaker than suspected.

TIP: Do not be quick to judge the news reaction; the shockwave may last several hours.

If you must trade the news, do use an execution tool such as www.forexnewsweapon.com. An invaluable reference is James Bickford's *Forex Shockwave Analysis* (McGraw-Hill, 2007). Mr. Bickford took the first step toward quantifying the chart patterns that form after a news announcement.

Going Against the Crowd

There are now quantified daily studies of Contrary Opinion in the currency markets. The most convenient is Jay Meisler's www.global-view.com weekly poll of professional traders. But it is not difficult to tell from the news where the public (read "retail traders") will be found and on which side of the market they will be trading.

The author's www.goodmanworks.com will soon offer a quantified Contrary Opinion tool for FOREX traders.

The logic of Contrary Opinion is flawless; gathering the information is the difficult part. Once everyone is bullish or bearish, everyone who wants to be on that side will already be in the market. Where will the orders come from to take the new positions required to continue to drive that trend? Remember, once buyers buy or sellers sell they have functionally no impact on the market until they offset their position.

Most FOREX traders lose money and are shown the door quickly. New traders tend to use the same trading techniques. This may tell you something. Of course, new traders lose predominantly because their attitude and money management techniques are suspect.

I was once bounced from an expert's forum because of my unconventional ideas about trading methods. In a discussion on support and resistance, I proffered the heretical idea that since so many traders used the same methods to calculate support and resistance, they could not possibly be of value. I want to find support and resistance areas that other traders ignore. That is where the money is, in my humble and contrary opinion.

This does not mean that conventional methods are taboo. It does mean to be aware that many others are using them and have read the same books you have. Conventional chart patterns have been around so long that I find it difficult to believe they can still be the basis of a successful trading program. Those who do use them seem to have found a twist that sets them apart from the crowd.

This also is about expectation. If too many traders expect an indicator or chart pattern to work, it will not; it cannot. Markets anticipate events. If everyone anticipates prices going to a certain price to form a head-and-shoulders chart formation, prices will never get there. Traders will anticipate that price and begin buying and selling on that expectation well before prices reach that level.

Markets also discount information. This means that information finds its way into prices before the event. "Buy on the rumor, sell on the news." Stock traders anticipate endless growth from a company. How often have you seen a quarterly report with a large increase in earnings, but the stock price drops? The market anticipated the report, and there is no one left to buy. Worse, while the earnings were good, the rate of earnings was lower than expected.

A weekly hour on the FOREX forums over the weekend will give you a good idea of upcoming expectations. Make a note of them, and see how the market actually reacts. I advise against perusing the forums during the week unless you are seeking specific information; it can be too unsettling. Everyone is quite sure they are right!

The Flyer

No, this is not a new trading method. I advise traders—once they have established some basic stability in the markets—to take the occasional flyer. Yes, I advised you to pick your tools and stick with them. But it is easy to get in a rut. Sometimes we need a self-push to see things from a different perspective, encourage our imagination to find new ideas, or joggle the subconscious into freeing an idea or solution tucked deep away.

If you are a scalper, try a day trade. If you use GSCS as a primary trading tool, try DiNapoli Levels or Drummond Point & Line. Trade a different pair. I traded FOREX eight years and never gave a second glance at the AUS/USD. One night I took a flyer on it. Now, it is one of my favorite markets.

Even a different look can encourage something good. Change the scale or colors on one of your charts for a day. Pick an indicator you have never studied from your broker-dealer's platform, and add it to a chart for a week.

Bathtub Analysis

Despite the intensive research of the markets using computers over the past 30 years, I am certain there is much yet to find; new methods, chart formations, tactics, and filters. Even new charting techniques are possible. Mr. Goodman's BoxCharts have never seen the light of day, nor Eugene Hartnagle's Pretzel charts. Mr. Goodman used what he called Bathtub Analysis. It is a form of what scientists call hypothesis testing. The logic is that if you are not looking for something, you will not find it and the best way to look is to ask questions and seek the answers.

Take a few dozen charts with you the next time you bathe or have a few moments of quiet solitude. An hour in the den with classical music in the background and two fingers of a good single-malt scotch also works! Form hypotheses—make them as wild and imaginative as you can; be creative. If the market opens higher and closes lower for three consecutive time units, what happens on the fourth unit? Look for patterns. Keep a notebook.

There are an infinite number of hypotheses to test. Some complex ones would require a computer, but many would not. If your bathtub analysis turns up something promising, drill down on a few dozen charts, and see if it holds up and/or can be quantified in some fashion. Still promising? Now test it on your demo account. At best, bathtub analysis will keep you sharp and train your mind to think proactively. At worst, the single malt will give you a pleasant buzz for a short time.

Ghost Trading

My trading method requires that I make price projections on the charts. I probably make 40 or 50 during a typical trading session. Charles Goodman called this "ghost trading." Most never happen. But when they do occur I know I am in sync with that market. The market has donated free information to my cause! Without projecting such "What Ifs" I would miss many good trades.

"If you don't look, you won't see." As you watch the markets *ask questions and make predictions*—even if they are silly ones. "What happens if the high of the last swing is taken out? The low? Only then, watch. You have gone interactive by asking a question. Waiting for the answer requires you to be more alert to what is happening in that market.

Chart formations always look great in the textbooks, but many of them do not work. We do not see them when they fail for two reasons: (1) A broken formation will not look like the formation at all—one has to be very objective and proactive to see them; and (2) we want to see only what we want to see, especially if we are only passive observers.

Trading Sessions

How long a session do you need to trade effectively? That depends on what Trader Profile you have chosen. A guerilla can come into his or her 5-minute charts and be trading in minutes. A position trader using 1-Day charts needs substantial time to see what is happening at his or her price level. As a day trader I try to make my sessions at least three hours in length and sometimes trade as much as eight-hour sessions. When you feel that you are losing your edge it is time to fold, even if you have only been trading a brief time.

TIP: The longer the time frame chart you trade, the more carryover information there will be from session-to-session and the longer it will take to get started each new session.

How many sessions do you trade in a year?

I trade four to five sessions a week typically; sometimes as many as 8 or 10. I always take a three-day weekend once a month and I take two full weeks off two or three times a year.

Finding a balance takes some effort. You naturally want to keep trading when you are in a groove—but things can change quickly if you overstay your welcome. You want to always be fresh and never trade tired or under duress. Know thyself.

Summary

Market environments can be used as a trading method, a back-testing algorithm, a money management tool, and as a performance analysis method or as part of your diagnostic heuristic. It is a methodology that allows the age-old Trending-Trading dichotomy to be quantified and studied scientifically.

Do not encumber your trading program with dozens of small tactical tricks. Stay focused on your primary tools and think Occam's razor, a time-proven maxim to keep things simple, never introduce complications for their own sake. But do be open to new and promising ideas, especially those that will complement your program and your trading style. Identify where they should sit in your trade plan and heuristic. Seek synergy instead of complexity. Test, verify, apply, retest. Or, per Hegel: Hypothesis –> Antithesis –> Synthesis –> Hypothesis.

Part

Extra for Experts

Options and Exotics

At the Interbank level, *options* have been an integral part of the FOREX landscape for many years. It is estimated that options may comprise up to 10 percent of FOREX market share, a substantial portion for hedging purposes by banks and corporations.

A bank may be at risk on an international loan for a short period of time. Hedging with currency options can eliminate that risk. Hedging acts as an insurance policy. If the bank is at risk on the long side of the EUR/USD, they can take the opposite position in options. A corporation might do the same while awaiting payment on a large sale. Loss on the business-side transaction is compensated by a profit in the hedge. For retail currency traders, speculative options trading has been the domain of seedy boiler-room operations until recently. There are now three domains in which you may trade currency options: (1) Two exchanges trade listed currency options; (2) you can spread-bet currency options at any of the spread betting operations mentioned in Chapter 13, "The FOREX Marketplace"; (3) several reputable retail broker-dealers now offer FOREX options on 10 or more pairs and with a wide variety of features. I now recommend traders who wish to work with currency options use a retail FOREX broker. The advantages and convenience of being able to trade spot FOREX and the corresponding FOREX options under one roof is substantial.

Exotics, currency pairs with the USD or EUR, and a small or exotic country's currency provide exceptional opportunities along with higher risks than the majors or top-tier crosses. They offer variety, have trading personalities all their own, and may be especially attractive if you have some knowledge or insight about the exotic country other traders do not.

Options

Options are not a simple investment vehicle and the terminology can be confusing.

Options can be used for speculation—to make a profit—or as a hedge—to protect a position maintained in the normal course of one's business. If you hedge a speculative spot FOREX position with options, it is considered a speculative hedge. It is only a true hedge if you are protecting a legitimate business transaction involving currency risk.

For speculation, options can be used as either a trading instrument or as a money management tool paired with spot FOREX trading.

I strongly advise new traders to become fully comfortable in the spot FOREX space before considering options. Because of the additional time value component, the matrix of possibilities and strategies can be enormously complex and mathematically heady.

In options time is not on your side. It is a constantly deteriorating (decaying) value. The price of the underlying currency must not just move in your favor to make money; it must move enough to compensate for the time decay. Every options trader has experienced this: The call is due to expire soon and suddenly the underlying vehicle (a stock, a commodity, a currency pair) begins to move up, sometimes dramatically. But the option is decaying even faster than the underlying vehicle is going up. The result: The price of the option continues to go down. In the meantime, the buyer of the spot pair has made a tidy profit.

An Options Primer

An *option* is the right to buy or sell the underlying currency at a specific price for a specified period of time. You can purchase an option or write an option. For speculative purposes, purchasing is most common.

The right to buy is a *call.* You have the right to *call* the position away from someone holding the spot equivalent.

The right to sell is a *put.* You have the right to *put* a spot position to someone.

You purchase a call if you believe the currency price is headed up. You purchase a put if you believe the currency price is headed down. An option is a contract between a buyer and a seller; the seller is termed the *writer,* the *buyer* is the purchaser.

Basic Options Terms

The *strike price* is the price at which the call or put may be exercised. It does not make sense to exercise a call or put (exchange it for a spot position) unless the call or put is *in-the-money*—trading above (call) or below (put) the strike price.

You may, of course, *offset* your option, buying it back (a put) or selling it (a call) before the expiration or even if it is not in-the-money. You have effectively transferred your contractual obligation to someone else. You might purchase a call out of the money and sell it out of the money and still profit thereby.

The expiration is the time frame of the option. In stocks and commodities, these are normally set for months. An option is said to expire in September, for example. In FOREX the expiration dates are closer since very few traders hold positions for months at a time.

The *premium* is the cost of the option. With options you are paying for the time-value as well as the price values. The underlying value of the option falls as time approaches the expiration—unless the price value increases at a faster rate. Options pricing, because of these twin values, can be complex and unpredictable. You can be correct on the price direction and still lose money because of decaying time values.

The intrinsic value of an option is what it is worth if exercised at any given time. When an option is out-of-the-money its only intrinsic worth is time value.

A call is in-the-money if the spot price is above the strike price; out-of-the-money if below. A put is in-the-money if the spot price is below the strike price; out-of-the-money if above.

The price of an option, or premium, is determined primarily by strike and expiration vis-à-vis the current price of the underlying currency. But there are other factors such as liquidity, speculative fervor, and volatility. For example, an out-of-the-money call is more valuable if the underlying currency is volatile; it has a better chance of going to in-the-money. Forecasting option prices—even knowing or inputting the price of the underlying currency—is far from an exact science. A small change in time value or price value may cause the option price to change by an inordinate amount. The various price factors appear to interact in a nonlinear fashion. Mathematic whizzes will find a similarity to the famous *n*-body problem.

A *vanilla option* is one with only the basic components of expiration date and strike price. An *exotic option* contains complicated features and complex payoffs that often are determined by outside factors. Exotic options are mathematically complex; going to the moon was easier than predicting exotic options in the author's humble opinion.

Traditionally, currency options have been of two types:

American-style: This type of option may be exercised at any point up until expiration.

European-style: This type of option may be exercised only at the time of expiration.

And they call us crooks!

If you trade with options, consider only American-style, vanilla.

The Pros and Cons of Options

Major pro: Buying options limits your exposure. The maximum you can lose is the value of the option, the price you paid for it.

Purchasing options as a speculative vehicle offers limited downside—you cannot lose more than the price you paid for the option—and unlimited upside, at least on a call. If you purchase a put, your profit is technically limited to the underlying currency going to zero.

The cost of the option may be less than the margin on the same spot position.

Major con: You pay for the time value of an option. In spot FOREX other than rollover charges (typically small), you do not pay for the time you hold a position.

Forecasting option pricing—even given the price of the underlying currency—is difficult.

If your option expires worthless, you lose your entire purchase price. This can occur from prices moving sideways and the time premium decaying to zero. If prices move sideways for the spot trader, he loses nothing and retains his margin funds. You may find prices of the currency moving in your favor but not fast enough to compensate for the time decay—a discouraging predicament most options traders have experienced more than once. If the time on your option expires and the option is out-of-the-money, its value is zero. (See Figure 19.1.)

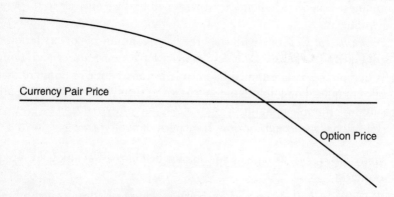

FIGURE 19.1　　The Downside of Options

The Four Basic Options Strategies

Terminology note: Be careful not to associate "buying" with calls only. You may also buy or purchase a put.

- Purchasing a call.
  Profit if prices to go up.
- Purchasing a put.
  Profit if prices to go down.
- Writing a call.
  Profit if the call buyer is incorrect.
- Writing a put.
  Profit if the put buyer is incorrect.

Purchasing and Writing Options

You may purchase either a call or a put, although it may sound strange to purchase the right to sell.

You may either purchase or write an option—either a call or a put. Remember, an option is a contract between a purchaser and a writer. An option writer collects the premium as income from the purchaser. The writer of a call must be ready to have his spot position called away or purchase a spot position if the buyer exercises his option. The writer of a put must be ready to purchase (or repurchase) the spot position from the buyer of the put.

If a writer holds a spot position when he enters an options contract, he is said to be a covered writer. If he does not hold a position, he is said to be uncovered or a naked writer.

Advanced Options Strategies

As I have mentioned, the mathematics of options is enormously complex. There are many high-level options strategies based on combinations of puts/calls, writing/purchasing, different strikes and expirations. They are not for the new trader!

Some of these have exotic names such as "condor" or "butterfly" derived from the graph of profit/loss calculations for the strategy. (See Figure 19.2.) I know, not much more impressive than the so-called Big Dipper constellation. But where would we be without imagination?

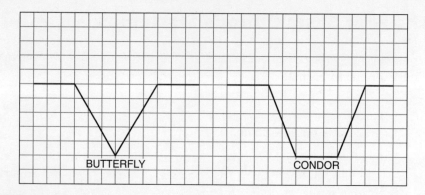

FIGURE 19.2 Exotic Option Strategies

The Greeks

A number of Greek letters have found their way into options terminology;
Delta, Gamma, Rho, and Theta.

> Delta is a measure of the change in the price of the option resulting from
> a change in the price of the underlying currency pair.
>
> Gamma is the change in Delta.
>
> Rho relates the options price to the prevailing interest rate.
>
> Theta is the change over a fixed time period with all other factors remaining unchanged.
>
> Vega, neither Greek nor Chevrolet, relates options price to implied volatility.
>
> Enjoy!

The Retail FOREX Options Landscape

There is a substantial *over-the-counter* (OTC) FOREX options market—this has
been around for many years. But it is only open to banks, institutions, and large
corporations. Fortunately large broker-dealers are beginning to tap into this
arena and offer it to their customers.

Spread-betting companies offer currency options, as well. See Chapter 13,
"The FOREX Marketplace," for a list of spread-betting companies.

I recommend you start with one of these if options appeal to you.

TradeviewForex www.tradeviewforex.com

TradeviewForex's Core Options Trading is a well-designed program.
TradeviewForex offers customer service a notch above most other brokers—

perhaps a handy feature if you are new to options and have questions along the way.

They advertise: Instant execution, accept request for prices on any date on any currency pair, Delta-based pricing, Market and Limit orders, State-of-the-art risk management.

PFG Best www.pfgbest.com

Best direct was originally an old-line commodity futures house. Options on futures have been around many years. Their no-double margin—combined margin for spot and options trading—might be a useful feature for the astute trader.

SaxoBank www.saxobank.com

SaxoBank was one of the first broker dealers to offer currency options; the program is now called the FX Options Trade Board. They have extensive information on their web site. Features: 40 currency pairs are offered with options, short date to one-year expiry, live streaming quotes, no dealer intervention. They also offer options on gold and silver.

Oanda www.oanda.com

Oanda offers a unique BoxOption. Traders define their own option by drawing a box on the currency chart whether they believe the exchange rate will eventually move to hit or miss the custom box. The trader also chooses the purchase price for their box. The system (I assume a complex algorithm) then calculates a payout based on the likelihood the box will be hit (open box) or missed (closed box). It is all or nothing. You collect if the box is hit (or missed) and forfeit the purchase price if the box is missed (or hit).

Here you are trading against Oanda's algorithm as well as the underlying currency pair. I am sure astute mathematicians are already at work attempting to reverse-engineer the algorithm. I am equally sure that if someone comes too close to achieving such an august aim, the algorithm will be modified before you can even say, "Send me my money!" See Figure 19.3.

Options for Trading

If you have concluded that a currency is going up or down in price, you may buy a call or buy a put on the currency. The number of pairs offered to retail

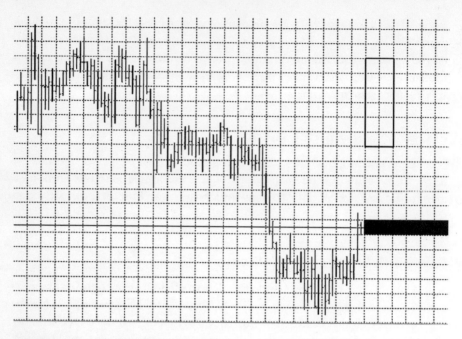

FIGURE 19.3 Oanda BoxOption
www.tradeviewfx.com and www.metaquotes.com

traders is growing quickly. Two or three years ago only the majors were available; today some brokers offer them on more than 40 pairs. You gain the advantage of limited risk but pay for that limited exposure. Much like an insurance policy, if you do not use it, it is lost.

Unfortunately, that limited risk tends to lull inexperienced traders into a false sense of security. They do not have to make a decision about getting out of a bad trade because of a margin call and are prone to let a losing trade ride until either the price of the currency is so far away and/or there is so little time value remaining that the option expires worthless. As a young trader in 1973 I watched my five Ford options slide from 11/2 to zero over a two-week period. "Tomorrow will be a better day." Tomorrow never came. Always keep in mind the basic options position. You may see the currency price go in your favor but the time value decays at a faster rate. The net result is that your option goes down in value.

Options for Money Management

Options for money management make a lot of sense but require significant study, experience, and discipline for the strategy to work properly. There are three basic strategies for money management with options but dozens of permutations on them. Remember, no matter how sophisticated your strategy is, you still must be correct about the price movement of an option to make a profit. There is no magic in the torturing of the numbers, friend.

These four strategies are based on long the EUR/USD.

Strategy 1: Perhaps you entered a market with extremely high volatility; long the Euro, short the U.S. Dollar (EUR/USD) just before an important news announcement is due. You might purchase a put on the Euro. Once prices begin to move in your favor, you can raise your stop to a break-even point and sell the put. Of course, you have lost money on the put, but you have bought time to allow your position to stabilize in your favor. If the trade moves against you instead, the option will cover at least a large portion of your spot trade loss.

Strategy 2: Perhaps you have a long-term trade in mind and plan to hold the position over several days. A put helps anchor your position against the risks and vagaries of a long-term hold. In FOREX the risks associated with long hold periods are substantial.

Strategy 3: In this scenario of a long-term hold, you could write a call against your position and collect income during the holding time from the purchaser of the call. You must calculate the value of the income versus the risk of having your spot position called away from you.

Strategy 4: You find a great trade, but the stop-loss would be too far away for your trading profile or perhaps a new report is pending. You can sell the spot pair and simultaneously buy a call option. As soon as your primary trade (the spot pair) reaches a point where you can place a break-even stop-loss, you cover (sell) the call option. You will lose some money on the option but if the pair performs according to your expectations, then being able to take the trade justifies the cost. See Figure 19.4.

Options are relatively expensive. You might think a good strategy would be buying both a short-term call and a put before a big news announcement would be effective. If prices move dramatically, the profit on one will more than compensate for the loss on the other. Others also have considered the idea. Option prices spike before such events, making a profit unlikely except for a quite extraordinary price move. There is no free lunch; sophisticated traders and researchers have almost certainly already studied and/or tried any strategy you may discover. Said another way—the markets are efficient.

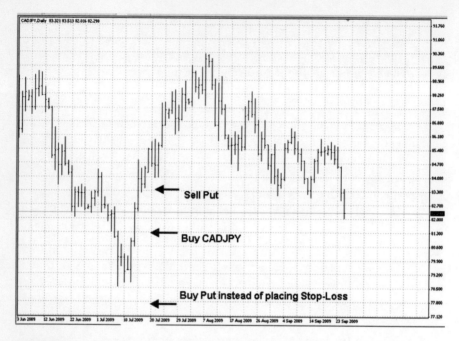

FIGURE 19.4 An Options Strategy for the Spot Trader
Courtesy Tradeview Forex, www.tradeviewforex.com, and MetaTrader, www.metaquotes.net

Exotics

Terminology is not consistent throughout the industry: a major is a pair consisting of currencies from the United States (USD), Great Britain (GBP), Japan (JPY), Europe (EUR), Australia (AUD), and Canada (CAD). An exotic is one of these (usually the USD or EUR) and one of the currencies shown in Table 19.1. A pair composed of two exotic currencies is called asking for trouble. Exotics may also be called *emerging*, although there is not a strict one-to-one relationship between the two.

Exotics are illiquid—there is much less trading in them than in the majors or minors. The degree varies; the Polish zloty is relatively liquid while the Thai baht is very illiquid. The lack of liquidity means that pip spreads are high and large orders may be difficult to execute. Risks are greater but so is profit potential.

Generally the best fills are during the appropriate session relative to the exotic: European session for the Zloty, Asian session for the Baht. Fills are an issue for exotic traders and make short-term trading difficult because such cost must be figured into the equation. Fifteen pips on a 50-pip swing is too rich but on an anticipated 200 pips it may be livable.

TABLE 19.1 Exotic Currencies		
Currency	*Name*	*Symbol*
BRAZIL	REAL	BRL
CHILE	PESO	CLP
CZECH REPUBLIC	KORUNA	CZK
HUNGARY	FORINT	HUF
ICELAND	KRONA	ISK
INDIA	RUPEE	INR
LATVIA	LAT	LVL
LITHUANIA	LITAS	LTL
MEXICO	MEXICAN PESO	MXN
MOLDOVA	LEU	MDL
POLAND	ZLOTY	PLN
SOUTH AFRICA	RAND	ZAR
THAILAND	BAHT	THB
TURKEY	LIRA	TRY
TURKMENISTAN	MANAT	TMM
URUGUAY	PESO	UYU
YUGOSLAVIA	NEW DINAR	YUD

The NFA has mandated that exotic currency pairs must be backed up with a minimum of 4 percent margin, yielding a maximum leverage of 25:1. Because of this limitation many exotic FOREX traders have moved their accounts to overseas broker-dealers to avoid this limitation.

Given a news event in an exotic country, prices may soar or dive, and exiting at any reasonable price may be difficult. Devaluations are uncommon, but when they do occur, overnight price changes of 20 percent or more can be either a disaster or a windfall.

Old-time traders will remember the devaluations of the Mexican Peso in the 1970s of 50 percent or more. Fortunes were made—and lost—literally overnight.

Trading Exotics

If you are interested in trading the exotics, buying call or put options may be an excellent idea. The advantages of options trading probably outweigh the risks involved in spot trading. Nonetheless, I believe that the new trader should first gain experience in the spot FOREX arena before attempting options, or exotics.

GFT FOREX, www.GFTFOREX.com, is a trailblazer in offering exotics to retail customers, but most other major brokers offer at least a few exotics. Notable are Gain Capital, www.gaincapital.com, and SaxoBank, www.saxobank.com. Visit web sites for a list of currencies traded by each broker-dealer. I must repeat: Be mindful of liquidity in exotics. If you think liquidity in the AUD/USD is poor at 12 P.M. Eastern, wait until you see the Thai Baht spreads! There is also the potential instability of these countries, causing their currencies to move suddenly and sharply. Requoting and ballooning spreads could be an issue, even for small traders. If you use an Electronic Communications Network (ECN) broker instead of a market maker to trade exotics, be doubly cautious. Remember, an ECN must find an order to match yours and does not act as a counterparty to your trades. If you place a market order to buy, prices will rise until a seller is found. Hopefully a rug merchant will need change to sell a rug to Aunt Martha and bail you out.

Begin trading exotics in mini-lots of 10,000 to get a feel for liquidity and other potential execution issues. Seek out broker-dealers who advertise exotics. Most brokers can get access to just about any currency pair—but liquidity becomes an even more critical factor if they have only one or two liquidity providers for that pair.

Summary

Options and exotics offer new possibilities for traders and open many doors to new and exciting trade opportunities. My advice: There is enough action in the major pairs and the top-tier minors and crosses in the spot market to satisfy most traders. Consider options as a money management tool more than as a substitute for spot FOREX. Trade options as speculative vehicles only after you have become experienced in the spot market of the major pairs and crosses. That said, currency option trading for speculative purposes is expected to continue to grow in the years ahead. The magnet of limited risk—whether rational or not—is appealing to many traders. As volume increases also expect a rise in the interest of sophisticated option plays as opposed to the simple buying and selling of puts and calls. If brokers see a market for a certain exotic they will offer it.

Exotics have real appeal to the experienced trader in my opinion. While liquidity is poor and fills on trades can be miserable, the trends tend to be long. If you can get aboard you might catch a nice long ride. When online retail FOREX first began in the 1990s the markets were inefficient; classical chart patterns that have not really worked well in futures or stocks for decades played out like textbook examples for two or three years. Alas, more traders arrived and with them the liquidity and the efficiency and the easy pickings disappeared.

There is a sense that because of the low interest—for now—in exotics the markets are still relatively inefficient. This market inefficiency can make them subject to better profit potential than the majors, *ceteris paribus*. I see clean classical chart patterns, for example, frequently on the longer-term EUR/PLN (Euro Polish Zloty) charts. But be cognizant of the minimum margin requirement of 4 percent for U.S. FOREX traders.

If you have the experience, time, and the inclination, spot FOREX exotics may well offer meaningful opportunities. Specializing in an exotic can offer a basic course in fundamental analysis, at the very least. Adopt a baht today.

Computers and FOREX

C omputers and FOREX is a match made in heaven. Without computers and the Internet there would be no online retail FOREX trading.

This chapter is optional for the novice currency trader, although investors with some trading experience will find it informative. All traders should at least be aware of advanced FOREX techniques using computers. The intense ongoing market research is destined to eventually impact even the smallest traders.

Technical Analysis

Technical analysis is the preferred trading method for many traders, big and small, institutional and individual. See Chapter 11, "Technical Analysis," for a summary of technical analysis ideas.

Computers are an obvious aid to doing technical analysis studies, both for finding new methods and testing old ones. A computer can help in two areas. Complicated ideas and data sets can be easily manipulated by a computer. A computer can test a trading method quickly and over an extensive set of historical data. This is a good check on the human mind's tendency to generalize with limited data.

A trader can create new indicators, for example, using a standard programming language such as Visual Basic 6, C++, or C# or he or she can use the languages built into trading platforms such as MetaTrader and NinjaTrader. The advantage of the latter is that the indicator may be both tested and applied to trading within the platform. If you program in an external language you must work with your broker's Application Program Interface (API) to port the program—and that can get messy.

The amount of research taking place in this arena is staggering. There are several forums online just dealing with the MetaTrader languages MQL4 and MQL5 and substantial activity in other scripting languages such as EasyLanguage (TradeStation), EFS (eSignal), and NinjaScript (NinjaTrader).

Expert Advisors

Expert advisors are combinations of indicators with a small rule set for determining specific buy and sell signals. They have become popular in the past two or three years. Some advisors can be quite complex and sophisticated. Others may be simpler: "Buy only when the 3-unit moving average is above the 10-Unit moving average *and* the Relative Strength Index is below 50 percent." The rule sets tend to be small in number and limited to a few Boolean operators such as AND, OR, NOT, and IF-THEN.

There are a few expert advisors available for sale to traders. Are they any good? If you found a system that worked well would you sell it for $199? Major institutions spend millions developing trading systems—and most wind up on the scrapheap of market history before they execute a single real-time trade. Professional team programming is expensive. Three specialists at $200 an hour might take 5,000 hours to develop a program.

Most expert advisors are tested first over a long historical data set. This can be misleading. Markets have a large number of environments and an expert advisor tested over a long period of time may either only do well on a small cluster of environments or the historical data used may not (in fact, probably does not) have an evenly distributed sample of all the environments. See Chapter 18, "Improving Your Trading Skills," for some of the applications of the Market Environment (ME) methodology, which attempts to overcome these deficiencies.

TIP: An expert advisor should not be confused with an expert system— though the two have similarities. An expert system is considerably more complex and has additional features such as attempting to learn from its mistakes and a procedure for "explaining" its decisions.

Automated Trading and BOTS

An expert advisor may be manually traded—the trader waits for the signal then executes the order manually, or automatically traded—the expert advisor executes the trade as it occurs. Computers do not get tired or hungry. They can make money for you 24 hours a day—if the program is good.

Automated trading has become popular with individual traders and institutions. Many retail brokers offer tools for and accommodate automated trader programs, even for small retail customers.

It may well be because I am older now but I simply do not trust these programs. At the institutional level I believe a reckoning is on the horizon. In my humble opinion an experienced trader can add synergy to any automated trading system.

High-Frequency and Ultra-High-Frequency Trading

These are all the rage today at the institutional level. As we go to press the Securities and Exchange Commission (SEC), concerned about the impact of high-frequency trading (HFT), has began an effort to at least slow its growth and regulate what it considers to be its excesses. Some practices involved are in legal gray areas, such as flash executions—stepping in front of a large order to garner a few pips as it pushes prices up.

HFT and ultra-high-frequency trading (UHFT) execute short-term trades—usually in seconds. In a sense they are not really trading as we know it. These computer programs are essentially watching for anomalies in the data set from the pool of large liquidity providers and attempting to predict—and profit—from what other automated programs are going to do. They wish to reverse-engineer the other online programs' decision-making processes via analysis of how and when they place orders.

I anticipated this in an article I wrote some years ago, "A Bust to the Markets" (Currency Codex, 1996):

> The investment markets will evolve into a war between several powerful computer programs, each seeking to develop new rules and information coding mechanisms and growing forecasts to "keep up" with the market's parallel behavior.
>
> But each computer will need to deal with another factor as well; a factor already noted in the markets. That is: What are the other players doing, or thinking of doing? What rules do they use to find the market's rules?
>
> Trading decisions will be made not on just what one concludes the market will do, but on what one concludes other systems "on-line" are likely to do. This becomes a problem for GAME THEORY, a

field of study likely to be soon dominated by self-organizing and evolutionary computing techniques such as cellular automata and Agent computing.

Computers in the market will make false moves to deflect the ability of other computers to know what it is planning to do and how it makes its decisions. (This will not sound at all futuristic to commodity floor traders who see the big interests routinely throw in false orders to deflect true intentions.)

This multi-dimensional game theory scenario, with a single technique periodically busting a market will, I predict, be the hallmark of the investment arena not long into the 21st Century.

This image of the market may not be to everyone's liking; especially old-timers like this writer who fondly remembers customer boardrooms alive with the comforting din of ticker tapes and clacker boards. But the fact remains, the markets will continue to exist even when a single technique dominates the action from time to time. Trading will become even more difficult and undemocratic, but also much more profitable for the few.

It will be most interesting to see how HFT and UHFT develop in the future. It should be said that at least in the short term they do add liquidity to the market, which is, of course, a positive factor. But in the long term they may well encourage questionable activities in the marketplace.

Into the Future of FOREX

Although it has lost some luster in this century, application of artificial intelligence (AI) methods has been seen in the FOREX arena. The three primary approaches are: expert systems, neural networks, and genetic algorithms.

I developed an expert system-neural network hybrid in the early 1980s, Jonathan's Wave, and used it successfully in the futures markets for a number of years. I moved on to exploring a cellular automata–based model, the Trend Machine (more on this in the next section). But the possibility of revamping Jonathan's Wave with modern techniques and computer firepower has rekindled my interest in artificial intelligence. The entire AI approach may have a second wind. I predict a resurgence of efforts by the large institutional traders.

Although there is intense disagreement on this subject, I have concluded AI methods are still primarily linear—no different in underlying structure than a moving average or relative strength indicator. Past market prices and data are manipulated to make forecasts, and curve-fitting remains the theoretical name of the game.

The search for a Philosopher's Stone—a method that will consistently beat the market—has been afoot from the inception of the markets themselves. In the mid-1900s many traders published (usually privately) small volumes with techniques to beat the markets. They typically looked good on paper—but failed when applied to real-time trading. Most were tested on simplistic market environments (trading markets, trending markets) and failed when the real-time market morphed into a different environment.

I am reminded of the secret system used by a trader I met in Hawaii in the 1980s. He believed that the random spread of ink spots from the news printer was actually hidden buy and sell signals from the floor traders. I do not know if he closed his account when the broker went to a digital printer.

The advent of computer analysis in the 1970s and automated trading in the 1990s encouraged traders to use this new tool to find the trading method over the rainbow. Much of the effort has been directed to using vast batteries of conventional techniques with deep mathematical and statistical twists. It is clear, after 30 years of effort: no linear method is going to beat the market, at least not consistently in all markets. As my late partner Jim Bickford would say, "You can torture the numbers, but you can't make them speak."

The Trend Machine

There is, however, exciting and promising research using nonlinear methods and modeling techniques culled from the sciences of complexity and artificial life (A-life). The underlying hypothesis is this: While the basic input datum of the markets—primarily prices—may be simple, the output can only be forecast with nonlinear methods derived from complexity theory. They do not use back-fit data or curve-fitting as do all conventional technical analysis methods. These include chaos theory, catastrophe theory, and cellular automata (CA). CA essentially grows a forecast from a seed using an algorithm or set of algorithms. Simple CA algorithms can generate complex behavior—just as the basic buy and sell orders lead to the great variety of chart formations. Whether it is possible to beat the markets with them remains to be seen. For an example, see "A Simple Cellular Automata Model for Predicting FX Prices" by Michael Duane Archer given to the Automata 2008 conference in the United Kingdom. A link to it is available on www.goodmanworks.com.

Figure 20.1 shows a 12-hour noninterpreted forecast for the EUR/USD in 1-Hour-minute increments from the Trend Machine. A 1 is a forecast for an Up bar; a 0 is a forecast for a Down bar.

FIGURE 20.1 Trend Machine Forecast

Source: TradeviewForex www.tradeviewforex.com and www.metaquotes.net

The forecast can be run in a stacked semaphore, with High, Low, and Close rather than just Close. It can also make forecasts interpreted to ME directional movement from −4 to +4, where −4 represents a steep downtrend and +4 a steep uptrend.

Arbitrage

Arbitrage, especially triangulation methods, is a perfect candidate for computer analysis and execution; it requires both deep and lightning-fast calculation. In general, arbitrage is the purchase or sale of any financial instrument and simultaneous taking of an equal and opposite position in a related market in order to take advantage of small price differentials between markets. Essentially, arbitrage opportunities arise when currency prices go out of sync with each other. There are numerous forms of arbitrage involving multiple markets, future deliveries, options, and other complex derivatives. A less sophisticated example of a two-currency, two-location arbitrage transaction follows:

Bank ABC offers 170 Japanese Yen for one U.S. Dollar and Bank XYZ offers only 150 Yen for one Dollar. Go to Bank ABC and purchase 170 Yen.

TABLE 20.1 Combinations of the Five Most Frequently Traded Currencies

Currency	Bid	Ask	Pip Spread
CHF/JPY	0.8514	0.8519	4
EUR/CHF	1.5676	1.5678	2
EUR/GBP	0.6915	0.6917	2
EUR/JPY	133.51	133.54	3
EUR/USD	1.2638	1.2640	2
GBP/CHF	2.2666	2.6674	8
GBP/JPY	193.02	193.10	8
GBP/USD	1.8275	1.8278	3
USD/CHF	1.2402	1.2405	3
USD/JPY	105.61	105.64	3

Next go to Bank XYZ and sell the Yen for $1.13. In a little more than the time it took to cross the street that separates the two banks, you earned a 13 percent return on your original investment. If the anomaly between the two banks' exchange rates persists, repeat the transactions. After exchanging currencies at both banks six times, you will have more than doubled your investment.

Within the FOREX market, triangular arbitrage is a specific trading strategy that involves three currencies, their correlation, and any discrepancy in their parity rates. Thus, there are no arbitrage opportunities when dealing with just two currencies in a single market. Their fluctuations are simply the trading range of their exchange rate.

In the subsequent examples, I refer to Tables 20.1 to 20.4 of currency pairs consisting of the five most frequently traded pairs (USD, EUR, JPY, GBP, and CHF) with recent bid-ask rates.

We omitted the other two majors, CAD and AUD, for the sake of simplicity and not because of lack of arbitrage opportunities in these two majors.

EXAMPLE 1: Two USD pairs and one cross pair (multiply).

First we must identify certain characteristics and distinguish the following categories:

USD is the base currency (leftmost currency in the pair):

USD/CHF	1.2402/05
USD/JPY	105.61/64

USD is the quote currency (rightmost currency in the pair):

EUR/USD   1.2638/40

GBP/USD   1.8275/78

Cross Rates (non-USD currency pairs):

CHF/JPY   85.14/19

EUR/CHF   1.5676/78

EUR/GBP   0.6915/17

EUR/JPY   133.51/54

GBP/CHF   2.2666/74

GBP/JPY   193.02/10

The fact that the USD is the base currency in two of the pairs (USD/CHF and USD/JPY) and is the quote currency in two other pairs (EUR/USD and GBP/USD) plays an important role in the arithmetic of arbitrage. We begin our investigation with just the bid prices. (See Table 20.2.)

The criterion whether to multiply or divide the USD pairs in order to calculate the cross rate is simple:

If the USD is the base currency in both pairs, then divide the USD pairs.

If the USD is the quote currency in both pairs, then divide the USD pairs.

Otherwise multiply the USD pairs.

To determine the deviation from parity for each cross pair, subtract the exchange rate from the calculated rate and convert the floating point decimals to pip values. (See Table 20.3.)

From Table 20.3, we can see that the EUR/JPY is out of parity by four pips. To determine if an arbitrage opportunity is profitable, we must first calculate the total transaction cost by adding the three bid-ask spreads of the corresponding pairs. (See Table 20.4.)

TABLE 20.2 Formulas for Cross Currencies

CHFJPY = USDJPY/USDCHF	85.14 = 105.61/1.2402	85.1556
EURCHF = EURUSD × USDCHF	1.5676 = 1.2638 × 1.2402	1.567365
EURGBP = EURUSD / GBPUSD	0.6915 = 1.2638 / 1.8275	0.691546
EURJPY = EURUSD × USDJPY	133.51 = 1.2638 × 105.61	133.4699
GBPCHF = GBPUSD × USDCHF	2.2666 = 1.8275 × 1.2402	2.266466
GBPJPY = GBPUSD × USDJPY	193.02 = 1.8275 × 105.61	193.002

TABLE 20.3 Calculations for Cross Currencies

Pair	Rate	Calculation	Deviation	Pip Values
CHFJPY	85.1556	−85.14	= +0.0156	+1.56 pips
EURCHF	1.567365	−1.5676	= −0.000235	−2.35 pips
EURGBP	0.691546	−0.6915	= +0.000046	+0.46 pips
EURJPY	133.4699	−133.51	= −0.0401	−4.01 pips
GBPCHF	2.266466	−2.2666	= +0.000134	+1.34 pips
GBPJPY	193.0023	−193.02	= −0.0177	−1.77 pips

TABLE 20.4 Transaction Cost

EUR/USD	2
USD/JPY	+3
EUR/JPY	+3

An eight-pip transaction cost to earn a four-pip profit is counterproductive (it amounts to a four-pip loss). If the parity deviation (the number of pips by which the three currency pairs are out of alignment) were greater, say 30 pips, then a definite arbitrage opportunity exists.

The trading mechanism to take advantage of this anomaly requires some consideration. First, determine what market actions are necessary to correct this anomaly. Assume that the EUR/JPY rate is currently trading at 133.51 and the calculated rate using the current EUR/USD and USD/JPY pairs is 133.81 (a 30-pip deviation). Parity between the three currencies will be restored if the following price action occurs:

- The EUR/JPY pair rises to 133.81, or
- The product of the EUR/USD and USD/JPY pairs drops to 133.51

Therefore the following trades are required to "lock" in the 30-pip profit:

- Buy one lot of the EUR/JPY pair.
- Sell one lot of the EUR/USD pair.
- Sell one lot of the USD/JPY pair.
- Liquidate all three trades simultaneously when parity is reestablished.

Warning: Executing only one, or even two, legs of the three trades required in an arbitrage package does not guarantee a profit and may be quite dangerous.

All three trades must be executed simultaneously before the locked-in profit can be realized.

EXAMPLE 2: Two USD pairs and one cross pair (divide)

The previous example uses the product of the two USD currencies to calculate the cross rate. An example of the ratio of the two USD currencies follows. Assume the EUR/GBP cross pair is currently trading at 0.6992 and that the ratio between the EUR/USD and GBP/USD pairs is calculated as 0.6952, a 40-pip deviation. Parity will be restored when the following price actions occur:

- The EUR/GBP pair drops to 0.6952.
- The ratio of the EUR/USD and GBP/USD pairs rises to 0.6992.

In order for the second action to rise, either the EUR/USD pair must also rise or the GBP/USD pair must decline (this differs in the previous example). Therefore the following trades are required to realize a 40-pip profit:

- Sell one lot of the EUR/GBP pair.
- Buy one lot of the EUR/USD pair.
- Sell one lot of the GBP/USD pair.
- Liquidate all three trades the moment parity is reestablished.

EXAMPLE 3: Three non-USD cross pairs

Technically the arbitrage strategy can be performed on three non-USD currency pairs also. In this example, we examine a straddle between the three European majors (EUR, GBP, CHF) where we focus on the EUR/CHF pair in respect to the two GBP currency pairs (GBP/CHF and EUR/GBP).

Assume the current rates of exchange are:

$$EUR/CHF = 1.5676/78$$
$$EUR/GBP = 0.6915/17$$
$$GBP/CHF = 2.2604/12$$

and their relationship is:

$$EUR/CHF = EUR/GBP \times GBP/CHF$$

Thus the calculated value for the EUR/CHF rate is 0.6915×2.2604 or 1.5631. The deviation from parity is $-.0045$ ($1.5631 - 1.5676$) or 45 CHF pips since CHF is the pip currency in the EUR/CHF pair. The trading strategy is:

- Sell one lot of EUR/CHF.
- Buy one lot of EUR/GBP.
- Buy one lot of GBP/CHF.
- Liquidate all three when parity is reestablished.

If all three trades are executed successfully, a profit of 45 CHF pips is realized. Subtract the three bid-ask spreads for the transaction costs (2 + 2 + 8 = 12) to see a net profit of 33 CHF pips. Now convert CHF pips to dollars (33 divided by USD/CHF rate 1.2402) to obtain 27 USD pips.

It should be noted in all the examples presented above that only three currencies are analyzed simultaneously. It is possible to add a fourth, or even a fifth, currency to the mix though this is normally left to the very serious arbitrage strategists.

The methodology for examining four (or even five or six) currencies at one time is to calculate every possible three-currency combination among the currencies selected. Rearrange them in magnitude of deviation from parity. Examine the deviations closely to see if there is a single anomaly or possibly even a double anomaly among the four currencies. This type of scrutiny will then determine if a four-currency arbitrage opportunity exists.

Specialized software is definitely required when dealing with four or more currencies in a single arbitrage package.

Pros and Cons of Arbitrage

Using triangular arbitrage strategies on the FOREX market has one very salient advantage: predetermined profits can be realized if the trades execute smoothly. Unfortunately, the disadvantages of this strategy are numerous:

- Higher transaction costs. The trader must pay the bid-ask spreads on three separate trades.
- Higher margin requirements. Roughly three times the margin is necessary to execute the arbitrage strategy and odd-lot trading may be required for the small capital investor.
- Precision timing is required. Arbitrage opportunities are usually short-lived.
- Multiple dimensions. The trader must thoroughly understand the arbitrage mechanism in order to determine which currency pairs to buy and which to sell. Each arbitrage package consists of two buys and one sell or one buy and two sells. Miscalculating any one of the three trades can cause disaster.

- Advanced monitoring techniques are usually required. This means calculating the above analysis on several pairs simultaneously in real time and will involve a software program that analyzes streaming quotes continually. It is possible to perform these tasks manually but the trader must have a high tolerance for tedium.

I must also mention that in the examples above, I intentionally simplified calculations by using only the bid price throughout. When executing an actual arbitrage trade, the investor must supply both bid and ask rate where applicable.

If you take a snapshot of all the major pair cross-rates at a given time and use transitivity to calculate from one end to the other you will find the whole is not the same as the sum of the parts. The trick is catching those anomalies as they stream along real-time.

Summary

Computers will continue to play a larger and larger role in FOREX generally and retail FOREX specifically. Like all technology, it is a sword that cuts both ways. The trader should consider both the pros and cons of any new applications and not accept them prima facie.

As my mentor Charles B. Goodman said to me when he saw my early computer trading models, "Remember, Dad, the next price can only be up or down." Whether you trade with a two-moving average crossover run on a Dollar Store calculator or a BOT executing a catastrophe model with an agent-driven genetic algorithm subroutine, I wish you success in the FOREX market.

How the FOREX Game Is Played

Market Makers and ECNs

There are two types of retail FOREX brokers: market makers and Electronic Communications Networks (ECNs).

ECN is similar in method to how the Interbank foreign exchange market works—orders are matched on a client-to-client basis. A large network of banks, institutions, and traders connect to the network, and orders are matched; there is no central clearinghouse for orders. If you wish to sell 50 million U.S. Dollars (USD) against the Euro (EUR), you place your order and wait for someone who wants to buy. Typically, because of the huge volume of foreign exchange business, transactions are instantaneous. The market is said to be liquid. Nevertheless, your order technically requires a counterparty to be executed.

ECN retail FOREX brokers build their own network and often tap in to the Interbank ECN.

A Peek under the Hood

Most retail brokers—especially the smaller ones accepting so-called mini-accounts—are market makers. Market makers act as a de facto central clearinghouse for their clients, a sort of mini-exchange. If you look closely at market maker web sites and their account documentation you will see a statement such as "XYZ-FOREX is the counterparty to all trades."

Market makers typically guarantee execution at the price you want, assuming their data stream touches that price. There are exceptions, however, as discussed below.

Market makers often trade against their own clients, acting as a proactive agent between their liquidity providers on one side and their clients on the other side. There is inherently nothing wrong with this; that is how they play the game. Trading against their clients performs three useful functions: (1) It provides liquidity; (2) it helps maintain an orderly market; and (3) it keeps their book from becoming too unbalanced. Because they are the counterparty to all trades, if they have 500 million USD on the buy side and only 50 million USD on the sell side (this is an exaggeration to make the point—balance is rarely off more than 5 percent) market makers are at risk if the USD should fall sharply. Market makers often hand off large orders to an ECN or the Interbank market to maintain balance.

Market makers are effectively bookmakers. In choosing a market maker broker, it is good to know how much net worth or liquidity they have in case they do suffer from an order imbalance. The Commodity Futures Trading Commission (CFTC) now requires a minimum capital requirement of $20 million for full-fledged retail FOREX broker-dealers.

Market makers are often accused of *running* or *harvesting* stop-loss orders. To a limited extent this is in pursuit of the three legitimate functions listed above. However, if a broker-dealer harvests stops primarily as a profit center, traders are not happy. It is difficult, if not impossible, to tell if a market maker is running stops at all and—if they are—the motive. Such is the capitalist experience. Because of the lax regulatory environment the inner workings of retail brokers is more opaque than it is transparent.

If you have access to multiple data streams, you can watch for stop harvesting. If one of the streams shows a sharp price spike resulting in a price several pips from the maximum or minimum of all the other streams, it is possibly a case of stop harvesting, especially if it is in an active market with good liquidity.

FOREX markets are said to be *fast* especially after the release of a major news announcement. This means there is a dramatic increase in price movement and/or volatility. Market makers often dramatically increase their pip spreads (ballooning) for a short period of time under these conditions to maintain order balance. Pip spreads have been known to balloon from 2 pips to as much as 50 pips for one or two minutes after a Federal Reserve announcement. Spreads often increase even before the news release as an effort to protect their book. If you trade the news—and I recommend against it for the beginning trader—use an execution tool such as www.secretnewsweapon.com.

There are horror stories of ballooning 100 to 200 pips. Spreads also balloon during inactive market periods when liquidity is low. Traders should either avoid trading during these times or at least be aware of this phenomenon. Ballooning spreads should be a legitimate market maker function, but many traders believe some market makers use it as a profit center technique. ECN spreads often balloon for the same reasons and under the same circumstances but typically not as much. It is unusual but not unheard of for a broker to simply not take an order or to quickly bounce it out of the system.

Guerillas and scalpers seeking small 5- to 10-pip profits may find it difficult to enter orders with a market maker. On occasion brokers will require traders to place pending orders—stops and limits—a minimum distance from the trade price, sometimes as much as 50 pips.

Although not as big a problem as it once was, requoting (or dealer intervention) has been the bane of market makers. In requoting, a broker gives you a fill at a price not seen on their official streaming data feed. More than any other factor, requoting has driven traders away from specific brokers and from FOREX generally. NFA Compliance Rule 2-43 has attempted to deal with the requoting issue but the competition of the marketplace has already done much to correct the problem in recent years.

Another form of dealer intervention that has frustrated retail FOREX traders is being "put on manual." This means that your orders are executed by hand at the dealing desk. Some reviews claim traders have been put on manual when they are making too much money (remember, the market maker is the counterparty to your trader). Some traders have claimed to have had their accounts frozen or closed for the same reason.

Brokers do seem to be getting the message. Requoting is much less an issue than it was in the past. But to a large extent, the damage is done and the term "market maker" has negative connotations to traders. To this end many brokers now advertise they have no dealing desk (NDD) implying that they are not market makers. What no dealing desk actually means and its functional effect is not clear. At the very least the line between market makers and ECNs is blurring, but the trend is certainly toward ECNs today. An NDD may simply refer to a fully automated dealing desk. It is certainly possible to imagine a broker profiting from traders without a dealing desk, by running them through an ECN of some kind.

Dukascopy, www.dukascopy.com, promotes a third way called a "centralized-decentralized" clearing system. An interesting article on this approach can be found on www.e-forex.com in the January 2007 edition.

Even on an ECN platform, executions in fast markets may be off your price by many pips. A five-pip slippage might not dramatically affect a day trader or a position trader, but it is a significant cost to the guerilla trader or the scalper. Although ECNs typically do not intervene between their liquidity providers and clients—acting only as a matchmaker—spreads from ECNs can also be heart-stopping. Without limits on order the price will rise or fall until a counterparty to your order is found.

At the highest level of foreign exchange trading, there are two games being played simultaneously. The first is simply attempting to determine what prices are going to do. There is a second, tactical level that is less visible, but real.

At the higher levels of FOREX trading, the players—typically large hedge funds—need to (1) know what the other players are doing or planning to do; (2) keep the other players from knowing what you are going to do; and, perhaps most interesting, (3) feed the other players false information so their conclusions about what you are going to do are incorrect. The typical retail FOREX trader need not concern himself with this tactical level, but should be aware of its existence. See the quote from the author's Currency Codex in Chapter 20 for more on this level of activity.

Most of the regulatory and order execution issues of interest to the retail FOREX trader stem from the fact there is no central clearinghouse for currency trading. It is difficult, if not impossible, to regulate an industry with no central locus. Consider the Internet as an example of that paradigm.

Many web sites offer broker-dealer reviews. When reading these reviews keep in mind: (1) Satisfied traders generally post less than unsatisfied traders; (2) the larger the broker-dealer, the larger its volume of complaints; (3) a small sample of reviews may not be meaningful; (4) seeing similar complaints on multiple web sites over several months increases the chances that the complaints are legitimate; and (5) small traders complain the most—and loudest—and the largest broker-dealers get the overwhelming share of newbies.

For reviews, see www.forexpeacearmy.com and www.goforex.net. For others, Google "FOREX broker reviews," "currency dealer reviews," "FOREX broker complaints," and permutations thereof. Such web sites seem to come and go quickly, which may or may not mean something.

Nothing here is meant to dissuade anyone from trading retail FOREX. If you know how the game is played, you have better chances of winning the game.

Appendix B

List of World Currencies and Symbols

Table B.1 is a list of global currencies and the three-character currency codes that we have found are generally used to represent them. Often, but not always, this code is the same as the ISO 4217 standard. (The ISO, or International Organization for Standardization, is a worldwide federation of national standards.)

In most cases, the currency code is composed of the country's two-character Internet country code plus an extra character to denote the currency unit. For example, the code for Canadian dollars is simply Canada's two-character Internet code ("CA") plus a one-character currency designator ("D").

I have endeavored to list the codes that, in my experience, are actually in general industry use to represent the currencies. Currency names are given in the plural form. This list does not contain obsolete Euro-zone currencies.

TABLE B.1	Symbol, Place, Currency Name	
AED	United Arab Emirates	Dirhams
AFA	Afghanistan	Afghanis
ALL	Albania	Leke
AMD	Armenia	Drams
ANG	Netherlands Antilles	Guilders
AOA	Angola	Kwanza

(continued on next page)

TABLE B.1 *(continued)*

ARS	Argentina	Pesos
AUD	Australia	Dollars
AWG	Aruba	Guilders
AZM	Azerbaijan	Manats
BAM	Bosnia, Herzegovina	Convertible Marka
BBD	Barbados	Dollars
BDT	Bangladesh	Taka
BGN	Bulgaria	Leva
BHD	Bahrain	Dinars
BIF	Burundi	Francs
BMD	Bermuda	Dollars
BND	Brunei Darussalam	Dollars
BOB	Bolivia	Bolivianos
BRL	Brazil	Brazil Real
BSD	Bahamas	Dollars
BTN	Bhutan	Ngultrum
BWP	Botswana	Pulas
BYR	Belarus	Rubles
BZD	Belize	Dollars
CAD	Canada	Dollars
CDF	Congo/Kinshasa	Congolese Francs
CHF	Switzerland	Francs
CLP	Chile	Pesos
CNY	China	Renminbi
COP	Colombia	Pesos
CRC	Costa Rica	Colones
CUP	Cuba	Pesos
CVE	Cape Verde	Escudos
CYP	Cyprus	Pounds
CZK	Czech Republic	Koruny
DJF	Djibouti	Francs
DKK	Denmark	Kroner
DOP	Dominican Republic	Pesos
DZD	Algeria	Algeria Dinars
EEK	Estonia	Krooni

TABLE B.1 *(continued)*

EGP	Egypt	Pounds
ERN	Eritrea	Nakfa
ETB	Ethiopia	Birr
EUR	Euro Member Countries	Euro
FJD	Fiji	Dollars
FKP	Falkland Islands	Pounds
GBP	United Kingdom	Pounds
GEL	Georgia	Lari
GGP	Guernsey	Pounds
GHC	Ghana	Cedis
GIP	Gibraltar	Pounds
GMD	Gambia	Dalasi
GNF	Guinea	Francs
GTQ	Guatemala	Quetzales
GYD	Guyana	Dollars
HKD	Hong Kong	Dollars
HNL	Honduras	Lempiras
HRK	Croatia	Kuna
HTG	Haiti	Gourdes
HUF	Hungary	Forint
IDR	Indonesia	Rupiahs
ILS	Israel	New Shekels
IMP	Isle of Man	Pounds
INR	India	Rupees
IQD	Iraq	Dinars
IRR	Iran	Rials
ISK	Iceland	Kronur
JEP	Jersey	Pounds
JMD	Jamaica	Dollars
JOD	Jordan	Dinars
JPY	Japan	Yen
KES	Kenya	Shillings
KGS	Kyrgyzstan	Soms
KHR	Cambodia	Riels
KMF	Comoros	Francs

(continued on next page)

	TABLE B.1 *(continued)*	
KPW	Korea (North)	Won
KRW	Korea (South)	Won
KWD	Kuwait	Dinars
KYD	Cayman Islands	Dollars
KZT	Kazakstan	Tenge
LAK	Laos	Kips
LBP	Lebanon	Pounds
LKR	Sri Lanka	Rupees
LRD	Liberia	Dollars
LSL	Lesotho	Maloti
LTL	Lithuania	Litai
LVL	Latvia	Lati
LYD	Libya	Dinars
MAD	Morocco	Dirhams
MDL	Moldova	Lei
MGA	Madagascar	Ariary
MKD	Macedonia	Denars
MMK	Myanmar (Burma)	Kyats
MNT	Mongolia	Tugriks
MOP	Macau	Patacas
MRO	Mauritania	Ouguiyas
MTL	Malta	Liri
MUR	Mauritius	Rupees
MVR	Maldives	Rufiyaa
MWK	Malawi	Kwachas
MXN	Mexico	Pesos
MYR	Malaysia	Ringgits
MZM	Mozambique	Meticais
NAD	Namibia	Dollars
NGN	Nigeria	Nairas
NIO	Nicaragua	Gold Cordobas
NOK	Norway	Krone
NPR	Nepal	Nepal Rupees
NZD	New Zealand	Dollars
OMR	Oman	Rials

	TABLE B.1 *(continued)*	
PAB	Panama	Balboa
PEN	Peru	Nuevos Soles
PGK	Papua New Guinea	Kina
PHP	Philippines	Pesos
PKR	Pakistan	Rupees
PLN	Poland	Zlotych
PYG	Paraguay	Guarani
QAR	Qatar	Rials
ROL	Romania	Lei
RUR	Russia	Rubles
RWF	Rwanda	Rwanda Francs
SAR	Saudi Arabia	Riyals
SBD	Solomon Islands	Dollars
SCR	Seychelles	Rupees
SDD	Sudan	Dinars
SEK	Sweden	Kronor
SGD	Singapore	Dollars
SHP	Saint Helena	Pounds
SIT	Slovenia	Tolars
SKK	Slovakia	Koruny
SLL	Sierra Leone	Leones
SOS	Somalia	Shillings
SPL	Seborga	Luigini
SRG	Suriname	Guilders
STD	São Tomé, Principe	Dobras
SVC	El Salvador	Colones
SYP	Syria	Pounds
SZL	Swaziland	Emalangeni
THB	Thailand	Baht
TJS	Tajikistan	Somoni
TMM	Turkmenistan	Manats
TND	Tunisia	Dinars
TOP	Tonga	Pa'anga
TRL	Turkey	Liras
TTD	Trinidad, Tobago	Dollars

(continued on next page)

	TABLE B.1 (continued)	
TVD	Tuvalu	Tuvalu Dollars
TWD	Taiwan	New Dollars
TZS	Tanzania	Shillings
UAH	Ukraine	Hryvnia
UGX	Uganda	Shillings
USD	United States of America	Dollars
UYU	Uruguay	Pesos
UZS	Uzbekistan	Sums
VEB	Venezuela	Bolivares
VND	Viet Nam	Dong
VUV	Vanuatu	Vatu
WST	Samoa	Tala
XAF	Communauté Financière Africaine	Francs
XCD	East Caribbean	Dollars
XDR	International Monetary Fund	Special Drawing Rights
XOF	Communauté Financière Africaine	Francs
XPF	Comptoirs Français du Pacifique	Francs
YER	Yemen	Rials
YUM	Yugoslavia	New Dinars
ZAR	South Africa	Rand
ZMK	Zambia	Kwacha
ZWD	Zimbabwe	Zimbabwe Dollars

Euro Currency Unit

O n January 1, 1999, 11 of the countries in the European Economic and Monetary Union (EMU) decided to give up their own currencies and adopt the new Euro (EUR) currency: Austria, Belgium, Finland, France, Germany, Ireland, Italy, Luxembourg, the Netherlands, Portugal, and Spain. Greece followed suit on January 1, 2001. The Vatican City also participated in the changeover. This changeover is now complete.

It is worth noting that any place that previously used one or more of the currencies listed below has now also adopted the Euro. This applies to the Principality of Andorra, the Principality of Monaco, and the Republic of San Marino. This applies automatically to any territories, departments, possessions, or collectivities of Euro-zone countries, such as the Azores, Balearic Islands, the Canary Islands, Europa Island, French Guiana, Guadeloupe, Juan de Nova, the Madeira Islands, Martinique, Mayotte, Réunion, Saint-Martin, Saint Pierre, and Miquelon, to name just a few.

Euro bank notes and coins began circulating in the above countries on January 1, 2002. At that time, all transactions in those countries were valued in Euro, and the "old" notes and coins of these countries were gradually withdrawn from circulation. The precise dates that each "old" currency ceased being legal tender are noted in Table C.1.

TABLE C.1 Official Fixed Euro Rates for Participating Countries

Old Currency	Conversion to Euro	Conversion from Euro	Legal Tender Terminus
ATS Austria, Schilling	ATS / 13.7603 = EUR	EUR × 13.7603 = ATS	February 28, 2002
BEF Belgium, Franc	BEF / 40.3399 = EUR	EUR × 40.3399 = BEF	February 28, 2002
CYP Cyprus, Pound	CYP / 0.585274 = EUR	EUR × 0.585274 = CYP	January 31, 2008
DEM Germany, Deutsche Mark	DEM / 1.95583 = EUR	EUR × 1.95583 = DEM	February 28, 2002
ESP Spain, Peseta	ESP / 166.386 = EUR	EUR × 166.386 = ESP	February 28, 2002
FIM Finland, Markka	FIM / 5.94573 = EUR	EUR × 5.94573 = FIM	February 28, 2002
FRF France, Franc	FRF / 6.55957 = EUR	EUR × 6.55957 = FRF	February 17, 2002
GRD Greece, Drachma	GRD / 340.750 = EUR	EUR × 340.750 = GRD	February 28, 2002
IEP Ireland, Pound	IEP / 0.787564 = EUR	EUR × 0.787564 = IEP	February 9, 2002
ITL Italy, Lira	ITL / 1936.27 = EUR	EUR × 1936.27 = ITL	February 28, 2002
LUF Luxembourg, Franc	LUF / 40.3399 = EUR	EUR × 40.3399 = LUF	February 28, 2002
MTL Malta, Lira	MTL / 0.429300 = EUR	EUR × 0.429300 = MTL	January 31, 2008
NLG The Netherlands, Guilder (also called Florin)	NLG / 2.20371 = EUR	EUR × 2.20371 = NLG	January 28, 2002
PTE Portugal, Escudo	PTE / 200.482 = EUR	EUR × 200.482 = PTE	February 28, 2002
SIT Slovenia, Tolar	SIT / 239.640 = EUR	EUR × 239.640 = SIT	January 14, 2007
SKK Slovakia, Koruna	SKK / 30.1260 = EUR	EUR × 30.1260 = SKK	January 17, 2009
VAL Vatican City, Lira	VAL / 1936.27 = EUR	EUR × 1936.27 = VAL	February 28, 2002

For convenience, and because their values are now irrevocably set against the Euro as listed in Table C.1, the XE.com Universal Currency Converter will continue to support these units even after their withdrawal from circulation. In addition, most outgoing Euro currencies will still be physically convertible at special locations for a period of several years. For details, refer to the official Euro site, www.europa.eu.int/euro.

Also note that the Euro is not just the same thing as the former European Currency Unit (or ECU), which used to be listed as XEU. The ECU was a theoretical "basket" of currencies rather than a currency itself, and no ECU bank notes or coins ever existed. At any rate, the ECU has been replaced by the Euro, which is a bona fide currency.

A note about spelling and capitalization: the official spelling of the EUR currency unit in the English language is "euro," with a lower case "e." However, the overwhelmingly prevailing industry practice is to spell it "Euro," with a capital "E." Since other currency names are capitalized in general use, doing so helps differentiate the noun "Euro," meaning EUR currency, from the more general adjective "euro," meaning anything even remotely having to do with Europe.

Appendix D

Time Zones and Global FX Trading Hours

The following table emphasizes the importance of the effect of time of day on FOREX market activity and volatility based on hours of operation around the globe. The top row is Greenwich Mean Time expressed in 24-hour military format. Banking hours are arbitrarily assumed to be 9:00 A.M. to 4:00 P.M. around the globe. See Figure D.1.

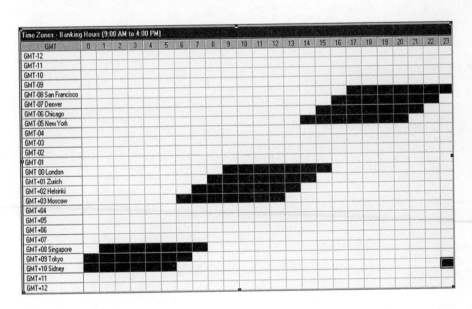

FIGURE D.1 Global Banking Hours

Examples of chart usage are:

- Locate Denver (row 6, or GMT less 7 hours). The first darkened cell in this row indicates when Denver banks open relative to other world banks.

- Move upward to top row to see that the concurrent time in London is 17:00 or 5:00 P.M., where British banks are now closed.

- A FOREX trader in New York must trade between 3:00 A.M. and 11:00 A.M. Eastern Standard Time in order to follow the heightened activity in central European markets (GMT + 1: Zurich, Frankfurt, Vienna, Copenhagen).

- San Francisco banks are closing while Sidney banks are opening, and so on.

The darkened areas in Figure D.1 accentuate the major banking centers. FOREX is a 24-hour market. You can trade 24 hours a day. Time of Day (TOD) can strongly influence trading volume, liquidity, and volatility.

The transition to the Asian session between 3:00 P.M. Eastern and 5:00 P.M. Eastern results in a quiet time when liquidity and volatility, *ceteris paribus*, are low.

Central Banks and Regulatory Agencies

A history of currency regulation is provided in Chapter 2, "A Brief History of Currency Trading," of this book. Traders interested in more details can visit the web sites listed in Table E.1.

Table E.2 is a list of affiliated central banks by country.

TABLE E.1 Regulatory Agencies	
Federal Reserve System	www.federalreserve.gov
Federal Reserve Bank	www.ny.frb.org
Securities and Exchange Commission	www.sec.gov
Commodity Futures Trading Commission	www.cftc.gov
National Futures Association	www.nfa.futures.org
Financial Services Authority	www.fsa.gov.uk
Australian Securities & Investments Commission	www.asic.gov.au/asic/asic.nsf
Bank of International Settlements	www.bis.org
Regulation in Canada	www.ida.ca/Investors/SecRegulation_en.asp

TABLE E.2 Central Banks

Argentina	Banco Central de la Republica Argentina
Armenia	Central Bank of Armenia
Aruba	Centrale Bank van Aruba
Australia	Reserve Bank of Australia
Austria	Oesterreichische Nationalbank
Bahrain	Bahrain Monetary Agency
Belgium	Banque Nationale de Belgique
Benin	Banque Centrale des Etats de l'Afrique de l'Ouest
Bolivia	Banco Central de Bolivia
Bosnia	Central Bank of Bosnia and Herzegovina
Botswana	Bank of Botswana
Brazil	Banco Central do Brasil
Bulgaria	Bulgarian National Bank
Burkina Faso	Banque Centrale des Etats de l'Afrique de l'Ouest
Canada	Bank of Canada
Chile	Banco Central de Chile
China	Peoples Bank of China
Colombia	Banco de la República
Costa Rica	Banco Central de Costa Rica
Côte d'Ivoire	Banque Centrale des Etats de l'Afrique de l'Ouest
Croatia	Croatian National Bank
Cyprus	Central Bank of Cyprus
Czech Republic	Ceska Narodni Banka
Denmark	Danmarks Nationalbank
East Caribbean	The East Caribbean Central Bank
Ecuador	Banco Central del Ecuador
Egypt	Central Bank of Egypt
El Salvador	The Central Reserve Bank of El Salvador
Estonia	Eesti Pank
European Union	European Central Bank
Finland	Suomen Pankki
France	Banque de France
Germany	Deutsche Bundesbank
Greece	Bank of Greece
Guatemala	Banco de Guatemala

TABLE E.2 *(continued)*	
Guinea Bissau	Banque Centrale des Etats de l'Afrique de l'Ouest
Hong Kong	Hong Kong Monetary Authority
Hungary	National Bank of Hungary
Iceland	Central Bank of Iceland
India	Reserve Bank of India
Indonesia	Bank of Indonesia
Ireland	Central Bank of Ireland
Israel	Bank of Israel
Italy	Banca d'Italia
Jamaica	Bank of Jamaica
Japan	Bank of Japan
Jordan	Central Bank of Jordan
Kenya	Central Bank of Kenya
Korea	Bank of Korea
Kuwait	Central Bank of Kuwait
Latvia	Bank of Latvia
Lebanon	Banque du Liban
Lithuania	Lietuvos Bankas
Luxembourg	Banque Centrale du Luxemburg
Macedonia	National Bank of the Republic of Macedonia
Malaysia	Bank Negara Malaysia
Mali	Banque Centrale des Etats de l'Afrique de l'Ouest
Malta	Central Bank of Malta
Mauritius	Bank of Mauritius
Mexico	Banco de Mexico
Moldova	The National Bank of Moldova
Mozambique	Bank of Mozambique
Namibia	Bank of Namibia
Netherlands	De Nederlandsche Bank
Netherlands Antilles	Bank van de Nederlandse Antillen
New Zealand	Reserve Bank of New Zealand
Niger	Banque Centrale des Etats de l'Afrique de l'Ouest
Norway	Norges Bank
Paraguay	Banco Central del Paraguay
Peru	Banco Central de Reserva del Peru

(continued on next page)

TABLE E.2 *(continued)*

Poland	National Bank of Poland
Portugal	Banco de Portugal
Qatar	Qatar Central Bank
Romania	National Bank of Romania
Russia	Central Bank of Russia
Saudi Arabia	Saudi Arabian Monetary Agency
Senegal	Banque Centrale des Etats de l'Afrique de l'Ouest
Singapore	Monetary Authority of Singapore
Slovakia	National Bank of Slovakia
Slovenia	Bank of Slovenia
South Africa	The South African Reserve Bank
Spain	Banco de España
Sri Lanka	Central Bank of Sri Lanka
Sweden	Sveriges Riksbank
Switzerland	Schweizerische Nationalbank
Tanzania	Bank of Tanzania
Thailand	Bank of Thailand
Togo	Banque Centrale des Etats de l'Afrique de l'Ouest
Trinidad and Tobago	Central Bank of Trinidad and Tobago
Tunisia	Banque Centrale de Tunisie
Turkey	Trkiye Cumhuriyet Merkez Bankasi
Ukraine	National Bank of Ukraine
United Kingdom	Bank of England
United States	Board of Governors of the Federal Reserve System
Zambia	Bank of Zambia
Zimbabwe	Reserve Bank of Zimbabwe

Central bank web sites may be found at www.bis.org/cbanks.htm.

Resources

Periodicals

Although the following monthly magazines focus on specific material, each frequently prints informative and timely articles on the FOREX marketplace:

Active Trader (TechInfo, Inc.)—www.activetradermag.com

Currency Trader (Online)—www.currencytradermag.com

E-FOREX (Quarterly)—www.e-forex.net

Forex Journal—www.forexjournal.com

Futures (Futures Magazine, Inc.)—www.futuresmag.com

FX Week—www.fxweek.com

Technical Analysis of Stocks & Commodities (Technical Analysis, Inc.)—www.traders.com

Books

The following list, although in no way complete, provides traders with FOREX library essentials:

Booker, Rob. *Adventures of a Currency Trader*. Hoboken, NJ: John Wiley & Sons, 2007.

Evans, Lewis, and Olga Sheean. *Left Brain Thinking: The Right Mindset and Technique for Success in Forex*. Inside Out Media, 2006.

Henderson, Callum. *Currency Strategy*. New York: John Wiley & Sons, 2002.

Horner, Raghee. *Thirty Days of Forex Trading*. Hoboken, NJ: John Wiley & Sons, 2005.

Kaufman, Perry J. *New Trading Systems and Methods*. Hoboken, NJ: John Wiley & Sons, 2007.

Klopfenstein, Gary. *Trading Currency Cross Rates*. New York: John Wiley & Sons, 1993.

Lein, Kathy. *Day Trading the Currency Market*. Hoboken, NJ: John Wiley & Sons, 2005.

Louw, G. N. *Begin Forex*. FXTrader, 2003.

Luca, Cornelius. *Technical Analysis Applications in the Global Currency Markets*. Prentice Hall, 2000.

Luca, Cornelius. *Trading in the Global Currency Markets*. Prentice Hall, 2000.

Murphy, John. *Intermarket Financial Analysis*. New York: John Wiley & Sons, 1999.

Person, John L. *Forex Conquered*. Hoboken, NJ: John Wiley & Sons, 2007.

Reuters Limited. *An Introduction to Foreign Exchange and Money Markets*. Reuters Financial Training, 1999.

Shamah, Shani. *A Foreign Exchange Primer*. Hoboken, NJ: John Wiley & Sons, 2003.

There are hundreds (if not thousands) of books pertaining specifically to technical analysis. A few of the most well-known books are:

Aby, Carroll D. Jr., PhD. *Point and Figure Charting*. Traders Press, 1996.

Archer, Michael. *Getting Started in Forex Trading Strategies*. Hoboken, NJ: John Wiley & Sons, 2007.

Archer, Michael D. *The Goodman Codex*. B.R. Jostan & Company, 2009.

Archer, Michael D., and James Lauren Bickford. *The FOREX Chartist Companion*. Hoboken, NJ: John Wiley & Sons, 2006.

Aronson, David R. *Evidence-Based Technical Analysis.* Hoboken, NJ: John Wiley & Sons, 2007.

Bickford, Jim. *Chart Plotting Algorithms for Technical Analysts.* Syzygy, 2002.

Bulkowski, Thomas N. *Encyclopedia of Chart Patterns.* Hoboken, NJ: John Wiley & Sons, 2005.

Bulkowski, Thomas N. *Encyclopedia of Candlestick Charts.* John Hoboken, NJ: Wiley & Sons, 2008.

Dobson, Edward. *The Trading Rule That Can Make You Rich,* Traders Press, 1989.

DiNapoli, Joe. *Trading with DiNapoli Levels.* Coast Investment, 1998.

Edwards, Robert D., and John Magee. *Technical Analysis of Stock Trends.* St. Lucie Press, 2006.

Kaufman, Perry J. *New Trading Systems and Methods.* Hoboken, NJ: John Wiley & Sons, 2005.

Lindsay, Charles. *Trident.* Trident Systems Publications, 1976.

Magee, John. *Technical Analysis of Stock Trends.* American Management Association, 2001.

Murphy, John. *Technical Analysis of the Financial Markets.* Prentice Hall, 1999.

Nison, Steve. *Japanese Candlestick Charting Techniques.* Hall, 2001.

Du Plessis, Jeremy. *The Definitive Guide to Point and Figure.* Harriman House, 2005.

Ponsi, Ed. *Forex Patterns and Probabilities.* John Wiley & Sons, 2007.

Ross, Joe. *The Ross Hook,* Traders Press, 1985.

Wilder, J. Welles Jr. *New Concepts in Technical Trading Systems.* Trend Research, 1978.

A fine resource for finding more titles is www.traderspress.com.

Web Sites

I encourage the trader to visit the following web sites as a brief cyber tour of currency trading. These sites are provided for research purposes. The amount of information on currency trading now on the Internet is enormous: A Google search finds more than 2.7 million entries for "forex." Inclusion here *does not* represent an endorsement of any kind. Suggested key words: "forex" "FX" and "currency trading."

Online FOREX Tour

www.global-view.com

www.goforex.net

www.fxstreet.com

www.forexfactory.com

www.goodmanworks.com

www.babypips.com

www.investopedia.com

www.forexpeacearmy.com

www.ninjatrader.com

www.dynexcorp.com

www.tradeviewforex.com

www.pfgbest.com

www.oanda.com

www.dukascopy.com

www.hawaiiforex.com

FX Calculation Scenarios

Calculating Profit and Loss

Scenario 1

USD Is the Quote Currency (Profit)
Currency pair. Select the corresponding currency pair from the dropdown list. The default is the EUR/USD pair.

Position. Choose either "buy" or "sell." The default is "buy."

Number of units. This is the individual number of units and *not* the number of lots or mini-lots. A full lot should be entered as "100000" and a mini-lot as "10000."

Entry price. This is the entry price regardless if the trade was a market order or a limit order. Include the decimal point.

Exit price. This is the liquidation price regardless if the trade was manually exited or a limit order was triggered.

Conversion rate. This entry is necessary to convert any profit or loss to U.S. Dollars (USD) if the quote currency (the second one in the pair) is not USD. In this example, USD is the quote currency. Enter the single digit "1" since we already have conversion parity. Other possibilities are explained later.

Click the "Calculate" button as shown in Figure G.1.

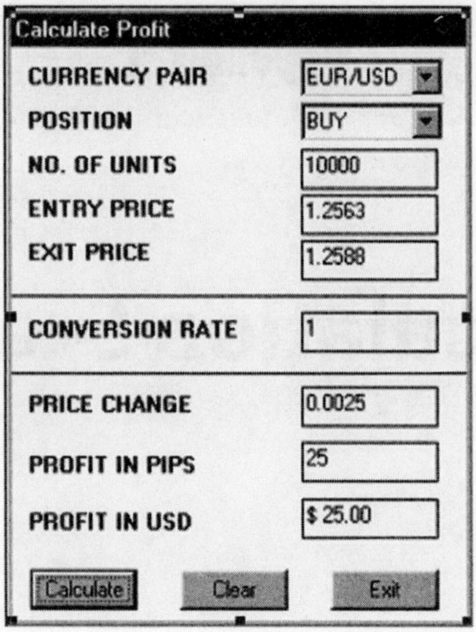

FIGURE G.1 A 25-Pip Profit in EUR/USD

In this example we bought a mini-lot (10,000 units) of the EUR/USD pair at 1.2563 and sold at 1.2588, netting a clear profit of 25 pips (price change times pip factor, or 0.0025 × 10,000). The price change is simply:

$$\text{Price Change} = \text{Exit Price} - \text{Entry Price}$$

The pip factor is the number of pips in the monetary unit of quote currency. There are 10,000 pips in one U.S. Dollar and, conversely, a single pip equals $0.0001. The pip factor is therefore 10,000.

$$\text{Profit in Pips} = \text{Price Change} \times \text{Pip Factor}$$

When the quote currency is the USD, profit or loss is calculated simply as:

$$\text{Profit in USD} = \text{Price Change} \times \text{Units Traded}$$

In our scenario, this equates to:

$$\$25.00 = 0.0025 \times 10{,}000$$

Many of you have just exclaimed, "Wow! That was painlessly simple. Show me one more!"

Scenario 2

USD Is the Quote Currency (Loss)   For those of you who exclaimed nothing or are staring blankly at this page, we will do it again, this time with the GBP/USD currency pair. See Figure G.2.

In this instance, we initiated a 30,000-unit short (sell) trade in the GBP/USD pair at 1.8863 and, sadly, it advanced against our hopes. We exited at 1.8883, losing 20 pips. Since the quote currency (the second currency) is USD, we know the conversion rate is 1. Thus using the profit formula

$$\text{Profit in USD} = \text{Price Change} \times \text{Units Traded}$$

we find that our profit is actually a loss:

$$-\$60.00 = -0.0020 \times 30,000$$

If the above calculations are still causing some confusion, I recommend that you take a break, then reread Chapter 5, "The FOREX Lexicon." As promised before, these calculations only require the four simple arithmetic functions: addition, subtraction, multiplication, and division. No exponents, logs, or trig functions. But this information must be completely clear before proceeding. Keep in mind that it is your money at stake.

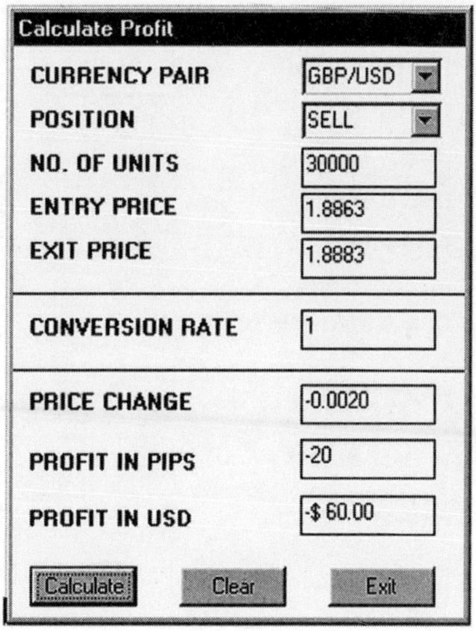

Calculate Profit	
CURRENCY PAIR	GBP/USD ▼
POSITION	SELL ▼
NO. OF UNITS	30000
ENTRY PRICE	1.8863
EXIT PRICE	1.8883
CONVERSION RATE	1
PRICE CHANGE	-0.0020
PROFIT IN PIPS	-20
PROFIT IN USD	-$ 60.00
[Calculate] [Clear] [Exit]	

FIGURE G.2   A 20-Pip Loss in GBP/USD

Scenario 3

USD Is the Base Currency (Profit)   If the quote (second) currency is not the U.S. Dollar, then profit or loss must be converted to U.S. Dollars. For example, a 35-pip profit in the USD/JPY pair means that the 35 pips are expressed in Japanese Yen (see Figure G.3). Therefore, one extra step is required to convert Yen to Dollars:

Conversion Rate. If USD is the base currency of the currency pair being calculated, then divide the profit or loss by the exit price. This simply converts the pip profit expressed as Yen to a profit expressed as U.S. Dollars.

Thus, when calculating currency pairs where the base (first) currency is the U.S. Dollar, the profit formula must be adjusted as follows:

$$\text{Profit in USD} = \text{Price Change} \times \text{Units Traded/Exit Price}$$

or, specifically:

$$\$33.09 = 0.35 \times 10,000/105.77$$

Obviously, all U.S. brokers perform this simple conversion to U.S. Dollars before adding profits to your margin account.

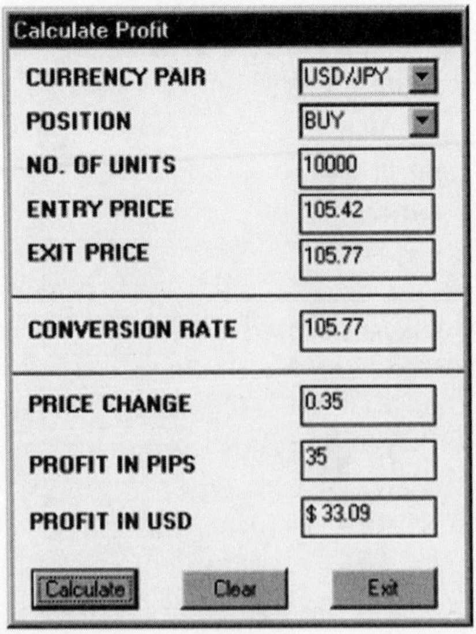

Calculate Profit	
CURRENCY PAIR	USD/JPY
POSITION	BUY
NO. OF UNITS	10000
ENTRY PRICE	105.42
EXIT PRICE	105.77
CONVERSION RATE	105.77
PRICE CHANGE	0.35
PROFIT IN PIPS	35
PROFIT IN USD	$ 33.09
Calculate Clear Exit	

FIGURE G.3   A 35-Pip Profit in USD/JPY

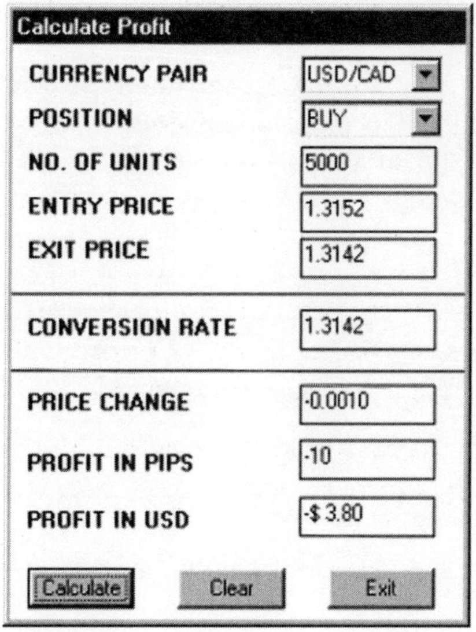

FIGURE G.4   A 10-Pip Loss in USD/CAD

USD Is the Base Currency (Loss)   This example is arithmetically identical to the previous example, except that a small loss is incurred. We purchased 5,000 units of the USD/CAD pair at 1.3152 and set a stop-loss limit order at 1.3142, which, unfortunately, was triggered (see Figure G.4).

Using the same adjusted profit formula as in the previous example,

$$\text{Profit in USD} = \text{Price Change} \times \text{Units Traded/Exit Price}$$

we find:

$$-\$3.80 = -0.0010 \times 5000/1.3142$$

Note: Always keep your losses small.

Non-USD Cross Rates (USD/Quote)   Most experienced traders can mentally perform the arithmetic in the above examples. It just takes practice. However, we must now tackle cross rates, currency pairs where neither currency is the U.S. Dollar. Obviously the profit in pips will be initially expressed in terms of the quote (second) currency of the *cross-rate* pair. The solution is simple: Look up the current price of the currency pair containing USD and the quote *currency* of the cross-rate pair, as shown in Figure G.5.

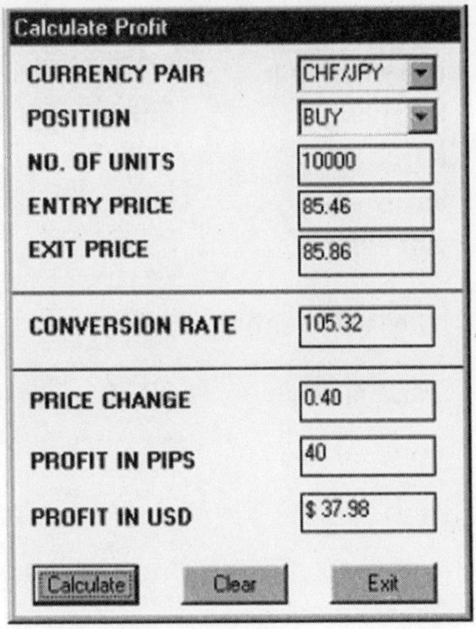

FIGURE G.5   A 40-Pip Profit in CHF/JPY

The Conversion Rate entry of 105.32 in Figure G.5 is actually the current price of the USD/JPY pair. The adjusted profit formula for this cross-rate trade is:

Profit in USD = Price Change × Units Traded/Conversion Rate

or

$$\$37.98 = 0.40 \times 10,000/105.32$$

A pattern is developing here . . .

Non-USD Cross Rates (Base/USD)   In the previous example, the USD was the base currency in the conversion pair (USD/JPY). In Figure G.6 USD is the quote currency of the conversion pair (GBP/USD).

The Conversion Rate entry in Figure G.6 is the current price of the GBP/USD pair. The reversal of the role of the U.S. Dollar in the conversion pair (GBP/USD) requires another change in the profit formula:

Profit in USD = Price Change × Units Traded × Rate

or

$$\$19.05 = 0.0018 \times 20,000 \times .8902$$

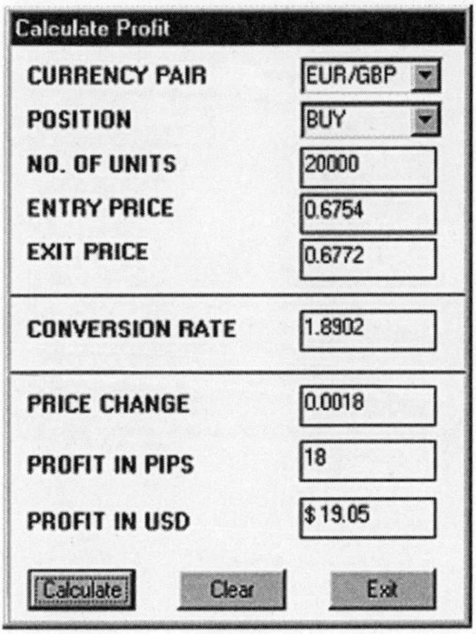

FIGURE G.6 An 18-Pip Profit in EUR/GBP

Remember that when USD is the quote currency of the conversion pair, you must multiply the rate. If USD is the base currency of the conversion pair, then divide the rate. Give yourself an A+ if you understood the previous examples on the first reading. You are destined for great things.

You may have noticed that there was no mention of transaction costs in the six scenarios given. The broker always subtracts the transaction cost at the moment the trade is initiated; therefore, transaction costs do not affect the above calculations.

Calculating Units Available

Before initiating a new trade, it is always advantageous to know the maximum number of units that you can safely trade without risking a margin call based on your current account balance. Most trading platforms provide an online utility that calculates this information, usually resembling what is shown in Figure G.7.

Enter the following data fields to calculate the maximum number of units to buy or sell:

- *Margin available.* This is the amount in your margin account you want to earmark for the current trade.

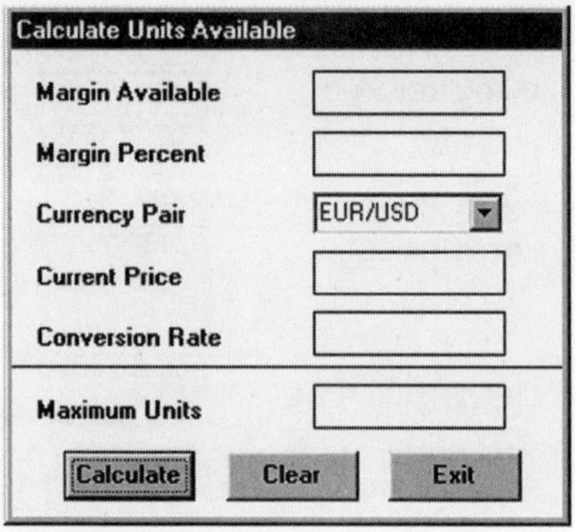

FIGURE G.7 Units Available Calculator

- *Margin percent.* This is your broker's margin percentage for leveraging trades.
- *Currency pair.* Select the corresponding currency pair. In this example, select EUR/USD.
- *Current price.* Enter the current ask price in the currency pair.
- *Conversion rate.* If the quote currency in the selected currency pair is USD, then enter "1."

Click "Calculate." (See Figure G.8.)

You can safely trade 15,000 units of EUR/USD in this example. In the next example (Figure G.9), we calculate the units available for a currency pair in

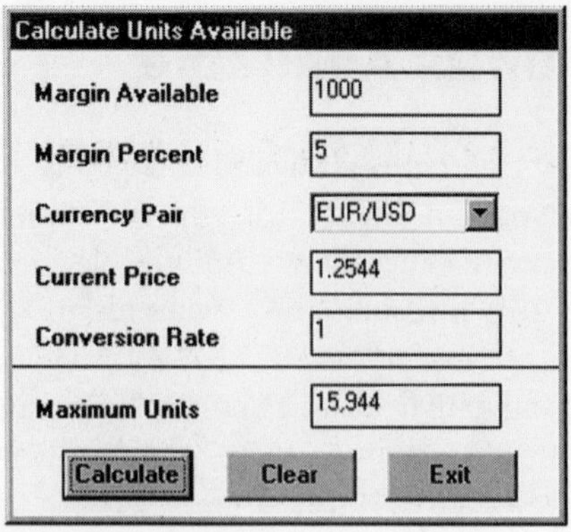

FIGURE G.8 15,944 Units Available

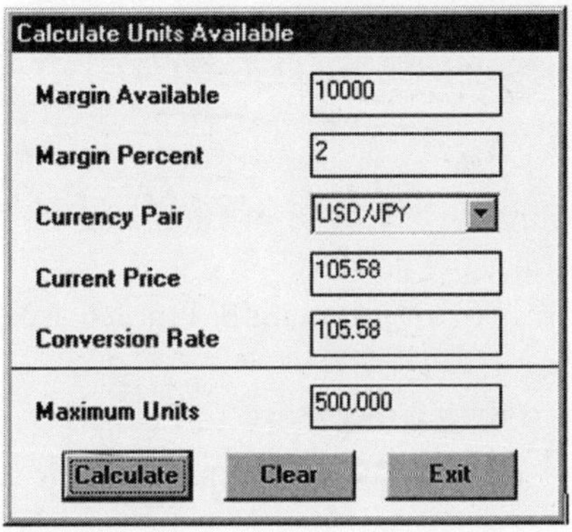

FIGURE G.9 500,000 Units Available

which the base currency is USD. Enter the first four fields as in the previous example. Since USD is the base currency in the USD/JPY pair, we must enter the current price as the conversion rate.

The formula to calculate the maximum units that can be traded is:

$$\text{Unit Available} = 100 \times \text{Margin Available} \times \text{Rate}/(\text{Current Price} \times \text{Margin Percent})$$

If USD is the base currency, then this reduces to:

$$\text{Units Available} = 100 \times \text{Margin Available}/\text{Margin Percent}$$

Cross rates can be handled in the same fashion by simply manipulating the conversion rate. Note: Always decrease the units available slightly to avoid a margin call. I recommend 10 percent.

Calculating Margin Requirements

Before executing any trade, you should always have a rough idea of how much of your account balance will be used as the margin requirement. Any trade whose margin requirement exceeds your existing account balance will not be executed. Trades whose margin requirements deplete nearly all the equity in your account are risky and may incur the dreaded margin call. The formula to calculate the margin requirement for a trade is simple:

$$\text{Margin Requirement} = \text{Current Price Units Traded Margin Percent}/100$$

Assume that your broker mandates a 5 percent margin percentage. You want to buy a full lot (100,000 units) of the EUR/USD currency pair, which is trading at 1.2538. Thus:

$$\$6,269.00 = 1.2538 \times 100,000 \times 5/100$$

This trade requires $6,269 for margin. Proceed accordingly.

Calculating Transaction Cost

Your broker will always calculate the transaction cost because that cost is automatically subtracted from your account balance the instant you initiate a new trade. Nonetheless, it is useful to know just how the broker computes this debit. See Figure G.10.

Remember that the ask price is used when the trader initiates a new buy (long) trade and the bid price is used when the trader initiates a new sell (short) trade. When the USD is the quote currency in the currency pair, the conversion rate equals 1, as seen in Figure G.11.

The basic formulas for the transaction cost in this instance are:

$$Spread \qquad\qquad = Ask\ Price - Bid\ Price$$

$$Transaction\ Cost = Spread \times Units\ Traded$$

$$\$3.00 \qquad\qquad = (1.2569 - 1.2569) \times 10,000$$

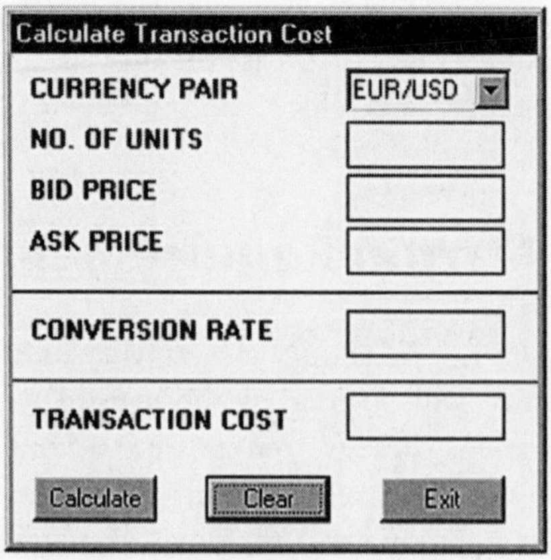

FIGURE G.10 Calculate Transaction Cost

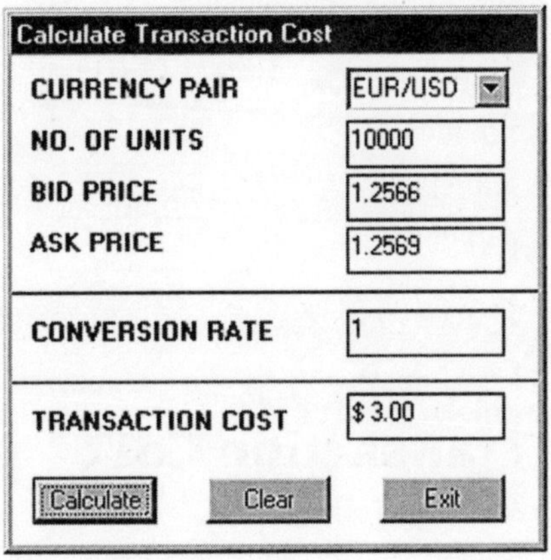

FIGURE G.11 A 3-Pip Spread in EUR/USD

Figure G.12 shows an example in which we calculate the transaction cost when the base currency is USD.

In this case, the formula becomes:

$$\text{Spread} = \text{Ask Price} - \text{Bid Price}$$

$$\text{Transaction Cost} = \text{Spread} \times \text{Units Traded/Ask Price}$$

$$\$3.24 = (1.2359 - 1.2355) \times 10{,}000/1.2359$$

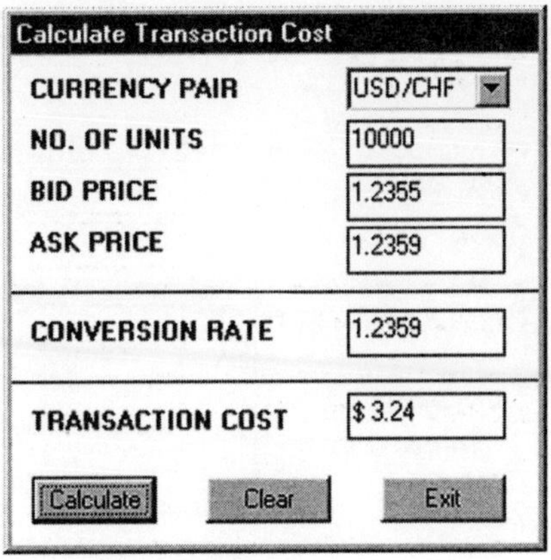

FIGURE G.12 A 4-Pip Spread in USD/CHF

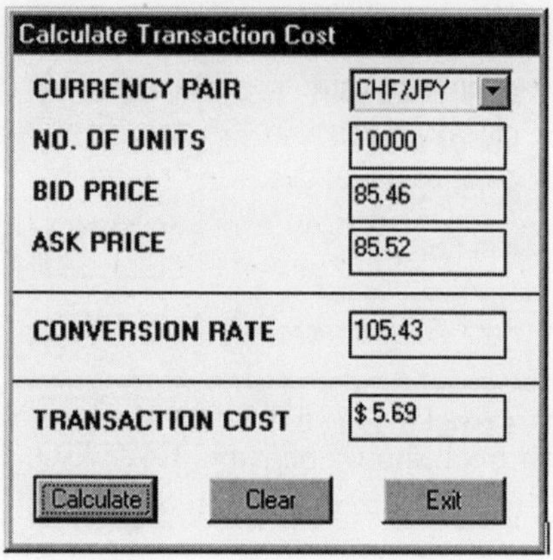

FIGURE G.13 A 6-Pip Spread in CHF/JPY

In our final example, we calculate the transaction cost in U.S. Dollars for a non-USD cross rate. We need to look up the current price of the currency pair containing USD and the quote currency of the cross rate pair (see Figure G.13).

In this case of non-USD cross rates, the formula becomes:

Transaction Cost = Spread × Units Traded/Conversion Rate

or

$$\$5.69 = (85.52 - 85.46) \times 10,000/105.43$$

Calculating Account Summary Balance

The Account Summary section of your broker's trading platform should look similar to what is shown in Figure G.14.

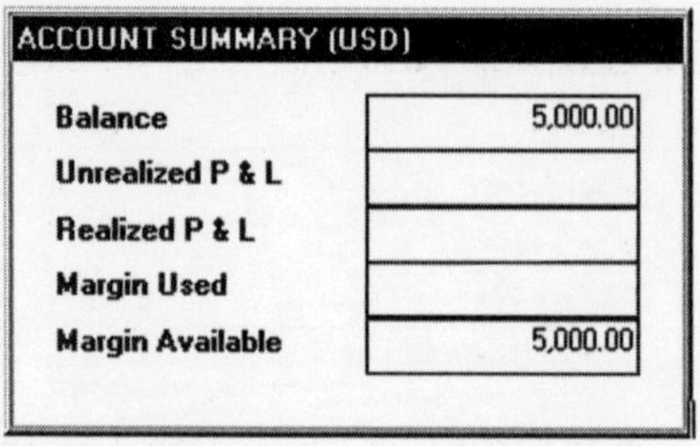

FIGURE G.14 Account Summary before First Trade

Let us say that your new broker offers 20:1 leverage, which means that you must "risk" 5 percent of the total value of any trade that you execute, long or short. Assume that you have analyzed, both technically and fundamentally, several major currency pairs and feel that the USD/JPY pair is overpriced and it will decline in the immediate future. You now execute a conservative entry order to sell 5,000 units of USD/JPY at a market price of 105.64. The transaction cost (the difference between the bid and the ask price) is three pips for the USD/JPY pair.

In Figure G.15 we see that the Balance and the Realized P&L entries are unchanged. Unrealized P&L show a negative 1.42 USD. This is the round-turn transaction cost, which is subtracted the moment a new trade is executed. Each pip in the USD/JPY trade is worth 0.4733 USD. Therefore:

$$1 \text{ pip } = 1/105.64 \times 50$$

$$1 \text{ pip } = 0.4733 \text{ USD}$$

$$3 \text{ pips } = 1.4199 \text{ USD}$$

The Margin Used entry shows 250.00 USD, calculated as follows:

$$\text{Margin Used} = \text{Total Cost of Trade} \times \text{Margin Percentage}$$

$$250.00 = 5,000.00 \times 5\%$$

The Margin Available entry has also changed:

$$\text{Margin Available} = \text{Balance} - \text{Margin Used}$$

$$4,750.00 = 5,000.00 - 250.00$$

After 10 minutes or so, we notice that your "feeling"—that the USD/JPY pair was oversold and would decline—has paid off. The USD/JPY has dropped

ACCOUNT SUMMARY (USD)	
Balance	5,000.00
Unrealized P & L	-1.42
Realized P & L	
Margin Used	250.00
Margin Available	4,750.00

FIGURE G.15 Account Summary after Market Entry

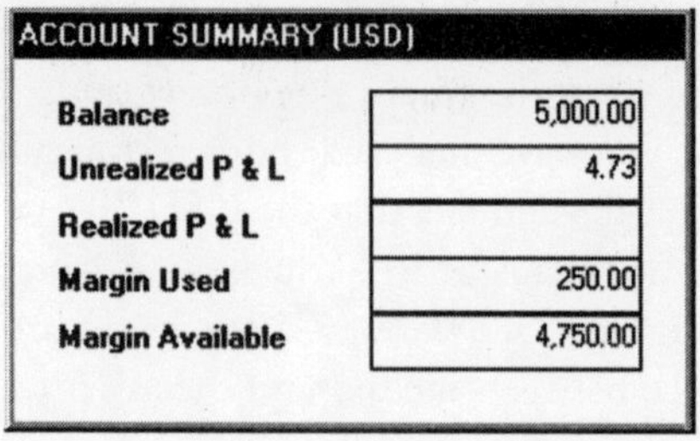

```
ACCOUNT SUMMARY (USD)

Balance                    5,000.00
Unrealized P & L                4.73
Realized P & L
Margin Used                  250.00
Margin Available           4,750.00
```

FIGURE G.16   A 10-Pip Profit

to 105.51. Not only have you recouped the transaction cost (minus three pips), but you gained a plus 10 pips in profit, as shown in Figure G.16.

At this point, market activity slows down and the price direction starts moving laterally. You decide that a plus 10 pips on your first trade is satisfactory and you close the trade. Essentially, this means purchasing 5,000 units of USD/JPY to offset your previous sale. Once your trade liquidation is logged at the broker's firm, your new Account Summary should resemble what is shown in Figure G.17.

The example, of course, is merely an illustration. Your first trade may be greater or smaller than the example.

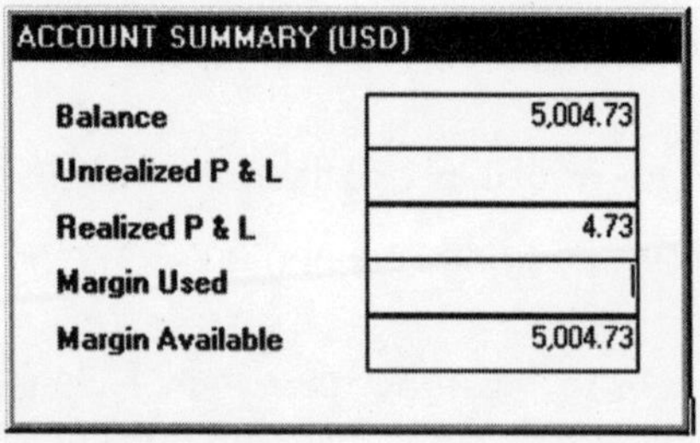

```
ACCOUNT SUMMARY (USD)

Balance                    5,004.73
Unrealized P & L
Realized P & L                  4.73
Margin Used
Margin Available           5,004.73
```

FIGURE G.17   After Liquidating First Trade

Glossary

algorithmic trading Trading by means of an automated computer program. Sometimes called Program Trading.

Application Program Interface (API) Computer code or routines for integrating trading programs to a broker-dealer's trading platform, most commonly used to allow a proprietary trading program to read and process a broker-dealer's data feed.

appreciation A currency is said to "appreciate" when it strengthens in price in response to market demand.

arbitrage The purchase or sale of an instrument and simultaneous taking of an equal and opposite position in a related market in order to take advantage of small price differentials between markets.

ask price The price at which the market is prepared to sell a specific currency in a foreign exchange contract or cross-currency contract. At this price, the trader can buy the base currency. It is shown on the right side of the quotation. For example, in the quote USD/CHF 1.4527/32, the ask price is 1.4532, meaning you can buy one U.S. Dollar for 1.4532 Swiss Francs.

at best An instruction given to a dealer to buy or sell at the best rate that can be obtained.

at or better An order to deal at a specific rate or better.

balance of trade The value of a country's exports minus its imports.

ballooning pip spreads The practice by market makers of increasing pip spreads during fast or illiquid markets. Spreads often balloon just before a news announcement or economic indicator is released.

bar chart A type of chart that consists of four significant points: the high and the low prices, which form the vertical bar; the opening price, which is marked with a little horizontal line to the left of the bar; and the closing price, which is marked with a little horizontal line to the right of the bar.

base currency The first currency in a currency pair. It shows how much the base currency is worth as measured against the second currency. For example, if the USD/CHF rate equals 1.6215 then one USD is worth CHF 1.6215. In the foreign exchange markets, the U.S. Dollar is normally considered the "base" currency for quotes, meaning that quotes are expressed as a unit of one USD per the other currency quoted in the pair. The primary exceptions to this rule are the British Pound, the Euro, and the Australian Dollar.

bear market   A market distinguished by declining prices.

bid price   The bid is the price at which the market is prepared to buy a specific currency in a foreign exchange contract or cross-currency contract. At this price, the trader can sell the base currency. It is shown on the left side of the quotation. For example, in the quote USD/CHF 1.4527/32, the bid price is 1.4527, meaning you can sell one U.S. Dollar for 1.4527 Swiss Francs.

bid-ask spread   The difference between the bid and offer price.

big figure quote   Dealer expression referring to the first few digits of an exchange rate. These digits are often omitted in dealer quotes. For example, a USD/JPY rate might be 117.30/117.35, but would be quoted verbally without the first three digits, that is, "30/35."

BLS   Bureau of Labor Statistics.

book   In a professional trading environment, a book is the summary of a trader's or desk's total positions.

box chart   A hybrid chart that boxes swings into bars using a specified boxing algorithm.

Bretton Woods Agreement of 1944   An agreement that established fixed foreign exchange rates for major currencies, provided for central bank intervention in the currency markets, and pegged the price of gold at US$35 per ounce. The agreement lasted until 1971, when President Nixon overturned the Bretton Woods agreement and established a floating exchange rate for the major currencies.

broker   An individual or firm that acts as an intermediary, putting together buyers and sellers for a fee or commission. In contrast, a dealer commits capital and takes one side of a position, hoping to earn a spread (profit) by closing out the position in a subsequent trade with another party.

bull market   A market distinguished by rising prices.

Bundesbank   Germany's central bank.

buyer   In options, the purchaser side of a put or call contract. (See writer.)

cable   Trader jargon referring to the Sterling/U.S. Dollar exchange rate. So called because the rate was originally transmitted via a transatlantic cable beginning in the mid-1800s.

call   An option to purchase a currency.

cambist   An expert trader who rapidly buys and sells currency throughout the day.

candlestick chart   A chart that indicates the trading range for the day as well as the opening and closing price. If the open price is higher than the close price, the rectangle between the open and close price is shaded. If the close price is higher than the open price, that area of the chart is not shaded.

cash market   The market in the actual financial instrument on which a futures or options contract is based.

central bank   A government or quasi-governmental organization that manages a country's monetary policy. For example, the U.S. central bank is the Federal Reserve, and the German central bank is the Bundesbank.

centralized market   Any market where all orders are routed to one central exchange. FOREX is not a centralized market.

CFTC   Commodity Futures Trading Commission.

chartist   An individual who uses charts and graphs and interprets historical data to find trends and predict future movements. Also referred to as a technical trader.

cleared funds   Funds that are freely available, sent in to settle a trade.

clearing   The process of settling a trade.

closed position   Exposures in foreign currencies that no longer exist. The process to close a position is to sell or buy a certain amount of currency to offset an equal amount of the open position. This will "square" the position.

CME   Chicago Mercantile Exchange, now CME Group.

collateral   Something given to secure a loan or as a guarantee of performance.

commission   A transaction fee charged by a broker.

confirmation   A document exchanged by counterparts to a transaction that states the terms of said transaction.

Consumer Price Index (CPI)   A weighted average of prices of a basket of consumer goods and services, such as food, medical, and transportation. The CPI is calculated by taking price changes for each item in a specified basket of goods and averaging them according to their estimated importance.

contagion   The tendency of an economic crisis to spread from one market to another. In 1997, political instability in Indonesia caused high volatility in their domestic currency, the Rupiah. From there, the contagion spread to other Asian emerging currencies, and then to Latin America, and is now referred to as the "Asian Contagion."

contract   The standard unit of trading in futures and options.

counter-currency   The second listed currency in a currency pair. See also *quote currency*.

counterparty   One of the participants in a financial transaction.

country risk   Risk associated with a cross-border transaction, including but not limited to legal and political conditions.

cross-currency pair   A foreign exchange transaction in which one foreign currency is traded against a second foreign currency. For example, EUR/GBP.

cross rate   Same as *cross-currency pair*.

currency   Any form of money issued by a government or central bank and used as legal tender and a basis for trade.

currency pair   The two currencies that make up a foreign exchange rate. For example, EUR/USD.

currency risk   The probability of an adverse change in exchange rates.

day trader   Historically a speculator who takes positions in currencies that are then liquidated prior to the close of the same trading session or day. In futures a day trader is considered a short-term trader. In FX a day trader—who holds positions across multiple trading sessions—is considered a long-term trader.

dealer   An individual or firm that acts as a principal or counterparty to a transaction. Principals take one side of a position, hoping to earn a spread (profit) by closing out the position in a subsequent trade with another party. In contrast, a broker is an individual or firm that acts as an intermediary, putting together buyers and sellers for a fee or commission.

deficit   A negative balance of trade or payments.

delivery   A FOREX trade where both sides make and take actual delivery of the currencies traded.

depreciation   A fall in the value of a currency due to market forces.

derivative   A contract that changes in value in relation to the price movements of a related or underlying security, future, or other physical instrument. An option is the most common derivative instrument.

devaluation   The deliberate downward adjustment of a currency's price, normally by official announcement.

directional movement (DM)   In technical analysis the net price change from one specified time unit to another specified time unit.

downtick   A new price quote at a price lower than the preceding quote.

econometric analysis   Using mathematical formulas or models to make trading decisions with fundamental information and data.

economic indicator   A government-issued statistic that indicates current economic growth and stability. Common indicators include employment rates, Gross Domestic Product (GDP), inflation, retail sales, and so forth.

ECU   European Currency Unit; see *European Monetary Union (EMU)*.

Electronic Communications Network (ECN)   A system in which orders to buy and sell are matched through a network of banks and/or dealers. See *market maker*, the other widely used method of order execution, and *NDD*, a hybrid.

Elliott Wave Theory   An old and well-respected technical analysis method based on a wave composed of five (1-2-3-4-5) swing—three in the primary direction (1,3,5) and two in the secondary direction (2,4).

emerging markets or currencies   Sometimes used to identify exotic currencies.

end of day order (EOD)   An order to buy or sell at a specified price. This order remains open until the end of the trading day, which is typically 5 P.M. EST.

Euro The currency of the European Monetary Union (EMU). A replacement for the European Currency Unit (ECU).

European Central Bank (ECB) The central bank for the new European Monetary Union.

European Monetary Union (EMU) The principal goal of the EMU is to establish a single European currency called the Euro, which officially replaced the national currencies of most member EU countries in 2002. On January 1, 1999, the transitional phase to introduce the Euro began. The Euro now exists as a banking currency, and paper financial transactions and foreign exchange are made in Euros. This transition period lasted for three years, at which time Euro notes and coins entered circulation. On July 1, 2002, only Euros became legal tender for EMU participants; the national currencies of the member countries ceased to exist. The original members of the EMU were Germany, France, Belgium, Luxembourg, Austria, Finland, Ireland, the Netherlands, Italy, Spain, and Portugal. As of February 2008, 27 countries belong to the EMU and 22 used the Euro (EUR) currency unit.

exotics A currency pair with the USD or EUR and a lesser traded currency such as the Thai Baht or the Chilean Peso. Considered riskier to trade than the majors or minors because of illiquidity and possible political unrest.

fast market A market is fast when it is hit with a large volume of orders over a short period of time. Markets are often fast after an unexpected news announcement.

FCM Futures Clearing Merchant.

Federal Deposit Insurance Corporation (FDIC) The regulatory agency responsible for administering bank depository insurance in the United States.

Federal Reserve (Fed) The central bank for the United States.

First In First Out (FIFO) Open positions are closed according to the FIFO accounting rule. All positions opened within a particular currency pair are liquidated in the order in which they were originally opened.

flat/square A trader on the sidelines with no position.

floating stop An automated *trailing stop*.

foreign exchange (FOREX, FX) The simultaneous buying of one currency and selling of another.

FOREX FOReign EXchange.

FOREX futures FOREX traded as a futures contract.

forward The prespecified exchange rate for a foreign exchange contract settling at some agreed future date, based on the interest rate differential between the two currencies involved.

forward points The pips added to or subtracted from the current exchange rate to calculate a forward price.

fundamental analysis Analysis of economic and political information with the objective of determining future movements in a financial market.

futures contract An obligation to exchange a good or instrument at a set price on a future date. The primary difference between a future and a forward is that futures are typically traded over an exchange (exchange-traded contracts—ETC), versus forwards, which are considered over the counter (OTC) contracts. An OTC is any contract *not* traded on an exchange.

futures FOREX Futures such as gold and silver traded as pairs by currency brokers. XAGUSD is silver and XAUUSD is gold.

FX Foreign Exchange.

G8 The eight leading industrial countries: the United States, Germany, Japan, France, United Kingdom, Canada, Italy, Russia.

going long The purchase of a stock, commodity, or currency for investment or speculation.

going short The selling of a currency or instrument not owned by the seller.

gold standard A monetary system where a country allows its monetary unit to be freely converted into fixed amounts of gold and vice versa.

Goodman Wave Theory A wave theory of prices, in the manner of Elliott Wave Theory. It differs in providing an integrated counting methodology and the fourth swing of a wave is connected to the entire previous 1-2-3 formation and not to just the third swing as in Elliott.

good till canceled order (GTC) An order to buy or sell at a specified price. This order remains open until filled or until the client cancels.

Gross domestic product (GDP) Total value of a country's output, income, or expenditure produced within the country's physical borders.

Gross national product (GNP) Gross domestic product plus income earned from investment or work abroad.

guerilla trader Similar to a *scalper* but trades in bursts of several small trades then recedes to the sidelines. Sometimes called a *sniper*. Discouraged by most retail brokers.

hedge A position or combination of positions that reduces the risk of a primary position.

high-frequency trading Trading frequently; scalping. A high-frequency trader uses tick data. See *ultra-high-frequency trading*. Almost always done with automated or algorithmic trading systems.

hit the bid Acceptance of purchasing at the offer or selling at the bid.

IB An *Introducing Broker*.

IMM International Monetary Market.

inflation An economic condition in which prices for consumer goods rise, eroding purchasing power.

initial margin The initial deposit of collateral required to enter into a position as a guarantee on future performance.

Interbank rates   The foreign exchange rates at which large international banks quote other large international banks.

intervention   Action by a central bank to affect the value of its currency by entering the market. Concerted intervention refers to action by a number of central banks to control exchange rates.

in the money   For a call option when the call price is above the strike price. For a put option when the put price is below the strike price.

Introducing Broker (IB)   Generally a small broker who relies on a larger broker-dealer to execute his trades and hold fiduciary responsibility for client funds.

King Kong syndrome   The emotional high that overtakes a trader when he or she does exceptionally well for a period of time, such as making a dozen consecutive winning trades. Usually followed by a large losing trade and a reality check.

Kiwi   Slang for the New Zealand Dollar.

leading indicators   Statistics that are considered to predict future economic activity.

leverage Also called margin. The ratio of the amount used in a transaction to the required security deposit.

LIBOR   The London Inter-Bank Offered Rate. Banks use LIBOR when borrowing from another bank.

limit order   An order with restrictions on the maximum price to be paid or the minimum price to be received. As an example, if the current price of USD/YEN is 117.00/05, then a limit order to buy USD would be at a price below 102 (that is, 116.50).

liquidation   The closing of an existing position through the execution of an offsetting transaction.

liquidity   The ability of a market to accept large transactions with minimal to no impact on price stability; also the ability to enter and exit a market quickly. See *thin*.

liquidity provider   Typically banks that feed bids and asks to broker-dealers. Sometimes ECNs act as liquidity providers for smaller brokerage firms.

long position A position that appreciates in value if market prices increase. When the base currency in the pair is bought, the position is said to be long.

Loonie   Slang for the Canadian Dollar.

lot   A unit to measure the amount of the deal. The value of the deal always corresponds to an integer number of lots.

major currency   Any of the following: Euro, Pound Sterling, Australian Dollar, New Zealand Dollar, U.S. Dollar, Canadian Dollar, Swiss Franc, Japanese Yen. See also *minor currency*.

managed account   Having a third party such as a professional money manager make trading decisions for you. Also called a discretionary account.

margin   The required equity that an investor must deposit to collateralize a position.

margin call   A request from a broker or dealer for additional funds or other collateral to guarantee performance on a position that has moved against the customer.

market environments   A method for quantifying "trading" and "trending" markets using paired sets of directional movement (net price change over time) and volatility (aggregate price change over time).

market maker   A dealer who regularly quotes both bid and ask prices and is ready to make a two-sided market for any financial instrument. Most retail FOREX dealers are market makers. A market maker is said to have a dealing desk.

market risk   Exposure to changes in market prices.

market-to-market   Process of reevaluating all open positions with the current market prices. These new values then determine margin requirements.

maturity   The date for settlement or expiry of a financial instrument.

mercury chart   A modified bar chart used in commodity futures. Each bar shows the price range for a time unit and changes in open interest and volume from the previous time unit.

minor currency   Any of the currencies between a major currency and an exotic, such as the Swedish Krona or Danish Krone.

money management   The techniques a trader utilizes to manage his money both in the aggregate and for specific trades.

money supply   The aggregate quantity of coins, bills, loans, credit, and any other liquid monetary instruments or equivalents within a given country's economy.

Mundo   A synthetic global currency calculated as the average of multiple ISO currency pairs. See Michael Archer and James Bickford, *Forex Chartist Companion* (John Wiley & Sons, 2006). The Mundo is useful for creating indices for studying relative strength and correlation between currencies and pairs.

NDD   A no dealing desk broker. Provides a platform where liquidity providers such as banks can offer prices to the NDD platform. Incoming orders are routed to the best available bid or offer. See also *market maker* and *ECN*. Similar to *straight-through processing*.

net position   The amount of currency bought or sold that has not yet been offset by opposite transactions.

news trading   The practice of attempting to profit from the price spikes sometimes caused by the release of news reports impacting a currency. Discouraged by most retail brokers.

NFA   National Futures Association.

NFA Rule 2-43   A set of compliance rules regulating retail FOREX in the United States.

offer   The rate at which a dealer is willing to sell a currency. See *ask price*.

offsetting transaction   A trade that serves to cancel or offset some or all of the market risk of an open position.

one cancels the other order (OCO)   A designation for two orders where when one part of the two orders is executed the other is automatically canceled.

open order   An order that will be executed when a market moves to its designated price. Normally associated with *good till canceled orders.*

open position   An active trade with corresponding unrealized P&L, which has not been offset by an equal and opposite deal.

option   A FOREX option is the right to purchase or sell a currency at a specified price for a specified time period. In futures it refers to any of the months in which a contract goes into cash settlement and expires.

order   An instruction to execute a trade at a specified rate.

over the counter (OTC)   Used to describe any transaction that is not conducted over an exchange.

overnight position   A trade that remains open until the next business day.

P&L   Profit and Loss; often used in reference to an account statement.

pips   The smallest unit of price for any foreign currency. Digits added to or subtracted from the fourth decimal place, that is, 0.001, for example.

point   100 pips.

point and figure charts   Similar to swing charts but use Xs to denote upward moving prices and Os to denote downward moving prices.

political risk   Exposure to changes in governmental policy that will have an adverse effect on an investor's position.

position   The netted total holdings of a given currency.

position trader   A trader who holds positions over days or weeks. Rare in the FOREX markets.

premium   In the currency markets, describes the amount by which the forward or futures price exceeds the spot price. In options, the cost of the put or call.

price transparency   Describes quotes to which every market participant has equal access.

profit/loss or p/l or gain/loss   The actual realized gain or loss resulting from trading activities on closed positions, plus the theoretical "unrealized" gain or loss on open positions that have been market-to-market.

programmed trading   See *algorithmic trading.*

Pugh chart   Swing charts categorized into four types: bear, bull, inside, and outside.

put   An option to sell a currency.

pyramiding   Adding to a position as the market moves up or down. Pyramiding a winning position is risky; pyramiding a losing position is suicide.

quant   Refers to the use of a mathematical or quantified method of trading, risk, or portfolio analysis.

quiet time   The period while the Asian sessions open, 3 P.M. to 4 P.M. Eastern.

quote   An indicative market price, normally used for information purposes only.

quote currency   The second currency quoted in a FOREX currency pair. In a direct quote, the quote currency is the foreign currency itself. In an indirect quote, the quote currency is the domestic currency. See also *base currency* and *counter-currency*.

rally   A recovery in price after a period of decline.

range   The difference between the highest and lowest price of a future recorded during a given trading session.

rate   The price of one currency in terms of another, typically used for dealing purposes.

reality check   A sudden, often unexplained, violent price move in a market. It generally occurs after a pair has been exceptionally orderly and predictable for a period of time.

requoting   The practice of a broker-dealer filling an order at a price not seen on their public price feed. Like *ballooning spreads* and harvesting *stops*, most typically associated with *market makers* and frowned on by traders.

resistance levels   A term used in technical analysis indicating a specific price level at which analysis concludes that people will sell.

revaluation   An increase in the exchange rate for a currency as a result of central bank intervention. Opposite of *devaluation*.

risk   Exposure to uncertain change, most often used with a negative connotation of adverse change.

risk management   The employment of financial analysis and trading techniques to reduce and control exposure to various types of risk.

rollover   Process where the settlement of a deal is rolled forward to another value date. The cost of this process is based on the interest rate differential of the two currencies.

round-trip   Buying and selling of a specified amount of currency.

running stops   The practice of market makers entering orders for the purpose of hitting customer stop-loss orders. Also called harvesting stops. Like *ballooning*, considered a negative practice by traders.

scalper   Someone who trades often. Trades are typically measured in minutes but sometimes seconds.

SEC   Securities and Exchange Commission.

settlement   The process by which a trade is entered into the books and records of the counterparties to a transaction. The settlement of currency trades may or may not involve the actual physical exchange of one currency for another.

shockwave   The mathematical description of price patterns during and after a news release.

short position   An investment position that benefits from a decline in market price. When the base currency in the pair is sold, the position is said to be short.

slippage   The difference in pips between the order price approved by the client and the price at which the order is actually executed.

spot price   The current market price. Settlement of spot transactions usually occurs within two business days.

spread   The difference between the bid and offer prices.

Sterling   Slang for British Pound.

stop harvesting   A practice purported to be practiced by market makers in which prices are artificially raised or lowered to execute client stop-loss orders placed in the market. See *running stops*.

stop-loss order   Order type where an open position is automatically liquidated at a specific price. Often used to minimize exposure to losses if the market moves against an investor's position. As an example, if an investor is long USD at 156.27, he might wish to put in a stop-loss order for 155.49, which would limit losses should the dollar depreciate, possibly below 155.49. Sometimes abbreviated as S/L.

straight-through processing   Orders are not stopped or massaged at a dealing desk but are sent straight through from liquidity providers to buyers and sellers.

strike price   In option trading the price at which a put or call may be exercised.

support levels   A technique used in technical analysis that indicates a specific price ceiling and floor at which a given exchange rate will automatically correct itself. Opposite of resistance.

swap   A currency swap is the simultaneous sale and purchase of the same amount of a given currency at a forward exchange rate.

swing chart   A form of charting connecting prices filtered by a minimum increment. Similar to point and figure charts. Pugh swing charts use vertical lines connected by short horizontal lines. Line swing charts use angular lines connecting price to price. Swing charts are said to be price-functional; the time frame is not a parameter.

Swissy   Market slang for Swiss Franc.

take-profit order   An order that liquidates a trade at a profit. Sometimes abbreviated as T/P.

technical analysis   An effort to forecast prices by analyzing market data, that is, historical price trends and averages, volumes, open interest, and so forth.

thin   A thin market is the opposite of a liquid market. You cannot enter or exit a market without adversely affecting the price, pushing it up with a buy order and down with a sell order.

tick   A minimum change in time required for the price to change, up or down.

trading market   A market that is moving more sideways than up or down.

trading session   Most commonly means one of the three eight-hour sessions for trading FOREX over a 24-hour period: Asian, European, and North American. Technically there are five sessions between Sunday evening and Friday evening: The New York exchange trades from 7:30 A.M. to 5 P.M. EST. The Sydney, Auckland, and Wellington exchanges trade from 3 P.M. to 11 P.M. EST. The Tokyo Exchange trades from 6 P.M. to 11 P.M., stopping for an hour-long lunch break then trading again until 4 A.M. EST. The Hong Kong and Singapore exchanges trade from 7 P.M. to 3 A.M. EST. The last exchanges trading are the Munich, Zurich, Paris, Frankfurt, Brussels, Amsterdam, and London exchanges. These all trade from 2:30 A.M. to 11:30 A.M. EST.

trailing stop   The practice of moving a stop-loss in the direction of the market's movement. Used primarily to protect profits. See also *floating stop*.

transaction cost   The cost of buying or selling a financial instrument.

transaction date   The date on which a trade occurs.

trending market   A market that is moving predominantly up or down as opposed to sideways (trading market).

turnover   The total money value of all executed transactions in a given time period; volume.

two-way price   When both a bid and offer rate is quoted for a FOREX transaction.

ultra-high-frequency trading   Trading extremely frequently. Typically used by hedge funds to catch anomalies in the data feed or predicting how other large algorithmic-based traders will act. Always done with automated or algorithmic trading systems.

unrealized gain/loss   The theoretical gain or loss on open positions valued at current market rates, as determined by the broker at its sole discretion. Unrealized gains/losses become profits/losses when the position is closed.

uptick   A new price quote at a price higher than the preceding quote.

uptick rule   In the United States, a regulation where a security may not be sold short unless the last trade prior to the short sale was at a price lower than the price at which the short sale is executed.

U.S. prime rate   The interest rate at which U.S. banks will lend to their prime corporate customers.

value date   The date on which counterparts to a financial transaction agree to settle their respective obligations, that is, exchanging payments. For spot currency transactions, the value date is normally two business days forward. Also known as maturity date.

vanilla   A normal option with no unusual or special conditions.

variation margin   Funds a broker must request from the client to have the required margin deposited. The term usually refers to additional funds that must be deposited as a result of unfavorable price movements.

volatility (V)   A statistical measure of a market's price movements over time characterized by deviations from a predetermined central value (usually the arithmetic mean).

Also, the gross price movement over a specified period of time given a minimum value unit. See also *directional movement* for net price movement.

whipsaw   Slang for a condition where any securities market begins moving laterally, exhibiting very little volatility.

writer   In options the seller of the put or call option.

yard   Slang for a billion.

Index

Vanilla option, 249
Van Treuren, R. David, 236
Vega, 252
Volatility (V), 69, 172, 208, 228, 231–232, 240
Volume, 153

Wave and swing analysis, 135–136
Websites, 45, 295–296

Whipsawing, 135, 208
Winner/loser ratios, 52, 53, 215
Writer, 248

Yap, Dickson, 177
Young, Jimmy, 176